AF394523

'I once sat up in The Corner with a BBC radio
producer at St James' Park where the noise was so
great it broke his tape recorder. This is the story of
a football club that not only breaks tape recorders,
it breaks hearts and mends them. In this case, two
hearts in one, father and son, Chris and Ewan.

'*No Complacency* is a brilliant memoir of a father's love
for his son and their shared love for a football club.'
Professor Robert Colls,
author (including *This Sporting Life*) and historian

'One of the best football books that's ever come my
way. Chris Bowlby's *No Complacency* offers a vivid,
multi-layered reading of the game, both past and
present, exploring how even as big football becomes
an increasingly amoral, rapacious industry, it
still retains its deep emotional charge; while as a
human story, it is profoundly affecting. Altogether,
a very notable addition to the sport's burgeoning
literature, and potentially a classic.'
David Kynaston,
author (including *Tales of a New Jerusalem*)
and historian

'I loved it. Brilliantly researched and eloquently
written.'
Paul Ferris,
former player and author
(including *The Boy on the Shed*)

NO
COMPLACENCY

NO COMPLACENCY

LIFE, DEATH, FOOTBALL, AND THE CATHEDRAL ON THE HILL

CHRIS BOWLBY

HERNE
BOOKS

First published in 2026 by
Herne Books
Unit 1, The Exchange
6 Scarbrook Road
Croydon CR0 1UH
info@hernebooks.com

This product conforms to the requirements of the European Union's General
Product Safety Regulations (GPSR).
EU Authorised Representative for GPSR:
Easy Access System Europe –
Mustamäe tee 50, 10621 Tallinn, Estonia
gpsr.requests@easproject.com

ISBN: 978-1-917665-12-4

A catalogue record for this book is available from the British Library.

Printed and bound in Great Britain by Bell & Bain, Glasgow

CONTENTS

1
A Moment When Everything Changes

THE MATCH NEARS ITS END, all seems in the balance, it seems the perfect scenario for viewers, listeners and excited commentators. As a football fan I may be excited too, but even if my team isn't playing I'm anxious about the words that may suddenly be said, and the memories that will suddenly intrude. It may be 'late drama', a 'game turned on its head', or, worst of all, a moment 'right at the death' when everything changes.

I love this sport, and always will, and it has played a constant role in my life. I'm looking forward to revealing and exploring why in this book, in ways that I think many may find surprising. And the first surprise will be painful. For when I hear those commentators' phrases now I sometimes flinch, briefly but powerfully paralyzed by the emotion of my most troubling football memory.

It happened not at a professional stadium, nor watching a game on TV, but on a meadow at the end of our street in east Oxford, on an early January day in 2012. The rest of our family was away so it was just me, my 16-year-old son Ewan, a ball and an expanse of rough grass. We knew this grass intimately; it had been our play space, our imaginary stadium, since Ewan had begun to walk. Our football bonding had begun within the playground in one corner of the meadow, surrounded by a hedge and a metal fence, its panels an ideal size for mini-goals at either end. All was a space well suited to a tenacious toddler fascinated by the unpredictability of a bouncing, deflecting, apparently anarchic ball – but a ball with which he could begin to try to control, move with, and do his own thing.

Ewan was taught at home by my wife Jane until the age of nine. I was whenever possible an assistant teacher specialising in outdoor sport, and this was our playing field. The meadow was never flat but I, as an ambitious father, maybe hoped its variability as a surface would foster the kind of skill famous players said they had acquired through endless practice dodging obstacles in uneven backyards or roaming with a ball out on the streets. As Ewan grew our game expanded into the wider world of the meadow, our search for footballing spaces combined with investigation of this landscape with all its seasonal variation. We navigated poor drainage in winter, marvelled at the exhilarating hardness of high bounce from the sun-baked summer surface, relished kicking through piles of autumn leaves. I like to think now, or perhaps dream, that we were like the Dutch who were said to have mastered the use of space in their total football because their frequently flooded landscape forced them to manipulate space in everyday life.

Football, everywhere, exists in so many landscapes and at so many levels, across families, age groups, neighbourhoods, clubs and institutions. Our adopted and invented space was just one of many others in the local football universe. Oxford University colleges over the river had pitches galore, their played-on grass kept however at some distance from the immaculate quadrangled lawns within the colleges themselves; mud and rougher ground did not belong with the high-minded horticulture of those great seats of learning. This was east Oxford, borderland between very different parts of the famous city, and very different kinds of football. In another direction was the road to Headington, where a professional team, Oxford United, played in Ewan's early years. On Saturday afternoons we could sometimes hear the drifting sounds of college choirs rehearsing from one side displaced by a roar of joy or dismay from the Manor Ground rolling down the hill from the city's north-east.

In another green space nearby stood Headington Hill Hall, where the publishing tycoon, Robert Maxwell, had run a business empire that included football clubs as entrepreneurial playthings. And then in 2001, as part of that growing transformation of football ownership and financial intrigue the intimate Manor Ground was demolished when a property developer moved Oxford United to a soulless stadium next to a car and retail park on the city's southern periphery.

Our pitch, our deeply personal football territory, remained; it had distinctly dodgy drainage but seemed less susceptible to the larger currents of social and economic change. Apart, that is, from the time when the college that owned the land suddenly decided to deny access and padlock the playground, once our mini-stadium. We resisted, called in the local press, confronted the college hierarchy with its supposedly charitable commitments, and won a satisfying victory. When part of the meadow later began to overflow with sewage after local developers and water companies failed to update their infrastructure, it was the destruction of playing space that proved the most telling way of shaming those responsible. We were now part of a football community, ready to defend our space fiercely when even our little patch proved vulnerable to the encroachment of distinctly unsporting outside powers. Football, I sensed – people's football – could matter and mean much more than many assumed.

The meadow's historic name was 'Angel and Greyhound'. 'Greyhound' suited well the speed with which the teenage Ewan could sprint and return the long passes I sent towards him. 'Angel' conjures for me the way he could time his headers perfectly, soaring upwards to meet the ball. Hundreds of times we had played together there, sometimes more seriously as Ewan became a competitive youngster, sometimes hilariously as we experimented with new moves and outlandish ball skills.

When my team, the team I had persuaded Ewan to support, Newcastle United, had done well we might try to re-enact glorious moments seen on TV. When, more often, they had dismally failed, our fantasy football attempted to replace the memory of disappointment with a better imagined outcome.

And it was more than just our space. My other son, Alfie, had joined in as soon as he was old enough in his wonderfully idiosyncratic way; a boy who had arrived in the world four months early and always enjoyed defying the rules, relishing most the performance of moments of gratuitous drama such as calamitous own goals. Then there were friends who, like us, found football a joyous release from the more confined pressures of life. I remember once heading for the meadow after a local concert with our friend Colin Carr, a brilliant cellist who adored Liverpool FC and was so happy to play riotously amidst the mud and winter evening darkness after hours of concert-hall concentration. At other times football worked its wider associational magic as random locals, tourists, visitors, sometimes even their dogs joined in our games on the meadow as the beautiful game spread its beneficent wings across Angel and Greyhound territory.

So that was where we were that January afternoon, Ewan and I playing with all that memory, all that reassurance of a familiar place from which we always returned feeling happier. Football had been a constant through his boyhood and he seemed no less enthusiastic now despite all the rival attractions in his increasingly rich adolescent life. He completed a balletic volley and grinned as I picked up the ball to conclude our game. Once that had been a controversial paternal act as football never lasted as long as he wanted. Early in his football watching he had clocked and championed the idea of 'extra time', not only in these games but also when faced with, say, going to bed. But that was long ago; such fathering was no longer needed. Once I had been the explainer of rules, the would-be coach, the voice of attempted authority. Now he was quicker, stronger, easily as knowledgeable as me; we shared football in affectionate equality. Beginning to walk towards home our words turned towards another favourite subject: what we would cook for tea.

Then, suddenly, a few seconds that mark the most abrupt rupture of my life, a line forever drawn between its before and its after.

I noticed Ewan's head jerk upwards; I thought at first he had spotted an unusual aircraft or was observing one of the red kites that glide imperiously over the Oxford landscape. But his head movements became increasingly unnatural and then he collapsed. My son, a few minutes before so full of vigour, now lay motionless. As I bent desperately over him dimly recalled first-aid lessons helped me turn him on his side, but he still showed little sign of life. I looked frantically around the meadow, but at that time there was no-one else there, no community of footballers or dog walkers nor anyone else to summon. I had no phone with me, as these outdoor games had always seemed a blissful escape from the tyranny of constant mobile communication.

I yelled out, but there was no response, and I remember grappling for a few moments with two of the deepest parental instincts in paralysing contradiction: the first, to stay with my son who suddenly seemed in such peril; the second, to fetch help. Then I ran towards home, appalled at abandoning Ewan yet desperate for medical reassurance. I grabbed my phone, rang 999 and after an eternity of minutes an ambulance drove onto the meadow; paramedics emerged with their professional calm to ease my parental panic. Up to the John Radcliffe hospital we rode, next to where Oxford United had once played. Accident and Emergency provided reassurance at least that his life was not in imminent danger; it was established that he had had a seizure, but its cause was unclear. It was, in fact, the first indication of the illness that, a decade or so later, would end his life. But to those testing him that day and in subsequent months, the idea that a boy seemingly so healthy, a boy taken ill after vigorous exercise, could be dangerously ill seemed implausible as other explanations were offered. And we were only too happy to embrace such diagnoses with immense relief.

Ewan resumed life, and football. As well as our games in the meadow he joined as many training sessions and teams as possible. His life had steadily filled with music, dance, chess, cookery, social life, travel. While others questioned whether football belonged with everything else he now did, Ewan with the omnivorous enthusiasm which I endlessly admired saw no tension. I had known that tension myself, that assumption that the playing and following of football would naturally be displaced by superior interests, and I was delighted he did not succumb.

Aged nine, he had won a choral scholarship to a nearby Oxford school which also, at junior level, played football. So on Saturdays I cheered him from the touchline, then hastily threw a choirboy cassock over muddy knees and saw him over the road to Evensong. There he sang with angelic purity, using the same voice that, shortly before, was calling raucously for a through ball or muttering darkly against the injustice of a referee's decision. For a few years we relished his and fellow-choristers' glorious sound, their talent taking them to venues including the Albert Hall. Ewan's favourite moment, though, was probably the day his choir team won the football tournament at a national gathering of singers.

And then came early adolescence which, for boy choristers, has a cruel audibility. The breaking of that beautiful treble voice – preciously preserved now in a few tantalising recordings – seems now to hint at the tragic fragility of a life that once seemed able to take on everything. After Ewan's first seizure we had hoped all was back on track. But the seizures kept occurring, often while he was playing football. On one occasion he collapsed in the school playground and his classmates told him later they thought they had been watching him die. On another day an ambulance was called when he was playing for the juniors of the main local amateur team, Oxford City. As a family, we now had a new sense of football time. The 90 minutes of a game were not primarily about the result or the performance, but simply whether Ewan could last without collapse, without the phone ringing yet again to tell us yet another emergency had occurred. For us football, supposed to be about leisure and relaxation, had become the location of constant fear.

Eventually the right tests were done, and a brain tumour was diagnosed. It was not initially malignant, but surgery was required to remove as much of it as possible. Long, mystifying waits in Accident and Emergency after yet another unexplained collapse were replaced with parental waits of an altogether more terrifying kind as Ewan had brain surgery in the JR hospital. I kept an occasional diary at the time, in which football somehow seemed to be the consoling framework within which I attempted to comprehend my fears:

> November 2012: Ewan is now in the recovery room after his op. And the image that's encouraging me in anxious, anxious times: a few days before, on Oxford City's pitch, I saw him waltzing through a defence to score a great goal. Behind, in the distance, was the huge JR hospital. An image to sustain us as we never know what the next moment can bring. It's a journey alternating between anxiety, elation and defiance. But he's faced it all with such spirit as he seems to dance around the obstacles in pursuit of his goals.

Despite that spirit, Ewan was beginning to face not only the immediate challenge of surgery, but also the psychological effects of living with such a troubling condition at a teenage time of changing self-consciousness. His gradual response began to shape what would become his extraordinary life's work, an exploration of how those afflicted by such conditions can face the greater questions it poses way beyond the coldly clinical. There was immense sympathy from family and friends. As he wrote later, after his first operation he returned to 'seeking release in sport and socialising' as 'the thrill and camaraderie of teams sports, particularly football' had long been 'a nourishing and uplifting part of my life'. But he noticed nonetheless how his condition meant he was perceived differently, in, for example, the comments he received when wearing a protective cap to protect his scarred and weakened skull. Illness, he realised, could mark you out, 'make you feel lonely while surrounded by people'.

The surgery to remove most of his brain tumour initially appeared successful as regular scans suggested no new growth. On he went to Cambridge University, prospering academically though he needed regular encouragement and emotional support as the implications of his illness intensified, the mental as well as physical scarring. At times he remained reclusive in his college room, shunning social life, but football thankfully drew him out. In the strangely fleeting and fragmentary world of Online remembrance I cherish the random appearance among search results of his academic work, singing and prowess at chess, a report of a 2014 cup upset when his college won 4-2 'with help from a superb hat-trick for Ewan Bowlby'.

Another period mercifully free of surgery ended shortly before his final university exams; yet again a seizure during family football sounded the alarm. On a visit home while playing with Alfie and me he felt what he described as familiar sensation of 'overwhelming heaviness'; a kind of irresistible weight, he felt, was dragging him onto the grass. Another ambulance, another wait in Accident and Emergency as harassed medics raced around dealing with overwhelming numbers and attempted rapid diagnoses to free up beds while we attempted to explain to them Ewan's underlying problem. Eventually – after he managed despite everything to perform brilliantly in his final Cambridge exams – further investigation revealed that the tumour had returned. This time he was going to have the most extraordinary intervention: an awake craniotomy, in which he would remain conscious throughout the operation so that surgeons could monitor his cognitive activity as they tried to avoid damaging vital brain tissue.

I sat with Jane for many hours in a corridor waiting for news, wondering not only how the surgery was going, but what on earth Ewan would be saying and thinking as his head was opened up. It all began, he told us afterwards, with the most bizarre of awkward small talk about weather or school until everything eased when Ewan let slip that he was interested in football. The surgeon's eyes 'lit up' and talk of teams and players flowed while as much tumour tissue as possible was extracted. Whenever I hear an exasperated football supporter claiming his team's performance is 'doing his head in' I sometimes think of Ewan joking about Newcastle United while holes were drilled in his skull. After many hours there was relief as the surgeon emerged to say that all has gone well. But our ease was cruelly short-lived as a few days later we were called back to another consultation to be told that a biopsy on the tumour tissue removed had shown that it was malignant. There was much baffling jargon and no mention of the C-word but eventually we all realised that Ewan now had cancer.

Instead of heading for postgraduate life at St Andrews University he faced months of punishing radiotherapy and chemotherapy. There was little or no energy for football, but one thing we could do for hours on end was talk. Walking to appointments, waiting during delays, passing the time as he sat feeling the effects of such powerful treatments, we had conversations about the most profound and the most trivial of subjects. And football, for us, would always feature prominently in both categories. It was in part a deliberate distraction from the severity of what Ewan was facing. But it was also part of a wider conversation about the living of life in all its variety that grew in importance as we gradually responded to the deep uncertainty of the future he faced. Well beyond gossip about the latest results, we were both fascinated by what the game seemed to tell us about the world we lived in, reflecting identities, moods and ambitions far beyond events on the pitch.

And as I spoke to Ewan I began to think more and more about why the game had been such a constant in my life, and how it had somehow linked and enriched so much of what I had done. We continued to exchange views, ideas and (if truth be told) bad jokes about our lives in football when he was able to move to Scotland and begin his research into cultural life, spiritual concerns and cancer care. When Newcastle were playing our conversations and messaging took on their own timetable and vocabulary and we settled on a slogan that became a motto for football, life and now, for me, grief: 'no complacency'. Even if our team was winning with minutes to go, still we superstitiously sent each other these words, perhaps in a desperate attempt to protect us against the crushing disappointment of the late equaliser, the sudden setback, the way life can, suddenly and bewilderingly, kick you.

Yet all the anxiety makes the moments of success so much the sweeter. In grieving for Ewan I cling to the times when he heard about or saw a wonderful piece of skill or goal and would celebrate simply with the word 'sublime'.

WHY FOOTBALL?

So why, in the end, do I find myself wanting to write about football of all things soon after the loss of my son? Why is it that in football I have found myself facing that loss more than in most other areas of my life? This framing of grief through football seems in some ways puzzling to me – sport is meant to be trivial release from 'real' life, yet it seems to have a presence and an influence that can extend way beyond what we might expect. And that comes, I see increasingly, from stories. Ewan devoted his research as he lived with cancer to understanding how we can use stories and culture to navigate life, and death.

So this book is based on the story I told Ewan about what football had meant to me, and draws then on our shared experience of football as it changed so radically in recent decades. In the next two chapters I explore how I first fell for the game, and Newcastle as a football city; and then how my football interests broadened and deepened as I moved away to live in different places, including abroad. One place that has influenced and engaged me hugely is Germany so its football, or rather Fussball, forms another chapter.

I watched on, both as fan and sometimes as working journalist, during the time when my club, Newcastle United, careered between dramatically different owners and eras. And the best way it seemed to me to capture that period and how I and Ewan saw it was through the themes that form the next chapters: the football shirt, the stadium and its culture, and (a subject especially close to Ewan's heart) how football became a kind of secular religion.

The most intense human side of football prompted two further chapters. First on men and their moods, and football's relationship with often struggling societies, focused on another club that has come to mean a lot to me and my family: Gateshead FC. Women's football also inspired us, which prompted an exploration – in a chapter called 'Lost Lasses' – of the shocking story of how the women's game that flourished a century or so ago in regions like the North East of England, now once again my home territory, was suppressed but has now revived. The final chapters return to the most personal of themes for me and my family surrounding Ewan's death. At first I questioned whether football could still be part of my life, until one game changed my mind. And then came broader redemption when my club Newcastle United succeeded as it had not done for decades, and I and many around me found a way of holding together celebration with commemoration of those who had not lived to see the day.

Football is a sport with an ever-increasing global presence and is constantly being reinvented and repackaged. Yet its history – personal and communal – runs stubbornly alongside, like a tenacious defender who won't let a highly-paid striker steal the show. Ewan's life and death at first shocked me into questioning whether I could or should ever engage again with football, but before long I wanted somehow to resume and take forward the conversation that he and I had begun back on our local field as we invented and explored our pitch and let the game into more and more of the landscape of our lives.

I can no longer talk with Ewan, nor run with him. But in what follows I want to celebrate what the game has given and still gives to me. I want to explore why it matters and where it might be going, and honour in his memory the way football can show us how to live without complacency and with compassion, valuing how people, a ball, and some space can become something bonding and magical across lives past and present.

2
DRAWN IN

IT IS 21 JUNE 1970, early evening, and my location is a sitting room in Croydon, south London. But my eight-year-old mind is far away in Mexico City sensing, despite the grainy black and white TV screen, the colourful passion of 100,000 people at the World Cup final between Italy and Brazil. And on the pitch is simply one of the most enjoyable, inspiring things this young boy has ever seen.

There was in those days very little football on TV. The first match I remember watching was the FA Cup final the year before, an intense contest between Manchester City and Leicester City. But this seemed very different, hardly the same sport. Most of the tactical subtlety will have passed me by, just as the Italian players were being bypassed with increasing Brazilian brio. Yet there was something about the style, the performance, that was mesmerising, especially once Brazil, 3-1 up, sensed victory was assured and they could now play for fun. The Brazilian players seemed to become artists not athletes; they danced rather than ran, pirouetted around tackles, caressed and conjured with the ball instead of kicking it. Until, that is, the scoring of the final goal, the one I have remembered vividly ever since. Most of the team joined in as they teased their way through the Italians. Pele then laid the ball off nonchalantly and Carlos Alberto, casting off all the instinctive caution of a full back, charged forward with perfect timing to propel it emphatically into the corner.

This was, I think, my first taste of the game's sublime

attraction, its potential offering of moments that can defy the confusion or blandness of routine recollection. Yes, I have probably added layers of memory having re-watched the match and that goal since, but I'm confident in recalling the simple sensation of a boy's wonder at how a game with rules could suddenly become a performance of such exuberant, spontaneous joy. There must have been many millions watching around the world who were similarly impressed. And so it began to bind me into the extraordinary global reach of this great British sporting invention. I headed outside immediately afterwards with my best friend from primary school, a Japanese boy called Kyozo, whose Dad had been temporarily posted to London, and we tried to reproduce those Brazilian moves in our mini version of the new global football enthusiasm.

We went to the local park on Duppas Hill, roaming across the grass expanse of a recreation ground where there had once been the Croydon workhouse. Its green space was now a welcome contrast to the flyovers and skyscrapers looming over the town centre. I played on pitches there with friends, for my school, the cub scouts – any team that would have me. We were out in most weathers, though shelter was sometimes necessary in mud-encrusted municipal dressing rooms that reeked of deep heat embrocation and the euphoria or despair of post-match chat. In places like that, far from the warmth of that Brazilian TV vision of sporting samba and endless celebration, I was perhaps beginning to sense that the game could replicate life's lows as well as its intoxicating highs. Yet that only deepened its potential hold. It would need defending against those who saw it as little more than casual exercise, nothing that mattered deeply.

My primary school was small, with many of its intake from a nearby children's home. The playground, set around a severe Victorian building with noxious outdoor toilets, was a tempestuous place in which football fought for space amongst other frenetic activity and the occasional fight. Headmaster

Mr Hatchard was an austere chain smoker who held a cane in his yellowed hands to inflict public corporal punishment. His chief educational enthusiasms were the repetition of times tables and the perfection of copperplate handwriting. When he sensed that I had academic potential he saw it as his mission to remove me from the playground and its sporting corruption, so summoned me to his smoke-filled study to offer me the role of library monitor.

I was however reluctant on two counts. Recently I had managed to become class milk monitor, only to have that prestige cruelly removed by Education Secretary Margaret Thatcher's decision to abolish free school milk. Like the milk itself on summer mornings, the attraction of monitoring jobs had somewhat soured. Much more importantly, library duties during break time would have taken me away from football. I declined, eliciting a sorrowful warning from the head about failing to realise my potential, a first indication to me that football would be seen as not the kind of thing superior people were meant to like.

For me, however, it seemed an increasingly promising field of potential achievement, as our school team progressed towards the dizzying heights of the 1972 Croydon Small Schools Cup Final. I'd like to say that we were supremely talented. But it was, if truth be told, more of an introduction to the tension between aspiring to play like Brazil while needing to secure results. Shouting from the sidelines was our Welsh coach, who I now believe modelled his brusque approach on the great outspoken manager Brian Clough. He drilled us in playing an offside trap – hardly the beautiful game, but highly effective against other teams who had never come across such ruthless tactics among ten-year-olds.

At the end of a tight semi-final I scored a late winning penalty and returned home to be told by my mother that I had passed the eleven plus exam and would be moving on to grammar school. She was I suspect somewhat surprised that I was far more interested in celebrating how I had held my nerve to place the ball beyond the keeper. But it was in fact a day of damaging football destiny. I was one of only a tiny handful from my class of over thirty who had succeeded in the exam. And it was only later that I realised this would open up what would be for me the most painful of divides: grammar school meant playing rugby and hockey, not football. Headmaster Hatchard would have been pleased; I would be furious.

For now I continued to play and watch as much as football as possible. My first visit to a professional game had been at Selhurst Park in 1969 to see Crystal Palace play Manchester United. I wish I had a clearer memory of the game and the players, as I know now that the great Bobby Charlton was there and scored. It is not what happens on the pitch that lingers in my mind, however, but rather an early sense of the aura around a stadium: the smell of cigarette smoke, the ebb and flow of communal noise and emotion, the way a changing mood can roll though a crowd with awesome intensity.

I decided at once that Palace would be my team and, in a foretaste of another wave that would roll through football, a commercial one, I rushed off to acquire their kit. My Mum, who had little or no interest in sport, was alarmed at the expense, seeing shrewdly how lucrative for clubs was the clamour for each season's new shirt. Next Christmas I acquired too my first proper football, a miracle, it seemed to me, of manufacturing as variously sized leather panels were somehow woven together to create a perfect globe. That first ball feels like a symbolic focus now as I think of the way in which football has been like a kind of global thread linking so many of the places and people in my life.

And I was drawn more into that new sphere of mental geography as I began to follow the professional game and the British leagues, waiting impatiently each Saturday afternoon for the music of five o'clock on the radio and the incantation of the day's results. Just as some felt a sense of national belonging by listening daily to the shipping forecast, so my sense of my own country's complexion was shaped by the fans' poetry of Albions, Rovers, Thistles and Academicals, juxtaposed with numbers: doom-laden nils were intoned alongside fantastical and upbeat fours and fives that would mysteriously shape the mood of many thousands of anxious listeners.

But my sense of football geography and local loyalty was soon to be upended. After a single term at my new secondary school in Croydon came a move that would transform my experience of what the game could mean. My family went from London to live in Newcastle upon Tyne, a city with an altogether more intense relationship to football and all that it could mean to a region, its identity and its mood.

Transfixed by the Toon

It was, in fact, a kind of return. I had been born in the North East of England but on Teesside not Tyneside. My father was then a clergyman in Billingham, a town dominated by the enormous Imperial Chemical Industries (ICI) enterprise. When I was there in the early 1960s its plastics production and brutalist concrete town centre still seemed to promise progress to its population – though the pollution from chemical production, the ubiquitous pipes above ground and clouds of strange vapours I remembered, was far less attractive.

I certainly seemed to find the town centre attractive as a toddler, alarming my parents by escaping there and ignoring all the safety talk I had supposedly imbibed at the local Tufty Club's milk and rusk mornings. Somehow I crossed a main road before being rescued amidst the shops where I later bloodily crashed my bike racing down a spiral walkway. Perhaps the ticking offs I doubtless received helped persuade me that the grass parkland and pitches I had crossed during my adventures were a better place for a boy to assert his independence.

ICI paternalistically provided jobs, housing and leisure, including a football pitch made exceptionally verdant with its finest fertiliser production; it was home to a team, Billingham Synthonia, named proudly after a chemical process. Teesside's football enthusiasts were internationally minded too, famously adopting the locally-based North Koreans during the 1966 World Cup. By the time that tournament was played, however, I had moved south at the age of five, too young to have absorbed anything of the North East's football enthusiasm.

Now in 1973 we were heading back north as my Dad had become Bishop of Newcastle. This meant, as I will reveal later, he could join a great tradition of episcopal supporters of the city's football club. His own sporting education at public school had focused on rowing and featured no football; he too had been in one of those parts of the education system that thought the game unsuitable for the higher-minded. I do have a faint memory of sitting in a pushchair on a touchline watching him leap for a header during a parish game in a Billingham park. But back trouble soon ended his sporting activity.

Once we had returned north, however, he began to tell me what football meant to our new region, and how he had first discovered that as a young clergyman in 1950s Sunderland. In the nineteenth century, young men from my Dad's educational and social background often promoted association football as 'their' game, designed to instil in young men the kinds of values and virtues threatened by urban industrial life. Clergymen encouraged football in the name of 'muscular Christianity'.

By the time my Dad became a clergyman, football as a professional sport was very different, and that kind of overt, top-down evangelism was no longer effective. 'Industrial mission' was the new Church focus, and he had spent months away from his theology textbooks learning what it was like to earn a living with a mind-numbingly boring job filing car parts. In that kind of environment football talk was all the more important as a distraction from the tedium, digesting what had happened the previous Saturday or looking forward to the next. When he moved to Sunderland he noticed that

Roker Park – the local professional football ground – seemed to be a place of profound communal worship. And the pastoral care he learned to offer in hundreds of home visits, time spent down mines and in shipyards and railway stations, hospitals and prisons could often be commenced through conversations about what was happening in the football world. I found the same thing when talking to the wide range of people who would turn up – some invited, some not – at our clergy home. On one occasion in Newcastle, while my parents were entertaining a local aristocrat in one part of the house, I was discussing in a back room great centre forwards of the past over a cup of tea with Norman, a 'gentleman of the road' and regular caller who had lost his job in the local shipyards.

Dad wasted no time on arrival in Newcastle in January 1973 establishing his episcopal-football credentials. He told the local *Evening Chronicle* that the postponing of his enthronement as bishop for a couple of weeks had a 'silver lining' as it would enable him to go to cheer on his 'new team' Newcastle against his 'old one', Crystal Palace. He had, moreover, 'told his 11 year old son, Christopher, to put away his Crystal Palace scarf for good'. I'm not sure I had been consulted about this media initiative and remember thinking initially that I would stay loyal to Palace.

My sister Anna remembers with amusement his charmingly naïve warning before the match that we might at the ground hear 'some words you haven't heard before'. We were of course already familiar with all the expletives, though not delivered with the vigorous intonation of Geordie fans in full cry. Newcastle won 2-0 which must have begun to test my loyalty. I held out for a while until deeper undercurrents in our new home city began to lure me towards a fateful change of allegiance.

Supporting the local team in a place like Newcastle is, for many, something you must be born into, a birthright and birthduty which only proper Geordies can ever properly appreciate. I am awkwardly aware that makes me a kind of dubious interloper who came late to the party and can never, in some eyes, really belong. That suspicion is reinforced in today's game by anxiety among longstanding supporters about how globally owned Premier League football is eroding the link between club, fans and place. In the pursuit of revenue from an ever more scattered yet lucrative international fanbase, clubs' attention is focused increasingly on occasional, high-spending 'tourist' visitors and TV subscriptions rather than 'born and bred' supporters who want to go to every game.

What I hope my story can suggest is an idea of adoption that relates well to the club's history and its players, allows generously for outsiders as well as insiders to join in, yet honours that extraordinary character which is so closely based on the place and the culture from which a football club emerges. It is also the story I told my sons many years later as I encouraged them to support what all the Newcastle locals call 'the Toon' even though, at the time, we were not living locally. I wanted them to feel the pull of a place and a team that stood for much more than an arbitrary result or a distant TV image that engaged little emotion or commitment. My son Ewan came through his illness to have a profound understanding of how 'stories' are the way in which we can navigate the roughest as well as the best places life may take us; and one of our running conversations was about how I was drawn into Newcastle football life.

The Moor that Made Me

Absorption into local football began for me not as a fan, but as a player – a player desperate to find what he was now denied educationally. My new school was the city's Royal Grammar School (RGS), located not far from St James' Park but keeping a distinct cultural distance. Had I known its history I might have realised how my prospects were now severely limited. In 1892, the year Newcastle United was formed out of the merger of two of the city's clubs, the then RGS headmaster had asserted his authority with comprehensive clarity: 'No Association Football', he stated, 'is to be played in this School in any form whatever.' In the school song we praised merchants who ventured boldly forth, 'wielders of sword and of pen'; a song dating back to the time when the school saw itself as training leaders for the British Empire. And it was notable, initially at least, that football did not prosper in many of the Empire's territories, though it would spread far and wide elsewhere on the back of British global trading and industrial activity. Our sporting curriculum was governed by attitudes well captured by historian Niall Ferguson: 'Soccer, the gentleman's game played by hooligans, was of course the country's most successful recreational export. But "football" was always a promiscuous sport, appealing to everyone from the politically suspect working class to the even more suspect Germans; to everyone, in fact, except the Americans.'

So while I would benefit hugely from my school's academic excellence, its sporting life was a major disappointment. I began resentfully to shiver on the wing of regional rugby grounds or (later) hockey pitches, frustrated at how restricting those sports felt compared to the football I loved. Nor did rugby have much of a local following. My favourite explanation is that of the author Harry Pearson, who suggests that North Eastern men never needed to prove their muscularity as they displayed that in their everyday heavy industrial work. Instead they wanted a sport that enabled them to show artistry, creativity; that idea, which I eagerly passed on to Ewan, was music to his choirboy-footballing ears. In those dying days of the direct grant scheme and local authority funded free places my grammar school had pupils from across the North East's communities, rich and poor, but the football those communities cherished was not to be part of our education.

We did manage some informal football in school break times. And playing on such rough surfaces proved useful preparation for when salvation came on Sunday afternoons as I discovered how profoundly football was rooted in the Newcastle landscape. I lived next to a huge expanse of open space right next to the city centre called the Town Moor. It covers around a thousand acres, much larger than, say, Hampstead Heath in London but far less famous. At first glance it may appear to be little more than grassland with footpaths and grazing cows. Yet the people of Newcastle have used and imprinted themselves onto this space in all kinds of ways, making it a kind of living canvas of the city's historical identity. On its territory there have been public executions, military exercises, isolation hospitals, asylums and cemeteries, huge political and trade union demonstrations, imperial exhibitions, an aerodrome, extensive allotment gardening, temperance festivals, and, to this day, a famous annual funfair, the Hoppings.

Its governance and accessibility as a public space has over the centuries been the subject of fierce debate, shaping the political philosophy of land ownership. The great radical thinker Thomas Spence, pioneer of the idea of the 'rights of man', cut his teeth on resistance to a proposal to enclose the Town Moor in the 1770s. One history of the city called the Moor 'the true People's Park, where one may roam without fear or favour'. In keeping the Moor's special character Newcastle had bucked the historical trend. As the author of *This Sporting Life*, Robert Colls, puts it, at the beginning of the eighteenth century 'for most of the people most of the time, a rough and ready space was always to hand. But as the towns grew the fields were lost and there was nothing to remember except perhaps in a name'. While so much open space, and so many playing fields, have been lost in Britain to urban development, Newcastle's Town Moor has mostly been defended, apart from the sacrifice of some space to one of the great gods of post-war development, the urban motorway.

One of the richest parts of the Moor's history, and its evolving civic significance, has been sporting. Historian Lynn Pearson has identified no fewer than 29 different 'sports and recreations' played in a place she calls 'the cradle of Newcastle sport'. They included 'pedestrianism', horse racing and special miners' games such as potshare bowling. A Newcastle United golf club was founded there (unrelated to the football club), celebrated in an article in *The Times* of 1919 headed 'Democratic Golf' as a place offering 'the cheapest golf in England' where teachers, shopkeepers and post office clerks could afford to play. Sport on the Moor was organised by all kinds of people as part of their daily routine. There was even in 1848 an Early Risers club which met at 6am to 'hear a lecture, play a little cricket, quoits or football, before repairing to a nearby inn for breakfast'.

I found my own version of this rich sporting culture in the form of a huge informal game of football on the Moor's eastern side which took place every Sunday afternoon. Anyone could turn up and then teams were organised by an older bespectacled man in baggy shorts who struggled to keep up with the swifter youngsters but presided with a kind of benign authority. Only later did I realise that this man was none other than the city's Lord Mayor, Hugh White, who during the week swapped his baggy shorts for civic finery and on one famous occasion welcomed the US President Jimmy Carter to our Civic Centre. There were players of greatly varying size and ability. At the appointed time the crowd which had turned up was divided into teams under Hugh's supervision in a way which subtly attempted to avoid a brutal form of Darwinian domination. I like to think of it now as a kind of last hurrah of 1970s Social Democratic redistribution, soon to be swept away in a harsher political, and sporting, age.

So this was what *association* football could mean, a game in which a city's people high and low could join spontaneously in a shared place to enjoy the game they loved. It became for several years my only source of regular football while, a short distance away, my school did its best to educate me into other sporting preferences. That was never going to succeed, however, as I was being lured increasingly towards another corner of the Moor, on which stood the Newcastle United stadium. The Moor had been crucial to the club's foundation. Grazing land on its edge – said to have been used for sheep awaiting slaughter – had been leased for a new stadium in the 1880s, and the modern football club reportedly still pays rent which helps to finance the Moor's upkeep. The drainage of the modern Premier League pitch is rather better than elsewhere on the Moor, though when I first went to watch Newcastle in the 1970s there was, after a period of poor weather, a struggle for quality amidst the quagmire. The St James' Park pitch does however still have a pronounced slope appropriate for moorland topography down which the home team likes to play in the second half of games.

During matches in harsh midwinter the floodlit stadium glowed like an enticing circus tent. Ecstatic shouts from its many thousands of devotees were broadcast siren-like across the Moor's expanses, and even those some distance away sensed how the Toon were doing as they heard roars of delight or detected drifting groans. In my first years of living there I was considered too young to go to matches on my own. But in observation and conversation I slowly began to realise how football, and this club, infiltrated itself into the city and surrounding region way beyond the stadium and its fans.

Even some players recruited by Newcastle United seemed almost alarmed by how much it all mattered to the locals. Striker Peter Withe joked that 'they say if you hang 11 Newcastle United shirts on a washing line, 20,000 fans will turn up to watch them'. Another famous goalscorer Andy Cole, who arrived from Bristol in 1993 commented:

'It was like being beamed up to another planet after my life in London. In the south there are other interests, other distractions. Up there ... it's football, football, and then more football ... It was such a culture shock. I was brought up to enjoy life, and football is always going to be very much a sport for me. Not to the Geordie boys. For them it's the whole point of their existence.'

Kevin Keegan, adored as one of the club's greatest players and managers, concluded: 'Newcastle inspires a culture and devotion that is truly unique in English football'. Others in, say, Merseyside or Manchester or north London would doubtless disagree. But few would deny that the allure of football in Newcastle is especially powerful. Paul Ferris, who came in the 1980s to play for Newcastle as a teenager from Northern Ireland, wrote of how 'the football club – its history, its heritage, what it meant to the people – was seeping into my bones'. 'The club, the city and its people,' he sensed, 'weave their way into your affections and once they get in they become a part of who you are.'

Although a fierce Geordie pride was at the heart of the club's identity, the club had in fact always been a great engine of integration in the region as many thousands of outsiders made it their home. When it first achieved national success in the Edwardian period most of its team was originally from Scotland. 'It was Scotsmen who set the game alight in the region,' concluded Arthur Appleton, 'football in North East England is a child of Scotland'. That tradition – of adopting footballers from everywhere as well as many kinds of migrants – has continued into today's global football age.

And yet there has been a difficult relationship between that idea of mobile footballing talent and the region's economic fortunes. The initial import of top players had begun when the North East was taking in many thousands to sustain its booming industries in mining, shipbuilding or chemicals. As those industries struggled after the Second World War, and Newcastle United stopped winning trophies, so it seemed that the region's finest football talent was often lured away by richer teams, just as many fans were forced to seek work elsewhere. Aggrieved fans watching those stars head elsewhere could sometimes lose sight of the generous openness to incomers that the region and its football had once celebrated.

My own life – moving back and forth between the North East and other places and countries – was an individual micro-part of the bigger economic and social story. I had even shifted teams from Crystal Palace to Newcastle. But from then on, the idea of changing allegiances never occurred to me. I can tell you to the minute when my bones told me my new loyalty was irreversible. Newcastle United had reached the semi-finals of the League Cup in January 1976. They trailed against Tottenham Hotspur after the first leg 1-0. I and a group of schoolfriends, now allowed by our parents to attend matches, entered St James' Park late for the second leg. We clutched tickets costing a steep 75 pence rather than the usual schoolboy 40, and peered from the back of the cavernous, densely-packed Leazes end, part of a crowd the son of the great Newcastle striker Jackie Milburn had once called '60,000 fanatical sardines'. Then after three minutes Alan Gowling, known variously as 'egghead' due to his university education and 'the galloping chip' because of his gangling appearance, used all his brainpower and athleticism to round the Tottenham keeper and score. The crowd surged, our feet became detached from the crumbling concrete terracing and we were swept in those barrierless days to the front. From there a 3-1 victory could be relished in close-up. Arthur Hopcraft, author of a famous account of *The Football Man*, suggested that 'in this incomparable entanglement of bodies and emotions lies the heart of the fan's commitment to football'. At the age of 14, I was now thoroughly entangled.

Only years later did I realise how dangerous those old grounds were, how close I and my friends were to catastrophe. The foundations of the concrete crash barriers on the St James' Park terraces had been discovered in the mid-1970s to be defective. One of our great heroes on the pitch at the time was a flamboyant centre forward, Malcolm Macdonald, who used to roar up the Great North Road near our house in his sports car after games. Every time he got the ball the crowd would surge some more. But looking back later, he was scathing about the state of the place where he played, with its ramshackle structures and crude, overflowing toilets.

> 'The only modernisation that had taken place was at the main entrance, which had a sort of new façade put on it. And that's pretty much what Newcastle United was at the time – a façade to hide the decay. Here … was a football club that was superbly supported but had done little to deserve that support. Not a thing had been done to the ground since it was built at the turn of the (twentieth) century, and if the supporters stood in three feet of pee, so what?'

A couple of years ago I came across a last relic of those most primitive of outdoor toilets at Carlisle United's ground, about to be redeveloped. They should perhaps have been taken to a museum, I thought, a bit like the Roman multi-seater lavatories preserved on nearby Hadrian's Wall, as a reminder of how football fans were once treated.

There was sometimes behaviour in those 1970s crowds as ugly as the physical surroundings: casual violence as drink-fuelled fans jostled for space, racist baying against non-white players and lurid harassment of the few women then at games as spectators or working in catering or for the police. That kind of behaviour was, at the time, dragging football down across the country. My wife Jane remembers how I rashly took her onto the St James' Park terraces during one of our first days out together. There were no other female fans visible, and she was understandably disturbed by the insanitary insanity, including a total absence of women's toilets. Somehow our relationship survived, helped by her generosity of spirit and previous encounters with football obsession in her extended family in Leeds. On our wedding day some of my male football friends mischievously presented me with a new football, to which was attached a pair of rubber washing-up gloves. This was interpreted by some as signifying a warning of domestic life interfering with football attendance. I took it as reminding me to do my duty before heading out. Jane may have thought, however, that rubber gloves, together with wellies, were what anyone heading for those terraces should wear as protection.

For some outsiders, Newcastle's passion for football was all part of an alien culture that set it apart from the rest of the country. John Ardagh, a veteran Francophile journalist who spent some time in the city in the 1970s, described St James' Park at the time I first started going as 'one of the most antiquated, unhygienic and uncomfortable in Europe'. For him, the local enthusiasm for football (despite such conditions) was part of what made it 'this strange self-absorbed tribal civilisation in this remote region of England'. His tone was at times that of a troubled Victorian explorer. 'Sometimes, in the back-streets of slums, amid football crowds, or in dismal pubs with their beer spilt on the tables and workers talking in a language I could not follow' he wrote, 'I even felt something of that Angst in the presence of an alien, vaguely menacing culture that I have felt in Moslem lands such as Iran or Algeria.'

I found Ardagh's account in my local library, one of the few contemporary accounts by an outsider of my new city to be found anywhere, and was baffled. Some of the conditions he described were real enough. But the overall alienation he felt was nothing like my experience. I was about to embark on a career in some ways like Ardagh's: Oxbridge, journalism, much time spent in Continental Europe. But that was not my grateful escape to a superior civilisation; I would always be looking back with yearning for the passion of St James' Park.

Forever Connected

By the late 1970s the end of my school career approached. I had thrived in the school's academic and cultural life, but wanted to register some final notes of protest at the belief that football was not part of a rounded Newcastle education. A single game of football was permitted at the school every year, between the prefects and the teachers, the one opportunity to demonstrate the talent the school was dismally failing to nurture. It was a tiny breach in the Victorian headmaster's decree that no football 'in any form whatever' was to be played.

Prefects had been created around the same time as his decree in order to 'bring a wholesome moral influence to bear upon the boys'. Having ascended the greasy pole to deputy head prefect in the autumn of 1978, I saw it as my duty to bring a different kind of influence to bear. I found myself involved in the selection of new colleagues. And my recommendations, I should now confess, may have been influenced as much by candidates' ability to shoot or tackle as by their broader moral qualities. This resulted in a team which, in December 1978, secured a thumping 5-1 victory over the staff. Due to a hard frost the venue had been switched from the school's rugby pitch to a more resilient place on the edge of the Town Moor, an auspicious moment for me as we were playing on what had become my Newcastle footballing home. The school magazine recorded the teachers quailing in front of a 'fiery and hostile' crowd of boys leaving them at the end 'shameful of their performance and with their pride severely dented'.

My final act of pro-football defiance came during school prizegiving day the following year when I was asked to give a speech thanking the visiting dignitary – an eminent man from London who began by saying how much he looked forward to visiting Tyne and Wear 'or, as we call it down south, Wear and Tear'. It was an uncomfortable moment for a school that, in some ways, had a reputation for preparing its pupils to 'escape' their economically challenged region as indeed I was to do having secured a place at Cambridge University. But there was one focus of local pride I could celebrate defiantly, ending my speech by saying I had been encouraged by my schoolmates to keep it short 'so that we can get to the second half at St James' Park'. The senior staff and dignitaries looked unamused, but the lads all laughed.

My school education was over, but I swiftly realised that all kinds of other education would now follow. I had most of a year to fill before Cambridge, much of which would be spent in Germany (see chapter four). First would come a few months of farewell to the city, and the Moor, that had made me love football. I worked as a volunteer decorator for Newcastle social services, offering paint and new wallpaper to pensioners who could not otherwise afford it. Our team consisted mostly of young lads on Community Service Orders, who wanted at lunchtimes to teach me how to break into Ford Cortinas. Our foreman was a former shipyard shop steward who had become a working-class Tory, revelling in the recent election as prime minister of my old milk monitor nemesis, Margaret Thatcher.

Our political debate was fierce; our football debate even fiercer, especially after Newcastle had lost and we tried to fathom why. One of our largest projects was in a tall block of flats overlooking the Moor where lived, I only realised much later, T. Dan Smith, the great visionary of North East regional development who had been imprisoned for corruption. Much has been made of his huge plans for the city's redevelopment, with urban motorways driven through the city centre and high-rise housing commissioned in dubious circumstances which proved to be far from the quality he had promised. Interestingly some of his thinking on regional development has undergone something of a rehabilitation recently as the North East continues to suffer from endlessly unfulfilled promises of some kind of 'levelling up'.

Less attention has been paid to Smith's sense of football's local significance, and his attempt to influence the development of Newcastle United. 'Football', he wrote in his autobiography 'is the ballet of Tyneside, every man understands it, and will go through thick and thin to watch it. His stoic and faithful thesis is that he will stand in the wet for 50 years to watch "the lads", provided something is dished up.' Smith was scathing about how the 'complacent' Newcastle United club, 'potentially one of Britain's wealthiest' had got away with 'second-rate facilities'. He hoped instead for a stadium to rival Real Madrid 'or even a modest Aztec stadium'. That was the stadium in which Brazil had entranced me with their 1970 World Cup win, and Smith's idea of Newcastle as the 'Brasilia of the North' could perhaps encourage the wild idea among Newcastle United fans that their team could, one day, include top Brazilian stars.

All that seemed a far cry from the St James' Park stadium I looked down on in 1980 as I repainted the interiors of flats high up in Spital Tongues. And running counter to all Smith's eloquent ambitions I could hear all around me one of the great flaws in his vision for Newcastle: the noise of frustrated children moved from terraced houses to high rise flats where they had no open spaces into which they could easily run out and play. Further afield I could see from on high the eastern edge of the Moor, where I had played on Sunday afternoons with the city's allcomers in a weekly association presided over by its mayor. And I know now how important that had been to my feeling of permanent connection to this place, these people and (despite the often infuriating way it was run) this club. I would soon be heading off to spend decades away, observing keenly from afar a history of almost constant frustration and disappointment. But the faith in eventual success, my fundamental football connection, would survive everything.

3
DRAWN AWAY

WITH ITS MANICURED LAWNS, ancient buildings and alluring mythology of gilded youth, Cambridge can seem an endlessly beautiful place. But to those there who face anxiety and disappointment rather than a sense of elite achievement it can feel as bleak as the winter's wind that seeps in from the eastern Fens. When my son Ewan was studying at Cambridge, not long after he had been diagnosed with a brain tumour, the implications of what he was facing began to feel overwhelming. I and his Mum Jane spoke with him almost daily on the phone. The point of those conversations was not to dwell relentlessly on his illness, worsening his anxiety, but more to offer the reassurance of constant sympathetic contact and the repetition of familiar, distracting themes. And for Ewan and me, that often meant football.

I found myself telling him football stories that would, I hoped, show helpful sympathy with wintry Cambridge depression. For I had experienced a much milder but still memorable sense of that bleakness after arriving as a student in the city in 1980. Newcastle United had visited soon afterwards to play the local team, in what I had hoped would bring a welcome reminder of home and triumphant demonstration of the footballing superiority of my club. It would, as I ruefully told Ewan, prove instead to be a foretaste of a very difficult decade for Newcastle, and football in general.

I had no recollection of the first defeat by Cambridge United in autumn 1980, other than the 2-1 result; perhaps some kind of benevolent memory filter was doing its best to protect me. But any such protection was limited. For I retained a far clearer recollection of a similarly dismal defeat the following second division season in February 1982. The reputation of football and its most unruly fans was, at that time, at a very low ebb. Outside the away end of the Abbey stadium the Cambridgeshire constabulary were in tense and sceptical mood. A self-professed Newcastle fan carrying bike lights and claiming to be a local student seemed to trigger alarm on their security profiling, and my lights were sternly confiscated as potential offensive weapons. Inside the ground my indignation merged into the Newcastle fans' mood in the deepening February gloom as our team laboured to a dismal 1-0 defeat.

Our team included a promising young player by the name of Chris Waddle. He should not have been bothered by that day's seasonal chill as he had been rescued from a life of sausage manufacture and part-time football when signed, for a reported £1000, from Tow Law Town, a high moorland club in County Durham reputed to have the coldest ground in England. (I have been to a game there and can report that the welcome is as warm as the winds are bracing.) Waddle's sullen body language, however, suggested that promotion to playing for Newcastle might also not be a joyous experience. It was, I joked later to Ewan, an omen, if only we had known. By the end of that decade we – together with multi-millions of England fans – would discover that while he was at times a brilliant player, bad Waddle body language could portend national disaster in an agonising penalty shoot-out against West Germany. And several decades later my longsuffering generation of Newcastle fans would also discover that shock defeats by Cambridge could continue to happen no matter how much money, and optimism, your club now had.

Newcastle's distinctly modest performances in the early 1980s did ironically match the painful discovery of my own distinctly second-rate footballing abilities. I had arrived at my Cambridge college, Christ's, hoping to become one of its football stars. But I swiftly realised that its first team was well above my level, moulded by an academic version of my cunning recruitment of school prefects. The team was coached by the head of modern languages, whose ideal candidate for annual college admission combined proficiency in irregular verbs with regular ability at goalscoring. Its star was Maurice Cox, who played professionally for Torquay United and admitted in TV interviews that his team-mates in the bus after matches were surprised to find him revising French poetry rather than playing cards. Faced with such superior levels of skill and élan, I had to settle mostly for the second eleven.

After Cambridge, and a year in the US almost entirely cut off from football (though, as I will explore in chapter 9, it gave me a first encounter with the potential of the women's game) I toyed briefly with the idea of an academic career. But a combination of pessimism about academia's future under government cutbacks and a desire to, somehow, be more at the centre of the political world then lured me in 1985 to a job in Westminster. From that vantage point I would watch football move from pariah through tragedy to new potential, but at a cost. Attending some of Newcastle United's visits to the capital during that period hinted at how the club, and football, was now caught up in wider turmoil.

In the Edwardian period, as the historians Richard Holt and Ray Physick record, Newcastle's football success had 'created self-confidence in a region far removed from London, the seat of parliament and monarchy and traditional bastion of culture, wealth and authority'. But games against London sides always 'gave a fresh lease of life to the north-south divide'. That divide seemed especially sensitive following the miners' strike between March 1984 and March 1985 when North East pit communities, their picket lines policed partly by reinforcements sent expensively from London, suffered what many in the region saw as a humiliating defeat. A sense of division had been reinforced too when movement between the region and the rest of the country had been crudely interrupted. I remember the shock of encountering roadblocks on the A1 as the police stopped and interrogated us, checking for flying pickets.

Mining had always had its emotional links with the North East's football clubs. One of Newcastle's greatest players, Jackie Milburn, recalled how local boys 'just disappeared into the ground to work for the rest of their lives as miners'. He had overcome his own claustrophobic fear of the dark and the danger to work early Saturday shifts down a pit, followed by a motorcycle ride to score goals at St James' Park. As recently as 1978 Alan Shoulder had suddenly emerged from night shifts in a County Durham pit to star in a cup run for Blyth Spartans and then become a much-loved Newcastle United forward. The rough treatment he received from robust defenders seemed trivial to someone whose previous working life had begun with a daily act of faith: 'You get into a cage that is going to drop 1,000 feet in about 50 seconds. If that bloke gets it wrong, you know you're dead'. The pits and other heavy industrial enterprises may have been a diminishing part of the North East's economy and society, but their workers and communities commanded a respect within the region that football fans echoed as they praised players who would always 'put in a shift'.

Newcastle United's fortunes in the 1980s had become as fragile and turbulent as the club's home region, facing all kinds of economic insecurity, social and political unrest. In the local press front page headlines desperately hoped for mines to be spared or shipyards revived, while the back pages yearned for a new era of United success. Such optimism had flared brightly in 1982 when Kevin Keegan, a miner's son, had arrived on the first of his messianic missions to rescue the club as a player, helping it return to the first division. But he left after two years and the momentum, like the local pits, swiftly disappeared from view, leaving only subterranean pride and defiance.

I was now observing much of this from afar but seizing moments to reconnect with my team when it visited London. Newcastle away games always prompted a gathering of the Northumbrian diaspora as so many had left their home region for work. Here are snapshots of my 1980s times following Newcastle in the capital, and what they revealed about the state not only of my club, but also of football itself.

QUEENS PARK RANGERS: PAINFUL POLICING

I had missed the previous season's Newcastle game at QPR in which the team's fragility had been woefully exposed. A Chris Waddle hat trick contributed to a 4-0 half-time lead; by the final whistle however the score was 5-5 and manager Jack Charlton called the second half performance 'a total embarrassment, absolutely diabolical....There are so many things wrong at Newcastle it is incredible'.

I was there for the same fixture in January 1986, as Newcastle succumbed to a tame 3-1 defeat. But it was what occurred afterwards that stuck far more in the mind. The away fans were kept in the ground while the home fans dispersed, and a large contingent of the Metropolitan police then formed a corridor through which the Newcastle fans were to be channelled on their way to the nearest underground station. (No provision was made for fans wanting to head in any other direction). The fans were mildly grumpy but resigned. Then some of the officers lining the street began to produce bundles of banknotes from their pockets, boasting that they had been earned as lucrative overtime policing during the pit strike in North East villages. Newcastle supporters were now incensed and I and my friends started to comment loudly on how the police were creating trouble out of nothing.

Suddenly two of us were hauled out of the crowd to be confronted by a Chief Inspector and threatened with arrest.

He was used, he said, to complaints by 'ignorant northerners' but could not stand 'f*!k*ng pseudo-intellectuals' criticising his men. It would have made for an interesting prosecution (I would of course have tried to argue that the use of 'pseudo' was an especially cruel form of regional prejudice). In the end we were shoved back into the crowd making its way home, the fans now far more resentful of police behaviour than their team's performance.

West Ham United: so bad it was good

Impotent anger had been the dominant emotion at QPR. Not long afterwards at West Ham United came an extraordinary display of resilience, defiance and simple good humour in the face of football adversity. It made out of an 8-1 defeat one of the most enjoyably memorable games I have ever been to. The West Ham goals started going in early and Newcastle players fell injured; it swiftly became clear this was just one of those days when the Fates were against the team, so there seemed little point in expressing disappointment or seeking to blame manager or referee. Defender Alvin Martin ended up scoring a hat trick against three different Newcastle goalkeepers, the last an emergency deployment of the 5' 8" Peter Beardsley which gave the final phase of the game the feel of the chaotic climax in a comic opera. And to match it all the Newcastle fans' singing intensified as every West Ham goal went in and continued into the half hour in which we were locked in the ground after the end, as bemused police officers looked on.

West Ham fans were generous in their admiration of such a display in defeat, which added to the sense of football community I had noticed when coming to the Docklands area of London regularly for five-a-side games with friends. We played next to a railway station romantically called Mudchute, but the pitches, and the old docklands community all around, were increasingly dwarfed by glitzy Canary Wharf developments racing upwards as a symbol of Thatcherite deregulation and financial services fever. Tyneside had plenty of former docklands and shipyard areas too, with their own struggling communities. But there was never any sign there of massed financial services HQs, fashionable cafes or eager yuppies riding to their rescue.

I was sad to hear later of West Ham's move from the old Upton Park to a stadium on another new east London redevelopment which, fans complained, sorely lacked a community atmosphere. How would you know such an atmosphere had returned? When your fans are still singing with rebellious joy at 8-1 down.

TOTTENHAM: A CRISIS OF FAITH

The worst day of my football supporting life came at Tottenham Hotspur in February 1987, at an FA Cup fifth round tie. It was a fairly even game, but Newcastle lost 1-0. The mood among fans was not helped by seeing Chris Waddle playing against us. His sale a few months before seemed to confirm an eternal truth of North East Life: that your finest creations, starting with the Lindisfarne Gospels via Stephenson's Rocket to the region's most talented footballers, would sooner or later be acquired by more affluent regions.

But what happened after the game had nothing to do with such historical grievances and made my mood far darker. There had been overcrowding inside the ground during the match, and some fans had to scale the metal fences that had been put in place to prevent pitch invasions – and which would later be the cause of appalling loss of life at in the Hillsborough tragedy. It is a memory now full of foreboding. But what would cause me immediate despair was the tension ratcheting up between belligerent Newcastle and Spurs fans as they came into closer contact.

As I walked away from the stadium after the game the north London street, full of Saturday afternoon shoppers and strollers, was suddenly overrun by gangs of rival fans in full chaotic combat. Women and children screamed, pushchairs were overturned, bottles were thrown and patches of blood could be seen on the pavements. Police officers were among those injured. Within minutes the rampage had passed through but left me with a deeply depressing feeling of shame. Association football seemed at that moment hopelessly associated with callous brutality, not any kind of caring community. And I knew the politicians were watching on.

WIMBLEDON: THE EMASCULATION OF GAZZA

We came in February 1988 to admire the latest stellar young Newcastle talent, a mercurial midfielder by the name of Paul Gascoigne. We left having witnessed a painful case study in the crushing of a football ego (and other sensitive things too). Plough Lane, home of Wimbledon FC, was a place known for agricultural defending and a fearsome team spirit that would bring a small unfashionable club some spectacular success, notably in that season's FA Cup. They had one player, Vinnie Jones, who saw it as his role to bring those of elevated reputation crashing down from their pedestals. The game lacked quality; 0-0 was always the likely result. Many in the crowd were drawn away from the lacklustre attempts by both sides to play flowing football, focusing instead on the war of midfield attrition between Gascoigne the would-be creative ball-player, and Jones who had very different ideas of what balls were for.

I cannot claim to have seen the moment immortalised by Monte Fresco's photo of Jones grasping Gascoigne's crotch, with the players' facial expressions eloquently expressing their respective determination and agony. But it certainly epitomised the afternoon's attrition well and hinted too at what would become one of the great and tragic running stories of English football: the hugely vulnerable genius of Gazza. Within months he became yet another high-profile talent transfer from the North East to London. And while Jones continued to ride confidently his fame in the capital on to a career as a TV and film star, Gazza would become the symbol of the naïve provincial party-boy who simply could not cope mentally with where his ability had taken him.

POLITICAL FOOTBALL

So those were some of my weekend and evening insights into one club's experience of the maelstrom of mid-1980s English football. During the week I was working at Westminster on the research staff of the House of Commons Library, specialising in international affairs. And well detached, one might assume, from the football world. In some ways, yes. Not much sport was discussed in the thickly carpeted and wood-lined rooms I occupied in the Palace of Westminster though the Whitehall fondness for referring to 'sticky wickets' and 'being on the front foot' hinted at the cultural dominance of cricket vocabulary in my new environment.

Part of my job was to scan the newspapers every morning and advise on the creation of a giant press-cuttings library on foreign affairs. My furtive glances at the back pages had to be disguised as far as possible. There was occasional joy at the discovery among my research materials of others who clearly suffered from my secret obsession. One day reading a sober article about the future of the Soviet economy in a distinguished think tank journal I suddenly came across this (to my mind) brilliant analogy:

'In my younger days I had the misfortune to support Newcastle United. The club had something in common with the Soviet Union. It was rich in natural resources, had a stirring decade under a ruthless and charismatic chairman and still had enormous pretensions; but team restructuring was undertaken by a series of indifferent managers, each one of whom was welcomed initially as a messiah.'

Ronald Amann was recalling standing on the windswept terraces of St James' Park as each new manager arrived, struck by the design of new strips, appreciating an increased work-rate 'but how one longed for the ball to hit the back of the net'. I'm not sure I had much luck persuading colleagues or MPs of the acuity of this analysis, but from then on I frequently thought of new Soviet leader Mikhail Gorbachev in the Newcastle dugout and wondered whether the club hierarchy would ever embrace the radical reform of *perestroika* or the public honesty of *glasnost*.

I did eventually discover the location of Westminster football enthusiasm, deep underground. In the pre-computer age the Commons Library held a vast quantity of paper documents relating especially to the United Nations and an organisation called the European Economic Community in which, at that time, few MPs took an active interest. It was another of my jobs as a new employee to descend into the basement of the Palace of Westminster to retrieve such documents, noticing as I went the worrying memos pasted on the wall explaining the evacuation procedure should the building be flooded by the Thames flowing alongside.

It was in these basement rooms that many of Westminster's key support staff were based, including technicians struggling to keep the largely unmodernised Palace safe from fire as well as flooding. (They are still there today.) There were also messengers responsible for moving around the mountains of papers and documents. Among these staff I swiftly discovered serious football expertise, and my journeys to retrieve obscure EEC documents on agricultural subsidies became suspiciously prolonged. When a Westminster five a side football tournament was announced the library's own support staff provided a superb core for our team and an impressive performance was assured – to the bemusement of the cricket-loving senior management.

There was, however, also a far more serious side to my encounter with football through the prism of Westminster.

There may not have been much personal interest in the game among many I worked with, but while I was there in the mid-1980s, football was becoming the focus of intense and hostile political attention. Historian David Goldblatt calls 1985 the 'nadir' of the game in England. A riot earlier in the year between Luton and Millwall fans had especially infuriated Margaret Thatcher, then at the height of her powers as prime minister. She was said to have watched footage of the rioting, initially broadcast live, over and over again. Thatcher had little or no personal interest in sport, but now focused on football as a threat to public order. As one of her biographers John Campbell observed: 'To Mrs Thatcher – as one of her colleagues who was interested in football noted – football fans, even when not rioting, were an alien breed, little better than striking miners, another face of the "enemy within".'

In May a fire at Bradford City's stadium, in which 56 fans died, exposed the appalling conditions of many grounds. The cause of the fire – rubbish accumulated underneath one of the stands – seemed grimly symbolic of the lethal complacency with which many clubs had been run. However, in the increasingly hostile media and political environment of the 1980s, the question of spectator safety attracted much less attention and sympathy than events highlighting some fans' misbehaviour. Weeks later in the Heysel disaster 39 mostly Italian fans died after a wall collapsed during rioting between Liverpool and Juventus fans at the European Cup final, leading to the banning of English teams from European competition for five years. Football, the *Sunday Times* declared, was now 'a slum sport played in slum stadiums increasingly watched by slum people'. Politically ambitious club owners like Chelsea's Ken Bates began to propose solutions such as electrified fencing around pitches, so that fans would be given a 'short, sharp shock' – the same language then being used about prison sentences. This football crisis now gave me a ringside seat in learning how public policy was sometimes made for understandable short-term reasons, but with catastrophic long-term consequences. My parliamentary pass as an 'Officer of the House' allowed me to stand at the back of the Commons chamber, where I could sense how political moods changed regardless of what was actually being said at the dispatch box. In similar vein I could see how such moods were reinforced well away from the public performance of politics in such crucial yet covert forums as the charged political atmosphere of the Commons tearoom.

The way football fans were now part of a deeper debate about the state of the country would be thrown into sharper relief for me in 1987 when my father-in-law, Tony Harrison, became embroiled in a media and political row over the publication and broadcast of his poem 'V'. He had written the poem after visiting his parents' grave in Leeds and seeing how it had been vandalised by aerosol-wielding fans on their way back from a match at the local football ground, Elland Road.

Tony's relationship with football had never been close. In childhood, he told me, his father had taken him to the cinema to enjoy James Cagney films but disappeared regularly on his own to watch Leeds United. Rugby league had become Tony's sport, reinforced perhaps by the cultural success of a local professional player, playwright and novelist David Storey. After moving to Newcastle in the late 1960s he had observed in a poem called Divisions the combination of braggadocio and vulnerability among tattooed local football fans.

> When next he sees United lose a match
> His bovvers on, his scarf tied round his wrist
> His rash NEWCASTLE RULES will start to scratch
> He'll aerosol the walls, then go get pissed...
>
> So I hope the TRUE LOVE on your arm stays true,
> The MOTHER on your chest stays loved, not hated
> But most I hope for jobs for all of you –
> Next year your tattooed team gets relegated!

Now, in the mid-1980s, Tony had written with a mixture of despair and deep sympathy in his poem 'V' about the Leeds fans whose team also lost regularly and who vented their frustrations on local memorials in his birthplace.

> Which makes them lose their sense of self-esteem
> and taking a short cut through these graves here
> they reassert the glory of their team
> by spraying words on tombstones, pissed on beer.

The Leeds (and Newcastle) club name, 'United', should have been about bonding. But football often seemed at that time to reflect division more than unity. Reflecting on the view as he looked in different directions from his family's graveyard high above Leeds city centre, Tony observed:

> the places I'd learned Latin, and learned Greek,
> and left the places where Leeds United play
> but disappoint their fans week after week.

There again was the idea that a grammar school, Classical education took you away from the football terraces to more elevated pursuits. But the letter V the Leeds fans often graffitied stood, Tony believed, for so much more in their lives and society than just football frustration.

> These Vs are all the versuses of life
> From LEEDS v. DERBY, Black/White
> And (as I've known to my cost) man v. wife
> Communist v. Fascist, Left v. Right

The poem went on to imagine a dialogue between him and one of the hooligans resenting all the jobs remembered on the gravestones to which he could not aspire. The dialogue contained multiple expletives and when the poem was about to be broadcast on Channel 4, the *Daily Mail* led its front page with the headline 'FOUR LETTER TV POEM FURY'. It warned its readers that the poem 'uses football hooligan slang' and quoted an outraged Tory MP describing Harrison as 'another probable Bolshie poet seeking to impose his frustrations on the rest of us'.

Many expressing outrage had not read the poem itself. Tony asked a *Daily Telegraph* reporter doorstepping him in Newcastle whether he had read it. 'Oh no, I'm news' was the indignant reply. The columnist Bernard Levin, revered by many Tory MPs, wrote a column in the Times praising 'V' as 'one of the most powerful, profound and haunting long poems of modern times'. But that kind of defence had limited political impact; this row was fuelled by football's now dire political reputation. At Westminster I was aware in the tea room of the simple ability of words like 'football hooligan', and 'obscenity' to feed an immediate demand for action.

What was unmistakeable in the mid-80s was the rise in relation to football of a wave of that formidable but dangerous political force: 'somethingmustbedone-ery', the demand, often under intense media pressure, that governments or indeed oppositions must propose swift action without much time spent thinking through potential long-term consequences. On the urgent need for improved ground safety, so horrifically exposed by the Bradford fire, I should perhaps not have been surprised that Parliament, operating out of an unmodernised Westminster building whose basements were crammed with fire hazards due to decades of complacency and negligence, would fail to act decisively. Most politicians were focused far more on public order rather than fan safety. And out of that, as I explored later in a BBC radio documentary, came the decision to build around the terraces tall metal fences, a kind of caging, to prevent pitch invasions such as that seen at Luton.

I discovered how there had been repeated enquiries into deaths at grounds due to crushing and similar problems since the early twentieth century, but nothing substantial had been done. Cosy relationships between local inspectors and clubs did not help. It also never occurred to those initiating the policy that fencing around the Bradford pitch would have led to many more deaths in that fire. One of the Thatcher government's sports ministers, Sir Neil Macfarlane, told me: 'I don't think we ever approached it in a very scientific way.' The imperative instead was 'reach out for a series of actions to be taken this day'. He admitted to me that he had never actually visited a fenced-in stadium.

The Hillsborough disaster of 1989 would prove how such fencing could pose a lethal danger as fans attempted to escape crushing. It caused the loss of 97 Liverpool supporters' lives. An official enquiry was led by Lord Justice Taylor, educated at my school in Newcastle and someone who, like me, had enjoyed as a teenager the St James' Park terraces. He described 'a general malaise or blight' over our national game 'due to a number of factors. Principally these are: old grounds, poor facilities, hooliganism, excessive drinking and poor leadership'. Taylor's report now led to the transformation of football's governance and economics and the creation of the Premier League.

'Complacency is the enemy of safety' was one of Taylor's most resonant conclusions. The new Premier League, with its transformed all-seater grounds, might have seemed like the product of a considered, enlightened commercial and technocratic decision with benevolent political supervision. But we should never forget, as I concluded in my documentary, that 'football's expensive transformation is built on foundations of grief and guilt'.

Finding World Football

My three years at Westminster were a fascinating political education but I was impatient, after a while, to escape its confines. It was, in theory, the 'centre of things' yet seemed in other ways frustratingly insulated from the wider world. Journalism and broadcasting in particular had long fascinated me and I applied to join the BBC World Service.

There are two things I recall about the interview. Asked to prepare a review of a radio programme beforehand I had chosen one about brain surgery, little suspecting that one day such surgery would play such an acute role in my family's life. The second moment I remember is one of the interviewers stating simply that: 'the best thing about this job is that you are paid to be curious about everything'. 'Hallelujah!' I felt myself responding inwardly and saw that as my new motto when I was fortunate enough to be selected. Curiosity about football too in all its reverberations would be fed by my new journalistic life.

As a World Service trainee, I was sent for several months in 1989 to Belfast. Not exactly exotic globetrotting, but I became fascinated by the contested identities of this place at the tail end of its terrible Troubles. It was part of my country, the UK, yet was as I swiftly discovered a place that most in Britain barely understood. The location that most absorbed me was Londonderry – or, depending on your identity, Derry – which seemed to dramatize the history, tragedy and yet defiant potential of Northern Ireland more than anywhere. And, as I slowly came to realise in subsequent visits, there was an extraordinary football subculture here too. Watching a march by the Protestant Apprentice Boys I saw the familiar bowler hats and Orange sashes, but among many younger men Rangers shirts were de rigeur, a proud association with the fiercely sectarian identity of Scottish football.

Their bitter opponents on the streets from a nationalist background often sported Celtic shirts. But in the traditionally Catholic area of the town next to the Irish border a local club, Derry City, was engaged in its own powerful and more subtle assertion of identity. Almost closed down by the Troubles, it had revived its fortunes in 1985 by joining the Republic of

Ireland's Irish League despite being located on the territory of Northern Ireland. Aided by players enterprisingly recruited from as far afield as Yugoslavia and South Africa, the club had won a treble of Irish titles and was about to host Benfica, no less, in European competition. I gradually sensed in my visits there that beneath the headlines of bombs and shootings there were often deeper currents to be seen in Derry flowing towards a different future. While football had been dragged at times into the worst of the Troubles, in other ways it had hinted at other ways of shaping the whole island's future. When I looked down from the ramparts of the old Protestant bastion to the Bogside I could see plenty of evidence of violent polarisation and knew the history of terrible events there like Bloody Sunday. But Derry City's Brandywell stadium somehow seemed to soften the harsh edges of this traumatised landscape.

Back in London I joined a department bearing the old-fashioned BBC title of 'talks writers' whose job it was to prepare material on each day's news for the World Service's multiple foreign language broadcasts. It was a department shaped overwhelmingly by the evolution of the Cold War, and the Soviet empire. In each morning's meeting I sat and listened to intense discussion of developments in, say, Kazakhstan, Estonia or Bulgaria which the department's veterans would then agree to write about. There seemed little space amongst this most erudite of journalism for football enthusiasm. But even here I eventually discovered – albeit restrained and somewhat hidden – that the top specialist on far-flung Soviet republics was also a passionate fan of Leyton Orient; and that a mysterious senior writer too grand to attend morning meetings was obsessed with two things: US congressional politics, and Arsenal FC.

My final training attachment was to a part of the World Service with a vastly different culture but with its own unique football enthusiasm: the BBC African Service. Bonding with my new boss was immediate when, noticing my Newcastle United scarf, he asked whether I was an admirer of Billy

Whitehurst. Whitehurst was a player characteristic of the United team of that era, an ex-hod carrier and now striker whose style was, shall we say, robust. The famous Liverpool defender and TV pundit Alan Hansen called him one of the players 'who frightened me most'. Whitehurst's footballing skills were not extensive. I remember hearing one exasperated fan suggest that he 'couldn't trap a bag of cement'. But he was nonetheless a cult figure for many supporters including those of his previous club, Hull City, which my new boss supported.

So from now on, to the bafflement of BBC colleagues, whenever we met in corridor, lift or canteen we would look at each other, express the words 'Billy Whitehurst', and shake our heads knowingly. No further comment was needed but colleagues listening in must have wondered whether this individual obsessing us was perhaps an emergent world leader or a mysterious political codename.

The main programme I worked on was *Network Africa* – a fantastically un-BBC combination of Radios 4 (news), Radio 1 (much West African high-life music) and sport. At one point my job was to work late shifts taking in reports recorded on quarter inch tape from the continent's football reporters as African teams strove to qualify for the World Cup. The phone lines to, say, Kinshasa or Nairobi were often patchy but the reporters cut through with their wonderfully exuberant style as every goal was described with amplified ecstasy. I sensed from our audiences how huge was the African interest in world football. And I began to find football spreading its influence in the most unexpected places. The first documentary I made for the BBC involved a trip to Sweden to investigate tensions in its post-war social and political model. Among the causes of debate was large scale migration from Africa, with some Swedes saying they saw little chance of successful integration. But there were exceptions. In a small town near Gothenburg I found a community of Eritreans who had escaped the famine and conflict then affecting large parts of the Horn of Africa.

They said that it was difficult to adjust to local culture and tradition and meet Swedes. Yet football, a truly shared culture, was already helping; and one day my own English club would benefit. For among the Eritreans then arriving in Sweden were the parents of one Alexander Isak who would later become one of the finest players I ever saw in a Newcastle United shirt. The club would also recruit Anthony Elanga, born in Sweden to a Cameroonian father.

And in 1990 it was Cameroon that was my focus in BBC programmes I produced. They progressed towards qualification for the World Cup in Italy, and our African reporters' excitement grew infectiously. I was delighted when, in their first game in Italy, they shocked the World Cup holders Argentina. The dancing celebrations of veteran striker Roger Milla and endearingly laid-back goalkeeping of Thomas N'Kono encapsulated a new style of football which I admired so much that when Cameroon faced England in the quarter finals, I was genuinely torn, not wanting to lose either team from the tournament. England prevailed – just – and then came the semi-final against West Germany. For a Newcastle fan, the England team felt gratifyingly familiar, yet also prompted unsettling anxiety. It was managed by a boyhood fan of our team, Bobby Robson, and contained three players we had all watched blossom at Newcastle and then leave: Chris Waddle, Peter Beardsley and Paul Gascoigne.

Gathered in a friend's London flat we observed anxiously through our special Toon-tinted low-expectation lenses as Gascoigne, the man of endless talent and vulnerability, brought England so close to victory yet starred in his own personal tragedy. He was booked and burst into tears, knowing he would have missed the final. And then, with the score level after extra time, came the dreaded penalties. The Germans moved ruthlessly ahead; Chris Waddle was next up for England and had to score. We were probably not the only ones among the millions who opted to retreat behind the sofa. Those of us who had known the Waddle body language since the early 1980s felt his huge football ability was sometimes suppressed by some deep kind of personal doubt. Or it often looked that way. His shoulders were as disconsolately hunched as they had been on a cold Cambridge afternoon a decade or so before, his expression looked beleaguered, and his left foot sent the ball well over the German crossbar.

Despite this disappointment, I remember telling Ewan that the 1990 World Cup had lifted the spirits of English football fans in so many ways: a soaring *Nessun Dorma* soundtrack suggested transcendence of the awful disasters of the 1980s and the relentlessly depressing sound of violent conflict, catastrophe and sustained political and media hostility. In one of the most improbable encounters of the era, Gazza was even seen embracing Mrs Thatcher at a 10 Downing Street reception as her husband, rugby referee Denis, looked on in bemusement. In his autobiography, Gazza claims that he asked Thatcher 'is it ok, pet, if I put my arm round you?' while saying of Denis 'your security bloke doesn't look too happy'. Not exactly a meeting of minds but compared with the visceral hostility to all things football I had seen in mid 1980s Westminster, it represented a kind of redemption.

And I was less bothered than most of my fellow English fans that we had lost to our 'old enemy', the Germans. For alongside my increasing absorption into Newcastle and British football was another strand that would shape my life, and my relationship with Ewan. It was about football in another place, with another mentality: Germany itself. And what I value now more and more as I grieve is how the game there has been part of the great transcendence of the most appalling history, both national and personal. The Germans have a special relationship with grief, and with football, from which I have been lucky enough to learn.

4

FUSSBALL

BRAZIL HAD BEEN MY FIRST international football heroes in 1970; Germany began that year as my demons. For the TV broadcast of the World Cup quarter-final in Mexico I had, in the spirit of burgeoning trade union power in Britain, negotiated with my vicar father an early release from Evensong in Croydon Parish Church for football-fanatical choirboys. All seemed blessed as England raced into a 2-0 lead, but then in a chastening early taste of how games can change capriciously the West Germans struck back to level the score.

On to extra time and an even greater personal shock: an extended game seemed to my parents to be an unwelcome surprise, an unknown concept, and an unacceptable threat to already stretched bedtime discipline. I was dismissed upstairs as the whistle blew for 90 minutes and had my first experience of that superstition common to many fans: that a result is somehow the fault of something you do that can have nothing to do with players or pitch but just seems, as far as you are concerned, to make you responsible and the loss even harder to bear. After hearing the result next morning I was convinced that my absence had meant Gerd Müller was bound to score the winner; and so my first resentful encounter with the footballing curse of Germany versus England was complete.

In time, however, I would come to know a lot more about Germany, its people, and the role *Fussball* plays, and has played, in their life. Unlike my falling for Newcastle, however, this was less about going to matches or supporting specific teams. It was more about learning to notice how the game was significant in everything from national memory to local community to architecture. And, of course, in that relationship with England, where the game had become tragically enmeshed with the trauma of war. When I became older and more deeply absorbed in Germany's language, culture, and distinctive football world I slowly realised why this antagonism had run so deep.

FRIENDS OR FOES?

As a boy I had little initial appreciation of how Anglo-German football rivalry was layered onto much more profound tension. In January 1973, arriving at my new school after moving to Newcastle upon Tyne, I entered the main building with my older brother and sat in its imposing hall. Having come from a term at a newly built school in south London, full of glass and light, what struck me first was the gloomy atmosphere and furniture in the main hall: heavy, wooden and dark, with lively, argumentative boys playing mysterious games involving shoving coins around long, uncomfortable benches. Then I glanced up at the stage where morning assembly took place; or rather mourning assembly. It was dominated by a 'memorial organ' inscribed with the names of the school's dead in two world wars. In raised letters below the organ pipes were the words: *Dulce et Decorum Est Pro Patria Mori* (It is Sweet and Proper to Die for One's Country). Every school day began, for those who chose to think about it, with a reminder of 274 former pupils who had mostly been killed fighting Germans.

Not that we ever did think or learn much about all that in our studies. This was a grammar school with some terrific teachers but still stuck, in many ways, in the mould of a Victorian academy for aspiring gentlemen. We were fed plenty of Roman military history as our Latin teacher, who doubled up as an officer in the Combined Cadet Corps, urged us heartily to 'bash on' with studying Caesar's *De Bello Gallico*. *'Dulce et Decorum'* was not one of our translation exercises; only later did I learn what it meant, and how Wilfred Owen's poem had begun to change the phrase's resonance just as this school memorial was being constructed in the early 1920s.

As for German history we duly absorbed Caesar's descriptions of Germanic barbarians and then leapt forward in time to study a few German subjects – Luther and the Reformation, as well as Bismarck and nineteenth-century diplomacy. For the 'O' level exam we attempted to memorise the intricacies of the Schleswig-Holstein dispute between Germany and Denmark in the 1860s. Good preparation, perhaps, for those of us who hoped to enter the Diplomatic Service but hardly contemporary. As Lord Palmerston famously put it: 'The Schleswig-Holstein question is so complicated, only three men in Europe have ever understood it. One was Prince Albert, who is dead. The second was a German professor who became mad. I am the third and I have forgotten all about it.' In our school we learned and then forgot about it in large numbers. (Or at least I did until many years later when a passionate fan of Hamburg Altona football club told me the one of the reasons that his district was so distinctive was because it had been Danish-run until, wait for it, the 1860s!) But our school historical studies never went beyond 1914, the moment when the British Empire in which so many old boys had prospered passed its zenith and the first of those two deadly conflicts with Germany began.

Otherwise, my childhood impressions of modern Germans came from a curious but characteristic mixture of sources for a 1970s British boy. Most easily available were war films and comics in which blond beasts shouted *'Achtung Schweinhund'* before being defeated by British and American soldiers. The imagery was little changed from wartime propaganda publications in which plucky Brits heroically defused bombs impertinently dropped on their playing fields or, armed with little more than cricket stumps, defeated wicked Nazis.

And when it came to German footballers there were subtler but equally pervasive stereotypes I could absorb from the British media. German wins – especially against England – were attributed more to their players' 'typical' hard work, discipline and organisation, rather than flair or skill: a sporting expression, perhaps, of the combination of admiration, envy and angst with which many Brits viewed West Germany's post-war economic success. As the German coach Helmut Schön had put it after another West German win in 1972, England 'seemed to have stood still in time' while the Germans were now 'far superior technically'. *Vorsprung durch Technik* could seem painfully visible on international football pitches as well as in car showrooms.

It was probably assumed by many however that my generation would leave all such old rivalry and tension behind, embracing a new European identity. I still have my version of a primary school essay we had written on 'Decimalisation Day' in 1971, a moment when, our teacher informed us, we should celebrate being part of the first 'metric generation'. Moving on from inches and shillings would help prepare us for impending British membership of the European Economic Community. I wasn't exactly entering into that spirit, however, as my essay stated that I had spent a good part of the day reading Paul Brickhill's account of the 1943 Dambusters raid on Germany.

It was hardly surprising that epic tales of military success were more appealing to a young boy than new weights and measures or something called the Common Market. I became a keen maker of models of Second World War aircraft, ships and tanks, and fought extended wargaming battles with my older brother Rick in which he took the German side and I the Anglo-American. He won constantly due to his superior tactical nous and knowledge of wartime weaponry; my frustration drove me to look for what I hoped would be the best defence against this repeated humiliation: history. Off I went to the local library and returned with volumes by Winston Churchill and others as I attempted to discover proof that, in the end, the Germans were the losers. Along the way my teenage viewing progressed from war films and *Dad's Army* to the extraordinary TV documentary series *The World at War*. I began to sense the enormity of what Nazi Germany had done in the Holocaust, and that the eventual defeat the Germans had suffered was about far more than armed forces and battlefields. Moreover its consequences – including a brutally divided country – were still visible, still shaped lives and lurked in millions of memories.

How, though, could a young Brit begin to appreciate the human side of modern Germany's past? My schooling did give me one essential tool: a start in speaking the language. Learning German also led to the offer of a school exchange, my first travel abroad. As far as most of my contemporaries were concerned, this was not a popular option. Whereas Berlin or Munich might be seen today as some of the coolest destinations in Europe, in the 1970s few went to Germany from Britain unless they had to. And certainly not to our destination: the heavy industrial town of Gelsenkirchen in the Ruhr. It was Newcastle upon Tyne's twin town, chosen presumably because it was assumed exchange visitors would feel at home amidst each other's landscapes of coal mining, steel, and chemicals. Arriving in 1975 there was plenty of superficial familiarity in, say, the winding gear of coal mines or the snaking networks of overground pipes alongside roads, just like those that had dominated the view in my birthplace on Teesside.

Yet the *Ruhrgebiet* or Ruhr region was a really good place to begin understanding one of the paradoxes of West Germany's people: that they seemed to be enjoying a hugely successful modern society, despite having emerged a few decades before from unimaginable chaos and horror. While there we were ostensibly bonding with our German hosts in the spirit of European integration but nationalism still lurked mischievously as we played fiercely competitive games of football against our hosts. We were taken to see the local professional team, Schalke 04, who had built mining culture into their identity in a way that Tynesiders could readily appreciate. Schalke's opponents for that friendly game in 1975 gave me another intriguing new taste of football's international reach. Dukla Prague came from the Czechoslovak capital in which I would one day live. But their deeply compromised Cold War history – later affecting one of my favourite Newcastle players, Pavel Srniček – was as yet unknown to me. I was slowly learning however about something called the Iron Curtain. It even surfaced in the first football book I acquired – *Soccer My Battlefield* by Nobby Stiles, a jumble sale bargain – which included intriguing accounts of Nobby attending nightclubs with Manchester United team-mates in East Berlin after European matches. And that city would become the focus of my full engagement with Germany, its history and its sporting inheritance a few years later.

I left school in 1979 with a place secured for the following year to study history at Cambridge. Before then, however, a year off before university would plunge me into a very different kind of education: about the personal history of the twentieth century, with conflict between Britain and Germany at its centre. In my first post-school job, as a social services decorator in Newcastle, that history emerged in the form of conversations with the old people whose homes we were renovating, and sometimes simultaneously revealing their hidden history. The day I remember best was in one of the terraced houses built on the steep banks of the Tyne in Scotswood, near to what had been the huge engineering and armaments factory founded by the great Victorian inventor and entrepreneur William Armstrong. We began our redecoration by removing all the existing covering from the small house's damp walls. It became a form of interior archaeology, as the layers revealed different kinds of materials from different eras and the abiding poverty of the house's occupants. The final, oldest layers were simply newspaper as there had clearly once been residents there who had no money for wallpaper or had used newspaper as extra insulation while trying to stay warm.

The lonely elderly man who lived there joined us in reading scraps of the newspapers we removed. Some mentioned football, prompting him to reminisce about the streams of men who would finish early shifts at Armstrong's on a Saturday and then head up the hill, via numerous local pubs, towards St James' Park. The emergence of Newcastle United as a major football power had coincided with Tyneside's booming arms production. The club's first league title in 1905 came in the same year that the Japanese navy, many of its battleships and guns supplied by Armstrong's, won a spectacular victory over Russia; Japanese sailors later visited St James' Park to celebrate the connection, with their anthem played before the match. Armstrong's had also established a naval and gun-making outpost at Pozzuoli near Naples, and I've always liked to think that the Tynesiders and others who went to work there may have had something to do with the emergence of that Italian city's passionate and creative football culture.

But the man whose home we were decorating had much more sombre memories too. He recounted that he had been working in these streets as a young boy in summer 1914, selling the newspapers that announced the outbreak of the First World War. Most of the people he had talked to that day were cheered by the news as it promised more jobs in munitions. As the war continued, however, and losses among local recruits to the armed forces grew heavy, the mood changed. Some of the other lads he knew were Post Office boys who had the awful task of delivering telegrams to homes announcing that their sons had been 'killed in action'. Neighbours watched with gnawing anxiety as they approached; the boys would knock on a door, make their dreaded delivery and move swiftly on, trying to escape the searing sounds of shock and grief as their messages were opened.

After a few months of this archaeological decorating I left Tyneside and moved on to another job – the one that would turn my growing interest in Germany into a lifelong personal and professional focus. I had applied for a Youth Exchange programme sending Brits and Germans to work in each other's countries and was given a job in West Berlin. Setting off via the North Sea ferry to Hook of Holland, I then took a long train journey east. On the first part of the route were familiar voices: unemployed Geordie building workers, later to be made famous in the TV series *Auf Wiedersehen, Pet*, heading for German sites, and also British army personnel. The British army of occupation in Germany, with its own BFBS radio station, would become my means of keeping up with English football results and commentary. That kind of link seemed reassuring once I realised I was moving to a strange, tense, Cold War island as my train trundled through communist East Germany and I entered the part of Berlin still occupied by British, US and French forces, surrounded by the Berlin Wall.

By the time my application to the Youth Exchange had been accepted the only work available was as a nurse in an old people's home; but that proved to be a blessing. While others headed for, say, multilingual schools or travel agencies my new place of work in a working-class Berlin suburb had virtually no English speakers, yet was full of extraordinary people and memories. I made good progress in speaking German as the old people were enthusiastic if exacting teachers and took special delight in affectionately mocking my mistakes while encouraging my Berlin accent and mastery of the impish distinctive local humour or *Berliner Schnauze*. Most importantly, I steadily began to win their trust, so that in conversations as I cleaned their washbasins or changed their bedsheets all kinds of personal histories would emerge. I was assigned to wards containing German men who had lived through one or both World Wars, the Great Depression, the Third Reich, and the Cold War division of their city. Casual conversation about their lives, their pasts, could never come easily where so much trauma and guilt lurked. I began to learn that such highly sensitive silence had, for many in these German generations, become a kind of instinctive reflex or survival mechanism when living with the crushing weight of what they had done or experienced.

There was one subject that often broke the ice: football. Yet even these memories were often shrouded in terrible history. There was the man who remembered games played while serving on the Eastern Front, and who later told me of the massacres he had witnessed; the Jewish survivor of death camps who never talked about that but readily recalled great players from his community in pre-war German and Austrian football; the younger man who remembered growing up amidst post-war rubble and hunger, and how the 1954 West German World Cup win had been the first time he could ever feel patriotic pride.

My oldest charge, a man in his nineties, had advanced dementia and often could not recall what he had had for lunch. But his long-term memory was, by contrast, sharp; he lived mentally and vividly in his adolescent world as a young First World War German army recruit. I needed to use military language, staff members explained, to reassure him as I shaved him each morning. And he too sometimes mentioned sport as part of the wartime life his mind could never escape.

TRENCH FOOTBALL

These living links with the World War generations were much on my mind when I returned to Britain and began academic study of history. While I tried to absorb the grand sweep of textbook narratives as I prepared weekly essays, I craved too the small human details. And one of the subplots I began to follow was how, when it came to Germany and Britain, football had been present even in the most terrible of twentieth-century circumstances. Researching the military history of the First World War I came across a haunting image in John Keegan's famous work *The Face of Battle*. He described a unit of the Northumberland Fusiliers known as the Tyneside Commercials who were charging across deadly no man's land on the first day of the Somme offensive in 1916. This was a unit which many young men who had been to my Newcastle school had joined. 'As they got out of their trenches,' Keegan recorded, they were 'following a football kicked by a well-known north country player.' It was the spirit of football that officers hoped would inspire their men to martial glory. The reality was more as recorded in a quotation from the *Newcastle Evening Chronicle*'s coverage of the fiftieth anniversary of the Somme when a medical officer from the Tyneside Scottish regiment looked across no man's land after the battle and said: 'It's just as though they'd shot up the crowd going to see Newcastle United.'

Later, in the war diary of the Northumbrian Brigade, I found unsparing description of what they had faced in, say, the Ypres salient: '... no green thing remained. Fifty square miles of filth and mud, from which every shell that burst threw up ghastly relics.' And yet regular references to football were inserted almost casually, as if in desperate attempt to preserve some sense of normality amidst the hell. Bavarian troops facing them in the trenches teased with calls to 'buck up Newcastle United'. One morning the brigade was 'roused by a distant cannonade which increased in fury as the day grew' but 'nevertheless, football went on'.

The fate of the many thousands of young men who died has painful new resonance for me now, facing the loss of my son. Among those killed at the Somme was Dan Dunglinson, born in what is now my hometown of Hexham in Northumberland, a railway clerk who had been recruited as a centre forward for Newcastle United before enlisting. He was 26 years old, and his body was never found. I discovered that every Remembrance Day in the village of Authuille near the Somme a box is opened containing replica football shirts, including one bearing his name. Reading such accounts makes me think too of my maternal grandfather, Robert Monro, who died before I was born but had been an army chaplain during the Somme offensive in units largely recruited from the East End of London. Had they too defiantly brought football into their muddy, fearful and deadly wartime world? I have sometimes tried to imagine what that trauma must have meant for him and his faith.

Now all the death that my school had commemorated as *dulce et decorum* had a much sharper focus for me, as did the difficulty of promoting Anglo-German reconciliation after the loss and pain of two world wars. I had also absorbed my father's story of how, as a teenage recruit in the British army of occupation in Germany in 1945, he had seen the mostly ruined city of Cologne, with the spires of its cathedral still standing. 'Suddenly' he remembered, he 'had a strong awareness of the appalling waste of all this conflict. I knew then that I wanted to do something with my life that might lessen the violence and hatred in the world in some small way'.

That spirit of reconciliation still seemed in short supply when I first came to know Germany, some decades later. In the 1970s and 1980s as English football grappled with its hooligan demons, a minority delighted in using matches against the 'old enemy' to recycle every kind of cliché about warlike, robotic Germans. Songs celebrating bombing were sung, and the media enjoyed using Blitz headlines and picturing England players in tin helmets. Whatever the noise from the terraces, meanwhile, the England team often found itself outplayed by its German rivals. Even when England's players seemed more competitive, such as in that 1990 World Cup semi-final, Chris Waddle's penalty misery seemed to confirm that this was fated to remain the most difficult of territory for England fans.

By then, however, Germany itself was in the midst of the most astonishing change as the Cold War ice suddenly melted. My main football memory of that miraculous first summer after the removal of the Iron Curtain came from a bizarre game I played in Vienna. Disappearing borders suddenly offered new opportunities for mingling in sport as in every other area of life. And for the football fan too, a new era seemed possible, the rediscovery of how the game could unite rather than divide and sustain a culture of community and celebration. My father-in-law Tony Harrison had followed his powerful and controversial mid-1980s poem 'V' about the nihilistic despair of Leeds United football fans with a new play, *The Trackers of Oxyrhynchus*. It was based on the discovery in papyrus fragments of an ancient Greek satyr play and dramatized the never-ending battle between ideas of 'high' and 'low' art. In Classical literature satyrs had been half-human, half-animal characters with a lust for life who had their own cultural aspirations yet were seen as vulgar and threatening by the keepers of high culture.

At the centre of Tony's cast was a chorus of actors billed as 'fellaheen (labourers)/satyrs/football hooligans', who clog-danced, drank copiously and sported enormous phalluses, but were put firmly in their place by the God Apollo:

> The scale of creation like a scale with notes
> Runs the whole gamut from gods to goats,
> And distinctly closer to the latter,
> Low on the scale of being, comes the satyr
> Earthbound in the way you dance and drink
> Goatish in your instinct and your stink.

Such Apollonian cultural disdain sounded not unlike the kind of abuse English football fans had been receiving in the 1980s as a minority's bad behaviour grew. When the satyrs were forbidden to play Apollo's lyre they became aerosolling hooligans, setting fire to the papyrus. As I talked to Tony and understood more about the play I saw that he was also thinking about a subject close to my heart. He wanted to challenge the idea that the arts and sport were somehow in opposition or mutually incomprehensible, that football could not, in its way, lay claim to culture, be it great drama, popular poetry or operatic passion. His play had its extraordinary premiere in the ancient open-air stadium in Delphi in Greece. And the use of a stadium rather than a theatre was deliberate, as Tony wrote in his introduction:

> 'I resolved to dispense with the platform and use the entire stadium space. This helped to dramatize a contemporary division in our culture between sport and art. In the Pythian Games with its athletics and flute contests, poetry and drama, held on this site, such a division would have been incomprehensible. As would the division between tragedy and satyr play, "high" art and "low" art. And in honour of our ancient wholeness we performed our piece, and we became Ichneutae, "Trackers" seeking in fragments of our past and present a common wholeness, a common illumination, a common commitment to survival.'

The play was staged again near Vienna in May 1990 and on the day after the performance the actors playing the satyrs, somewhat hungover, had time to spare. In keeping with Tony's ideas, sport seemed like a good way to follow their theatrical performance. Many of them were working class English northerners and accomplished footballers; a former school friend of mine now at the British Embassy in Vienna said he knew of diplomats who could provide an opposition. It turned out that they were the staff of the local East German embassy, representatives of a country, the communist German Democratic Republic, which I had visited regularly while living in Berlin. In that summer of 1990 the GDR still technically existed but was swiftly being superseded by the emerging reunified German state.

As we chatted after the game these diplomats, previously

the most secretive of Cold War operators, spoke with open bewilderment about how their jobs were disappearing, and wondered what they would now do. But they were grateful for a game of international football that suggested they would not be seen by all westerners as pariahs. The satyrs, after all, knew what it was like to be permanently excluded. I thought of those bewildered eastern Germans a few weeks later when the team making its last appearance as West Germany beat England on penalties and then went on to win the World Cup itself. It was clear that in football, as well as in everything else, the western Germans were still very much taking the lead.

RELATIVES AND RECONCILIATION

And football would also have its uses as the new reunified Germany sought to prove that it was not a new threat, but had moved decisively on from the terrible past and wanted to complete reconciliation with wartime enemies. My son Ewan, born in the 1990s, would become fascinated with that idea of reconciliation, beginning with discovery of his own family's German roots. My wife's grandfather, Herbert Dietzsch, a market gardener, had been a communist in 1930s Germany, was imprisoned by the Gestapo after the Nazis took power, and had then escaped and made his way via Czechoslovakia and Poland to Britain. After the war he returned to 'build socialism' in the new East Germany, where we visited him during the Cold War, but he became increasingly disillusioned by the sterility of Soviet occupation.

With the Berlin Wall down he made his way to visit us in Britain, and we also took Ewan and his siblings on a return visit to Herbert's home in Zwickau. With his mischievous humour defying old age and all he had suffered, great-grandfather or *Uropa* Herbert swiftly became a family favourite. My children absorbed through that link that the idea of all Germans being somehow bad or fascistic or anti-British could not be true. My daughter Laura went on to study German at university and play cello at a Leipzig conservatoire; Ewan sang German music and followed German football with enthusiastic interest as did my other son Alfie, who with characteristic individuality adopted 1 FC Köln – and its mascot goat – as one of his favourite teams.

We established another family link with Germany when I made a BBC programme about an extraordinary story of post-war reconciliation in a village near the southern town of Pforzheim. After the area had suffered huge loss of life in a 'firestorm' air raid in 1945, several RAF aircrew who had bailed out were lynched a few days later. But decades afterwards the villagers sought forgiveness, and the pilot of the plane whose crew had been murdered, together with another of the crew who had escaped the lynching, began to visit the village and bond with its people over their shared wartime suffering.

I became close friends with a Pforzheim couple who had fostered the reconciliation, Renate and Gotthilf, and they in turn adopted Laura and Ewan as honorary godchildren. When Ewan went to visit he had long conversations with Gotthilf embracing the extraordinary contrasts in his life: how he had served as a German soldier on the eastern front near Moscow in 1942, surrounded by tanks and facing a Russian winter without much food or clothing. He had somehow survived, became a British POW later in the war and then returned to Pforzheim, where he saw its bombed devastation as a punishment for his compatriots' pre-war Nazi enthusiasm. Then he had become an artist, his creations out of shattered and re-formed glass capturing light in defiance of darkness.

And so as Ewan became a football fan and faced England-Germany encounters he was always going to find the old hype and casual hostility somewhat puzzling. Equally puzzling, I should confess, must have been my anxious paternal attempts to pass on my own deep pessimism, ingrained since 1970, about how such matches would go. The first full encounter we watched together on TV was the World Cup qualifier in Munich in 2001. Seeking to pre-empt his likely disappointment I suggested soothingly beforehand that the almost inevitable away defeat would not be terminal for England's prospects. As England's fifth goal went in, sealing a 5-1 victory, Ewan gave me a look that cruelly but justifiably marked a major breach in his six-year-old's belief that Dad always knew best.

In one of the first major tournaments we watched together, the 2004 European Championships, we enjoyed another kind of family football bonding. The Greek team enjoyed an astonishing triumph, with Newcastle defender Nikos Dabizas in their team. And they were coached by a German, Otto Rehhagel, who relished this stunning success. 'We were outsiders in the entire world of football. But as the Greeks teach us, the Gods always have their own plans.' Rehhagel, whom the Greeks dubbed 'King Otto', was seen by many as a figure of reconciliation between countries affected by the memory of wartime occupation and modern economic tensions. And for him, football had been his route out of the misery of a Third Reich childhood. Born in 1938 he survived wartime bombing as a child and learned his football in the tough early post-war environment of the Ruhr region, the first part of Germany I had known. He had wanted, he said, to be '... away from these ruins, hunger and poverty. The only way was football'.

And for one summer at least I like to think that my father-in-law Tony, who spent much of his creative life thinking about the Greeks and their Gods, allowed himself fleetingly to become a proper football fan. He happened to be in Greece when they won the tournament and he returned home with a huge Greek flag and enthusiastic reports of satyr-like celebrations. Like Gotthilf with his glass, however, such moments of brilliant Greek light always vied in his mind with shadow and darkness. Tony had spent much time in his work brooding about how the world could best confront and transcend the horrors of the twentieth century, with Germany and the Holocaust at their centre.

A Stadium Reborn

When Germany was chosen to host the World Cup finals in 2006 it brought to the forefront the role of football in modern German identity, and in its pursuit of a new international image As always, I was fascinated by how the country sought to use such an opportunity to exorcise historical ghosts. Once I realised that the tournament final would be played at the Olympic Stadium in Berlin I knew that would be the perfect focus for a radio documentary exploring how the past could be transcended in such a high-profile sporting event.

I had first encountered the stadium and the area around it in the very different atmosphere of my time in the city in 1980 when the Cold War, and the legacy of Nazism's defeat, seemed deep frozen into the landscape. On days off from work at the old people's home I had sometimes gone to wander around the stadium complex built for the 1936 Olympics, drawn by its historical power yet feeling small and lonely amidst its huge avenues, massive stone architecture and imposing statues of muscular Aryan figures. Not all areas were accessible. After the Second World War, British occupation forces used much of the site for offices and accommodation, with their lawns and cricket pitches a curious kind of culture clash amidst the gigantic 1930s stone statues. Inside, one former army officer revealed, the buildings had been 'crawling with spooks'.

The stadium's original architecture, historian Wolfgang Schäche told me, had been meant to overwhelm – to fascinate on the one hand but to subdue at the same time. It was also meant to motivate young people to be ready to fight for people and fatherland and, when necessary, to die. That death cult was expressed in the tall tower and Langemarck hall to the rear of the stadium, commemorating a First World War battle in which many young German soldiers had died. Hitler himself had felt a close personal connection with that battle and the Third Reich built a whole mythology around it, incorporated into the stadium design and 1936 Olympic ceremonies.

Sport in the 1936 Games had been partly a gratifying success for Hitler and his regime, with Germany winning the most gold medals. However the athletics had been most memorable for the medals won by the brilliant black American athlete Jesse Owens, in defiance of the Nazi assertion of Aryan supremacy. Something else I noticed about the 1936 Games as I came to know the stadium better was that medals had also been awarded in those early-twentieth-century Games for the arts, including literature and music, echoing that Classical idea of the link between culture and sport.

In one corner of the Olympic complex in 1980 I also discovered the *Waldbühne*, literally 'the stage in the forest'. It was constructed in the style of a Classical Greek amphitheatre, with steeply raked stone rows of seating. The Nazis had intended this place as a temple to Aryan culture, and it was first named after an anti-Semitic writer, Dietrich Eckart. After the war no-one had been sure what do with this tainted stone inheritance. While the Olympic stadium was still used for sport and many buildings around were commandeered by British occupation forces, the *Waldbühne* staged only occasional events such as a notorious Rolling Stones concert in 1965 where fans battled with the police. It seemed, in short, still spooked by its origins.

Reggae superstar Bob Marley's appearance there in June 1980, in what turned out to be one of his last concerts, marked a nervous attempt to reinvent the venue's reputation. I can remember being surprised by the heavy police presence as we arrived for the concert, uniforms standing out starkly amid the kaleidoscope of exuberant colour worn by around 18000 fans from many nationalities. Eventually Marley, a slight but magnetic figure (and, incidentally, great football fan) came onto the stage and into the spotlight, and the rhythms from his band and backing vocalists began to echo around the amphitheatre. He sang of 'No More Trouble' and Zimbabwean freedom and time to 'Lively Up Yourself'. Before long his positive vibrations seemed to animate everyone there, softening the stony severity of the venue itself. No one stayed sitting, everyone was swaying even, eventually, the previously rigidly watchful police. In a place where once the self-styled Aryan master race had celebrated what they thought would be their endless domination, someone very different was demonstrating real cultural power. And I have thought of that evening so often since, especially whenever I hear Marley's 'Redemption Song' of freedom and emancipation from mental slavery. The *Waldbühne* was redeemed that evening, and I began to realise how sometimes awful history in Germany could be overlaid with something much more positive.

The main Olympic stadium still awaited its final redemption, which football would facilitate. It had come back into use for football in the 1960s as a home for the Berlin club Hertha BSC and was now to be the centrepiece for the World Cup final, seen by multi millions around the globe. PR consultants talked excitedly about all this accelerating the 'image transfer' of Germany. In preparation for 2006 the Germans added it to the long list of buildings they were trying to transform after the fall of the Wall, while avoiding the charge of sweeping away and concealing dark history.

Often this extensive reconstruction involved building with supposedly transparent, democratic glass while shunning the heavy stonework of the authoritarian past. In the case of this stadium the emphasis was on keeping most of the original structure while adding lightness and illumination on top. Hundreds of limestone elements originally added by Hitler's favourite architect, Albert Speer, were removed, numbered, washed and restored. But most impressive in the renovation was a new roof, full of dazzling new technology; but a conspicuous gap was left to allow the view through to the Langemarck tower to remain. Sobering history, in other words, the linkage of sport with a death cult, was not forgotten.

And that seemed especially appropriate when I met Reinhard Appel who had been a member of the Hitler Youth assembled outside the stadium as the Red Army approached in 1945. He and his fellow teenagers had been told by their commander to 'regard the forthcoming battle for Berlin as a chance for sacrificial death, for such a death was a heroic one'. Many of them had died in a pointless charge towards Russian machine gunners when the war was already lost. On a hill nearby was a poignant memorial to many other teenagers who were shot for desertion in the same period.

So when I watched on TV the World Cup games coming from that stadium, and spotted that gap in the roof, I was taken back to that story of the tragedy of football caught in twentieth century carnage – a story also embracing *dulce et decorum est* at my school, and young Northumbrian soldiers running towards death at the Somme, following a football. And yet for all the heavy inheritance there was something joyous about Germany's ability in 2006 to stage the tournament with style, openness and enthusiasm as thousands of fans arrived from around the world. There was doubtless some exaggeration of all this as politicians took note of the game's potential power. When I made a profile of the German Chancellor Angela Merkel I discovered that, previously uninterested in sport, she had now become an enthusiast for football, regularly dropping in on the German national team's dressing room, debating tactics and mastering the details of the offside law with the characteristic thoroughness of her scientific training. She struggled to restrain diplomatically her triumphal joy at a summit with the new British prime minister David Cameron as they watched on TV together a German demolition of England in the 2010 World Cup.

The German football team had also become an embodiment of hopes for a more relaxed approach in the country to migration and integration. I visited Germany regularly to report on this issue, especially in the aftermath of Chancellor Merkel's bold decision to admit a million asylum seekers in 2015. Just as I had discovered in Sweden much earlier, football was seen as one of the areas in which contact between migrants and locals could proceed most amicably and effectively. But I was also covering the first stirrings of newly influential populist politics. There were hints of what would become a very different mood in an ugly row following comments by a politician from the emerging far right party, the AfD. He said most Germans would not want the black defender Jerome Boateng, new star of their national team, as a neighbour.

OLD ENEMIES, NEW FRIENDS

Full football reconciliation between England and Germany seemed meanwhile to be proceeding rapidly. When two German clubs contested the Champions League final at Wembley in 2013, I wrote a piece entitled 'Is Fussball coming home?'. I enjoyed discovering how, when the game first arrived in Germany in the nineteenth century, some local patriots campaigned to stop the 'foot-louts' infected by what was called 'the English disease' from playing a game that was 'absurd, ugly and perverted'. Gymnastics, it was argued, would better prepare German men for military service. Football survived in Germany but sadly that link between sport and war would feed the horrors of twentieth-century history. Now the game could be shared in a far more peaceful era and thousands of fans of Bayern Munich and Borussia Dortmund poignantly made their way along Wembley Way, partly built by German POWs in the 1940s.

To encompass all their football history the Germans now created a new national football museum in Dortmund which I visited with my family. There was a touching early reference to Britain as football's 'motherland'. And in the spirit of modern German internationalism an interactive display inviting visitors to judge whether the third England goal in the 1966 World Cup final had really crossed the line showed a large majority saying Yes, despite the fact that we were the only Brits there. West Germany might have lost that game but elsewhere in the museum were displays of the multiple trophies they had won, glittering like the treasure chamber of an acquisitive medieval ruler. Due attention was also given to the history of football in East Germany. There were the communist secret police chiefs who tried to manipulate matches, and the clubs seeking to retain key players in a consumption-starved society with bonuses such as sausages or washing machines. In museum displays it is often the smaller details that linger most in the mind. My favourite part of that section was an invoice sent by the Dynamo Berlin club to the Ministry of State Security for over 1200 tickets supplied for one game to Stasi secret police officers. That was one way to ensure minimal crowd trouble.

The ability of the East German authorities to influence players with the most modest of consumer goods seemed light years away from today's elite global football, dominated by ridiculous levels of expenditure and wealth. I also grew to admire increasingly, as did Ewan, the way German football across the reunified country offered a different kind of club system in which fans kept more influence and the game was more affordable for all. As Uli Hesse, historian of German football told me, whereas German fans had often been admirers of English clubs, admiring the atmosphere in their stadiums, things were changing. Due to the commercialisation of the British game he had noticed that now, in many ways, 'the English want to be more like the Germans'. Just as many British politicians had admired the way German industry was run, with long-term ownership and workers enjoying seats on the board, now British football fans were casting envious eyes towards German clubs.

WALTER SHOWED THE WAY

My education – at school and university, and in the hands of 'ordinary' old people – took me deep into the German history of appalling evil followed by, in many ways, great redemptive recovery. In my professional career as a journalist and documentary maker I would pursue that theme in all kinds of ways in all kinds of places. I might have assumed my interest in football would offer a complete distraction from such compelling but troubling interests. But I came to realise instead that German football was also part of this story; and there is one life that perfectly encapsulate that for me.

Recently I was asked to write an obituary for the *Times* newspaper of Walter Frankenstein. In 1943, as a young Jew living in Berlin, he had defied the prospect of imminent deportation to a Nazi death camp by going underground with his young family. And somehow, against all the odds, they survived the war. He had then understandably wanted nothing to do with Germany and went to live in Israel and then Sweden. Later, however, something had drawn Walter back – a belief that a new, different, better Germany had emerged, and a desire to rediscover some of the things that he had most enjoyed before the Nazis had attempted to eliminate him. Among his greatest passions was football. He had begun to support the Berlin team Hertha BSC as soon as he arrived in the city in the 1930s and continued to go defiantly after Jewish attendance was banned by Nazi law, only stopping when his wife persuaded him it had become too dangerous.

When he returned to the city long after the war he was delighted to resume attendance at Hertha games, now played in the stadium where he had first gone to watch the 1936 Olympic Games; the place I had come to know, and which was to be refurbished for the 2006 World Cup. Walter said he was proud of the way in which Hertha became one of many German institutions to confront, albeit belatedly, the way in which it had been complicit in Nazi persecution of Jews and others. In 2018, as its oldest fan, he was made an honorary club member.

After his death was announced, Hertha's 'ultra' fans displayed in his honour a banner at their next match. It displayed the answer he had given when asked how he and his family had survived the Holocaust. There were four pillars, he had replied, on which that survival was built. 'Impudence, no fear, good friends and a lot of luck.' 'Ultra' fans might conjure up in many non-German minds an assumption of racist thuggery; here were fans in Germany showing a very different face. As I will describe in chapter 9, I would discover too that German football's sense of solidarity and communal identity had helped create a project exploring the powerful links between football and grief – a project I could draw on after the death of my son Ewan. He would have so admired Walter's story, in which football might have seemed a trivial concern, but had made its own contribution to the defiant impudence, rejection of fear, and celebration of good friends that had helped one individual win through the darkest of days.

And Newcastle, I was also delighted to discover, had its own version of this story to set against the pain of so many young local lives lost in wars fighting Germans. Werner Oscar Maier, from a Jewish background, born in Berlin a mile from the Olympic Stadium, had escaped the Third Reich in the 1930s, come to my school in Newcastle, overcame anti-German prejudice, prospered in the Tyneside clothing industry and was, for many decades, a season-ticket holder at St James' Park. He was still attending in his nineties. Another, very special, adopted fan; another story I treasure; another piece I can weave into my global football story.

5

BEARING OUR STRIPES

GERMANY HAD BECOME PART of my football world. But whatever my international interests, Newcastle United would always remain the primary focus. In the 1970s I had been drawn into the club's compelling orbit, and from the 1980s I had felt its force field even when living far away. As the 1990s began, with the English game itself entering a new era, freer of some of the worst aspects of owner neglect, fan violence and political hostility, there was much to keep me absorbed. But I was again spending time abroad, witnessing a new global era emerge, affecting every kind of place and institution. The demands of work and life with a young family also meant I would not manage to get to many games; I became instead part of the rapidly growing TV audience, whilst keeping an intense interest in how my club and the football world was faring. As a journalist I remained transfixed by the Toon drama and took every opportunity to cover key figures and issues in a turbulent period.

It seems to me that my best way to begin to make personal sense of Newcastle United history from the 1990s onwards is not through more conventional headings of, say, league seasons but rather through three symbolic themes that came to preoccupy me and, once he was drawn in, my conversations with Ewan. So my next three chapters will be based on: the stadium as a place with its own special culture; the way football came to resemble a kind of secular religion; and first, how the story of something as apparently simple as the Newcastle shirt could reveal much about how the club, and the sport, was changing.

We treasure the collection of football shirts Ewan left us; his brother Alfie has his own too. They remind us of a sometimes thrilling, sometimes bewildering time of changing club ownership, fluctuating fortunes, a growing battle between club tradition and commercial innovation. In all of this we and every other fan had to work out how we would fit into everything that was happening.

Covering our Bellies

Ask the outside world what a male Newcastle United fan looks like, and the answer may well be: large of belly and wearing no shirt whatsoever. In any televised match featuring Newcastle you can rely on the director cutting at some point in the action to a close-up of Toon fans, one of whom will be conspicuously topless, regardless of the weather. The commentator will then sagely remind the audience of the reputation these supporters have for a passion which is, by implication, wildly exaggerated and recklessly exposed. I have never myself met a bare-torsoed supporter in Newcastle crowds, which has occasionally led me to wonder whether visiting TV crews, desperate for what is regarded as the essential Toon Army shot, bring a professional exposer with them as part of their essential matchday kit. Cameras – tick; lighting gear – tick; telegenic Geordie beer belly – tick.

People talk of football supporting as akin to a kind of tribal loyalty, but ultimately every fan chooses individually how he or she adorns themselves. That choice is now about not only support for their team but also, in more recent times, how they relate to their club's commercial partners. Nowhere is the identity of the football fan more interestingly revealed than in observing their top halves, and Newcastle knows it. In the city's

Great Museum of the North, close to St James' Park, amidst anthropological collections exploring global identities there is a cabinet containing Fijian grass skirts, nose ornaments from the Pacific and a Newcastle United shirt under the caption: You Are What You Wear.

Until a few decades ago, no one thought of the football shirt as a key consumer product. Match day mascots might have covered themselves from head to toe in team colours; but the vast majority of fans, overwhelmingly male, wore nondescript coats and similar hats or cloth caps. Scarves were a far likelier badge of belonging; shirts were what you worshipped on the pitch. Now, as part of the financial revolution transforming professional football, clubs began to want their fans to, in every sense, buy into the shirts' identity, preferably every season. I had been an early enthusiast for this retail revolution, queueing outside a Croydon shop in the early 1970s to acquire the new season's Crystal Palace kit. My Mum, sensing vulnerability to commercial pressure, seemed anxious about my craving and tried heroically to keep me on a more traditional supporters' path by knitting me a scarf in Palace colours. I was unimpressed, churlishly preferring the glamour of Umbro nylon to the virtues of homely wool, and responded like Private Pike in *Dad's Army* when his mother arrives fussily at Home Guard parades with emergency knitwear protection against winter chills.

After moving to Newcastle I clung for a while to my expensively procured Palace shirt, until transferring my allegiance to the black and white stripes. My initial hesitation may have been reinforced by the contrast between Palace's alluring claret and blue and what seemed to be the disappointing austerity of Newcastle's colours; or rather *lack* of colours. An all-white kit, like the great Real Madrid or the then triumphant Leeds United, might have been more appealing. But black and white stripes seemed somehow unsettling, a stark statement of contrast rather than coherence, and perhaps symbolic of a club whose glory days lay stuck in a more monochrome era rather than that of modern Technicolour.

Only slowly did I realise how black and white stripes seem so appropriate for Newcastle's history, psychology and regional appeal. There are various ideas as to where these stripes originally came from. Dan Jackson, brilliant historian of Northumbrians and their culture, mentions theories including the habits worn by Dominican monks who lived near to one of the club's founding teams, the arms of the Cavendish Dukes of Newcastle and a famous Northumbrian plaid worn by shepherds. Arthur Appleton, earlier chronicler of the region as a 'hotbed of soccer' suggests that one of Newcastle clubs that merged to form Newcastle United had a strip that was 'country jerseys of black-and-white vertical stripes'. The latter certainly seems appropriate for a club with a catchment area for players and supporters that has always extended well beyond the city of Newcastle to embrace urban and rural expanses in Northumberland, County Durham and beyond. As the poet Wilfrid Gibson, born in my home town, expressed it:

> Heatherland and bentland,
> Black land and white,
> God bring me to Northumberland,
> The land of my delight.

The black and the white together symbolise powerfully the great contrasts that live side by side in the region, defying attempts by outsiders to characterise it as uniformly bleak and depressed or wildly hedonistic. The region's economic history is of course suffused with much heavy industry, the relentless blackness of coal, and the dense and dark emissions of ironworks, chemicals and heavy engineering. Yet there is a completely different story of enlightenment and illumination that can be told of places that produced the glorious Lindisfarne Gospels, and became a major centre of book publishing, great engravers and glassmakers. In the carboniferous nineteenth century that still shapes the culture and reputation of the North East, it is often overlooked that the region also sparked the global electrical age by inventing the light bulb, the turbine and the power distribution network.

The people of the region lived daily with these sometimes stark contrasts, hoping that, however dark things might seem, there was at least the potential of future light. Buildings in North East cities and towns did become grimy with industrial pollution, but more recently their glorious stonework has often been cleaned to stand proudly alongside the lighter construction of new development. Industry, or now the remains of industry, was often located amongst stunning countryside. The North East weather can be dull or stormy, but can also, even in winter, offer the most brilliant light which brings profound psychological relief. As the cultural historian Peter Davidson puts it, 'northern summer is as prodigal of light as the winter is starved of it. Much of the melancholy of the north arises from the impossibility of saving one minute from the long light against the approaching darkness'. It is not hard to see why the great winter gathering at floodlit football matches could be so appealing.

Having light to set against the darkness was not just about psychology, but also survival; seafarers facing peril depended on lighthouse navigation, while those working underground had to have reliable illumination. Miners have been among the most enthusiastic footballers and supporters, men who spent so much time underground, recovering for the benefit of the nation tons of fossilised sunlight. They lived daily with prolonged darkness and always relished the brightness and fresh air of their gardens and sports. I have played club cricket on a ground near Newcastle that sits on top of a former mine, where the grass stains on my whites were mixed in with coal dust. England and Newcastle manager Bobby Robson, formed by a County Durham mining and Newcastle-supporting family, spoke of being 'born into a black and white world ... The murky gloom of the pit, the blinding gleam of the floodlights – they are the dominant shades of my life'.

The black and white may also be the right psychological combination for fans of a club which has oscillated between shining talent and success but also prolonged gloom. Many bear the scars of the latter; and wags might suggest that stripes, whether Newcastle's black and white or Sunderland's red and white, are apt for a region where football supporting has often been associated with a kind of self-flagellation. But the story of Newcastle United's last few decades has been about something more. The stripes have remained, though their design has been varied; the club's crest, linked to the city of Newcastle's iconography, has been fairly constant too. Increasingly prominent, however, and in eye-catching colour, have been the symbols of changing ownership, sponsorship and branding superimposed onto the deep tradition of the stripes, like the shiny new buildings traded by restless property developers which now stand on former colliery sites. The club's fortunes on the pitch have been impossible to separate from the attempt to make large fortunes off it; and the shirts, with all their stripes and symbols, have been where we can observe that contest.

Here is how four recent eras of shirt-led Newcastle style have looked to me.

Keegan and Hall, high fliers and hangovers

The North East's love of alcohol has been bemoaned by those conscious of its consequences for those who overindulge, while celebrated by others who see it as part of a vibrant, Carnivalesque culture. From the moment I began supporting Newcastle, the link between boozing and football supporting was loudly apparent. My approach to matches at St James' Park was across the Town Moor, a relatively quiet and sober place though the scene once a year of a giant bacchanalian funfair called 'The Hoppings' (which had, long ago, been a Temperance Festival). Most fans made their way to the ground via at least one of the numerous city centre pubs, and the results of such indulgence were evident in the ground's less than attractive aroma as primitive terrace toilets overflowed.

Across the road from St James' Park was a large brewery producing the famous Newcastle Brown Ale, and the company became the club's first ever shirt sponsor in 1980 with a logo featuring a blue star and an image of the Tyne Bridge. Then came what seemed like the greatest of footballing and sponsorship coups in 1982: the signing of England international striker Kevin Keegan. His reported £3000 a week wages, huge in those days, was underwritten by Newcastle Breweries. Excitement peaked when he played his first home match at St James' Park that August; his winning goal against QPR, he claimed, had been 'sucked in' by the Gallowgate End. Following the win there was another giant sucking sound across Tyneside as thousands of fans imbibed in celebration.

Such alcoholic highs always have to be slept off, however, and sustained success took time. 'People talked about the club being a sleeping giant,' said Keegan, 'but at times, I wondered whether it was actually in a coma.' Keegan and his team-mates did gradually stir things, and Newcastle were promoted back to the top division in 1984. And yet, as so often in the club's history, euphoria was followed by another painful hangover. Keegan retired, manager Arthur Cox left, and the club returned to another decade in the doldrums. Shirt sponsorship transferred to a different brewer, Greenalls.

A few years later change was in the air, in football and society. Cheshire-based Greenalls decided old style brewing supplying mostly all-male pubs was in terminal decline and moved into leisure and hotels; Tyneside begged to differ. Football itself, after the disasters of the 1980s, was beginning a new era of stadium transformation funded by TV revenue. Newcastle's version of that change, however, would resemble one of the rollercoasters I sometimes walked past in the Hoppings Fair, a thrilling but ultimately chaotic attempt to ride the wave of fans' traditionally passionate support while driving the club into a new era of commercialism and retail. That tension – between tradition and modernisation – has been playing out ever since. In 1990 the Newcastle Breweries' blue star returned as shirt sponsor, but at first the club, like a Saturday night ten-pint reveller on the Newcastle Quayside, tottered close to its greatest ignominy as relegation to the third division approached. That was averted after another dose of the intoxicating Keegan charisma, when in 1992 he reappeared on Tyneside as manager. First contact had been made by a brewing executive from the club sponsors, and the press conference announcing his appointment was held at the Newcastle Breweries Visitors' Centre.

Keegan summed it up simply: 'Newcastle had a famous history, an iconic shirt and a tradition of passionate support. What they didn't have was a decent football team.' Nor, he discovered, did they have decent training facilities, with 'horrendous' pitches, a gym covered in a layer of grime, and overflowing bins. As for the bright whiteness alongside the black stripes in that iconic shirt, clean-cut Keegan lamented that there was no washing machine so players had to take their dirty kit home. Many used the wrong wash settings so ended up playing for Newcastle not in black and white but 'dishwater grey'.

Money to clean up the club and improve team and laundry was to be arranged by its new chairman, prominent local property developer Sir John Hall. I would follow his career with particular interest, as he had a plan to weave together the history, the shirt and the passion to consolidate his own retail fortune while promoting regional regeneration. Here was a new embodiment of the nationally famous North East visionary following the collapse in disgrace of the career of T. Dan Smith, entrepreneur and politician convicted of corruption in the mid-1970s.

After the 1980s strikes and closure of most of the mines, shipbuilding and heavy industry, the region was groping for a new source of inspiration, jobs and prosperity. Hall, like Smith and Keegan a miner's son, had worked as a Coal Board surveyor, but believed after visiting the US that the North East could be rescued through shopping. In 1986 he opened the giant Metrocentre on the site of the ash tip of a decommissioned coal-fired power station on the south bank of the Tyne. It was a retail development on an unprecedented scale for Britain and Europe. When I first went there I came across an enthusiastic coach party from Hungary who had insisted on making a special visit. For locals in well-paid work it was highly attractive; for others it could be tantalisingly unaffordable, and security was tight. Local teacher and novelist Jonathan Tulloch described a kind of other-worldly quality: 'The Metrocentre sprawls over the flat, drained, marshy ground by the Tyne. It is unbelievably vast. It has many roofs and towers and buildings. It is like an immense cathedral with vast precincts. It is like a city ... like a gigantic hive of bees.'

Gone was the state-led planned economy of the early post-war decades, so prominent in North East life. Hall had made extensive use of special development regulations – or rather, lack of regulations – introduced by the Thatcher government, as well as its funding of a rerouted Great North Road near to the Metrocentre site. He was much praised by the prime minister as a kind of urban redevelopment alchemist. 'In a little over two years,' she marvelled, Hall 'has turned an area of marshland and industrial waste into a focal point for a community.' But the region was still resentful of recent economic shocks including the bitter miners' strike; and Hall sought shrewdly to maintain a reputation as a local patriot, insisting: 'The Geordie nation, that's what we're fighting for! London is the enemy! The South-East is the enemy! You exploit us, you use us, you take everything you can from us but never recognise our existence.'

That kind of language played well with local football fans long used to losing their best players, from what Bobby Robson called their 'thick seam of Geordie talent', to the south, just as millions of tons of North East coal had once been shipped from the Tyne near the Metrocentre site to warm London homes and power its businesses. Hall knew about football's hold from his upbringing near Ashington, birthplace of Bobby and Jackie Charlton as well as the great Newcastle striker Jackie Milburn; and his influence began to grow as he campaigned for control of Newcastle United and enthused about why the club was different. 'It's difficult for anybody to take in the mystique and the passion of soccer, but it can absorb your life. In a way it is a family; the club has a camaraderie, a ritual. The intellectual will never understand the passion of the Geordie for his football.' That passion was also profitable as fans flocked to buy Newcastle shirts in Metrocentre outlets. It was never entirely clear how far Hall's vision of the leisure and retail revolution meant challenging the old cliché of women going shopping on a Saturday while men went to the match. But the Metrocentre and other retailers could certainly benefit from the reported sales of up to half a million shirts a season. Unemployment was well above average, but North Easterners with steady jobs were eager spenders.

Newcastle fans were also famous for wearing club replica shirts not only at games but everywhere they went. As Joe Sharkey explains in his fascinating discussion of Geordie mentality, this sartorial habit has been attributed by some to an admirable desire to display solidarity, but by others to a 'sheep-like conformity' in sporting the stripes of the old Northumbrian shepherds' plaid. What such mass shirt wearing definitely did was expose fans to the outside world's applause when their team was popular, and ridicule when things went horribly wrong. Both responses would be prominent in the next few tumultuous football seasons as the Keegan managerial adventure gathered pace.

I had watched the first stages of the Hall/Keegan revolution from Prague, where I had moved to be the BBC's correspondent in 1992. It had recently undergone its own revolution – against communism – and was embracing the sudden arrival of Western consumerism with huge enthusiasm, delighting in junk mail and sporting every kind of branded plastic bag. Many of its young people, meanwhile, were heading West for new opportunities now the Iron Curtain was no more. One Czech migrant I watched closely was Pavel Srniček, a goalkeeper who had joined Newcastle in 1991. He had played briefly for Dukla Prague, one of the first foreign teams I had seen play in the mid-1970s, and near to whose ground I now lived. Its history was deeply compromised however as it had been supported in communist times by the Czechoslovak secret police and army. Srniček explained that he had originally gone to play there 'because a general asked for me'.

After arriving in Newcastle he had swiftly felt an affinity with local fans having grown up in a Czech mining area where he grafted as a teenager. He once had to 'slave for a month' helping to build a crematorium before he had money for a pair of jeans. Now on Tyneside he felt that 'everyone was together: the team, supporters and the city. You would walk the streets of Newcastle and it felt like you were part of this great big family'. Srniček's exuberantly colourful goalkeeper shirts attracted much attention. But the moment that would forever endear him to local fans was after Newcastle had won the second division championship and he took off his top to reveal a T-shirt underneath bearing the words: 'Pavel is a Geordie'. Here was the latest addition to the great Newcastle tradition of adopting talent and enthusiasm from far and wide. Yet Pavel's popularity also hinted at fans' respect for an individual who proudly retained his own identity beneath whatever the club required him to wear.

Momentum built under Keegan, at the club and all around it. 'There was something intangible enveloping the city, yet at the same time you could almost touch it', Srniček enthused. 'Music, culture and politics were changing and we were part of that zeitgeist.' There were other inspired signings. Keegan was a bit put out when he rang a young Bristol City striker called Andy Cole to say that Newcastle had bought him for £1.75 million so could he get the next flight north? Cole replied he had 'got something on tonight' which turned out to be his regular laundry evening. Lucky that the club now boasted its own washing machines as well as a team that would create endless scoring opportunities. When cleanly clad Cole did arrive he began an extraordinary scoring spree, 41 goals in one season, commenting casually: 'I just caressed the ball into the net.' Caressing was often all that was needed after elegant team-work that began to win admirers well beyond the North East for attacking finesse and a devil-may-care approach to defence. Keegan claimed, perhaps a little implausibly, that some travelled from as far away as Cornwall and Dorset just to watch them train.

Gabby Logan, now a top TV sports presenter, fell in love with Newcastle United during this period while studying at Durham. 'It felt,' she recalled 'like we lived in the United Kingdom of Newcastle. Only a cold-hearted football-hating fool would have spent their Saturdays in a Durham bedsit writing essays on employment law when they could have been in the cathedral of football being seduced by the black and white army.' When her career took her away to London a few years later there was much regret. 'I have never felt as strongly about a place as I felt about Newcastle right then. I think there is an indomitable spirit that runs through the very DNA of the place … in that moment, I felt I had at least belonged somewhere.'

Indomitable Newcastle fans scarred by decades of disappointment still sensed uneasily that national interest in the Keegan revolution was not just about the quality of the football – or the new cleanliness of the shirts – but rather a fascination with the club's continuous potential for unexpected drama. And sure enough, in January 1995 Keegan suddenly decided his team was becoming too predictable and that he wanted to sell Cole to great rivals Manchester United. TV crews assembled outside St James' Park as did hundreds of angry fans (angriest of all, perhaps, were those who had just painfully acquired Andy Cole tattoos or named their new babies after their striking idol). While directors backed off Keegan went out to talk to the crowd, their faces, he recalled, 'contorted with anger and hurt'. A robust debate took place, and Keegan concluded that, 'I cannot think of another club in England where the same would have happened.'

He increasingly felt the pressure, recalling revealingly that 'my transfer-market strategy for Newcastle in the Premier League was simple: we were creating a monster which we had to keep feeding'. The fans' mood improved when, in time for the 1995-6 season, new signings included striker Les Ferdinand and winger David Ginola. Both were not only talented players but extremely elegant men, and Ferdinand modelled the club's new clothing on a St James' Park catwalk. Sir John Hall was now at the height of his reputation and success. When I made a profile for BBC radio I visited his new home at Wynyard Hall, where the son of an Ashington miner was relishing living in what had once been the grand residence of the Londonderry mine-owning aristocrats. He and his associates also saw themselves as having deposed the hereditary elite which had run Newcastle United for decades, described in one account as composed of 'blood stock and acquaintances of directors and shareholders who passed control from generation to generation'. Hall told me his ambition for Newcastle United now went well beyond the football team as he hoped to create a 'sporting club' like that in Barcelona embracing everything from rugby to ice hockey and athletics. He gave me a slightly alarming example at the time of how he wanted the club to represent the region abroad: 'they'll have this little badge of Newcastle to carry the message of the North-East – exactly what the East Germans did, but without the drugs'.

Sporting success was meant to move in step with regional regeneration. The plan was to attract new international investment. 'We want the footloose companies that are travelling the world' Hall added. And Samsung – its executives wooed with seafood, avocado and lamb on a visit to a match at St James' Park (as well as the promise of multi-millions in government start-up grants) – had agreed to build an 'electronics city' near Wynyard making computer monitors, TV tubes and microchips. The jobs were desperately needed. In my birthplace on Teesside a few miles away thousands of jobs had evaporated as the ICI chemicals giant was broken up. Koreans had a special reputation on Teesside – when the North Korean team was based there for the 1966 World Cup the locals had adopted them. But there was scepticism about how long the South Koreans would stay. When I asked Sir John about this he replied with indignation. 'They may not stay very long? What nonsense!' However footloose Samsung did indeed scale down its plans a few years later, and the plant closed altogether in 2004.

By then the dream of Newcastle United as a championship winning team seemed distant too, but only after a season, 1995-6, that seemed to encapsulate all the hype, hope and hard landings that supporting this team could mean. My son Ewan had been born early in 1995 so my mood that year was full of the promise of new beginnings. The club's national influence seemed to surge in the autumn when Kevin Keegan was pictured at the Labour Party conference doing keepie-uppies with Tony Blair, whose constituency base was close to Wynyard. Blair was way ahead in the opinion polls and heading inexorably for his general election landslide. By early 1996 Newcastle seemed similarly predestined, 12 points clear in the Premier League; but then, in the cruellest period of any Newcastle fan's experience, they began to crumble. The key match was at home against closest rivals Manchester United. I was not a Sky TV subscriber and this was the pre-smartphone and Internet age so I sat at home in Oxford, with toddler Ewan in a Toon romper suit dozing on my lap, anxiously checking the Ceefax score update in between watching an episode of the epic TV drama *Our Friends in the North,* which featured much dashing of North East dreams.

In the first half at St James' Park Newcastle attacked relentlessly but the Manchester United goalkeeper Peter Schmeichel seemed unbeatable. In the second half, French striker Eric Cantona applied the counter-attacking *coup de grâce.* I grew rigid with despair. Why did arbitrary electronic news of an event far away over which I could have no influence affect my mood like this? That was a mystery I would discuss with Ewan when he too was afflicted.

Momentum was now lost; doubt set in and I began to stare morosely at the league tables in a permanent pessimism of worsening permutations. Even sunny Pavel Srníček seemed to lose his nerve, replaced for the final games of the season; and Newcastle fell short on the final day. Les Ferdinand believed Keegan never really recovered from this failure: it was 'almost as though a light had gone out in his head'. The football had ultimately failed, but won much admiration, as had that season's shirts, now seen as the classic of the Brown Ale blue star era and regarded by leading kit historian John Devlin as 'exquisitely crafted' and 'the greatest ever set of kits'.

Again the club responded with bravado. That summer, top England striker Alan Shearer arrived for a record £15 million fee. He was the last hurrah of the old school Newcastle Number 9 hero, muscular son of a sheet metal worker from the city who turned down offers from Manchester United among others in order to return home. He now appeared outside the stadium in the famous shirt and the adoring crowd, so angry the previous year when Cole was sold, reassembled to revive their euphoria. There were moments when the disappointment was banished.

Manchester United were thrashed 5-0 at St James' Park, a triumph encapsulated when Belgian centre back Philippe Albert, another hugely popular adopted Geordie, chipped the no longer unbeatable Peter Schmeichel with supreme self-assurance for the fifth goal.

But they were only moments. In the background, down in the economically all-powerful south and distant from what was happening on the pitch, more disruptive change was in motion. The Hall family and their associates decided to float the club on the London stock exchange. As with any flotation, what remained submerged could still be crucial. Financiers from far away became key figures in the club, and as far as Keegan was concerned, 'it had become a totally different organisation'. Keegan lived on the Wynyard estate but neighbour John Hall seemed increasingly to keep his distance, preferring a retreat in Spain to his grand northern residence. In January 1997 Keegan, faced with demands over his commitment linked to the flotation, resigned. Both prime minister John Major and Tony Blair felt obliged to comment, and the national media had another episode for their favourite sporting soap opera, picturing weeping fans in Toon shirts outside St James' Park.

This time the hangover was prolonged as the club seemed to be retreating into the old pattern of permanent footballing underachievement. Under new manager Kenny Dalglish Newcastle did manage to finish second in the Premier League but then Les Ferdinand and David Ginola joined the long list of Newcastle exports to Spurs. The leading figures in the club were now meant to be John Hall's son, Douglas, and an ambitious director, Freddy Shepherd. But in the first of series of incidents that made supporting Newcastle increasingly hard to stomach Hall and Shepherd were recorded in March 1998 in one of the 'Fake Sheikh' stings by the *News of the World* describing Geordie women as 'dogs' and mocking Newcastle fans as 'mugs' for buying the club's shirts at a huge mark-up from their manufacturing cost. They stepped down temporarily after a huge backlash, though Shepherd managed to return as chairman not long afterwards.

My mind was on other things at the time as my second son, Alfie, was born four months prematurely in Oxford in February that year, weighing around 600 grams, and spent many weeks in hospital as we watched him struggle for life. In his special care unit monitors beeped incessantly, alarms would go off, and on one occasion treatment of Alfie continued while in another corner of the room a priest read the last rites over a tiny body. My daughter Laura and Ewan would visit but Ewan sometimes found the heat and atmosphere unbearable, and we would head for a nearby playground and a kickabout to relieve the tension. Football found its way into Alfie's care when one of his nurses, who had grown up on Tyneside, knitted him a tiny black and white kit to wear on the day Newcastle played the FA Cup final in May. While the match was on we took him in a pram equipped with an oxygen supply for his first taste of the outdoors. Our team slumped to another of their many cup final disappointments but we remained exhilarated that day as Alfie breathed in his first outdoor air and his survival seemed assured. He too would become for me a great football companion.

After Dalglish left Newcastle in 1998, former star Dutch player Ruud Gullit arrived with the promise of 'sexy football' but swiftly discovered that few of Newcastle's players could manage his technical and tactical requirements, let alone a more arousing style of play. There was another tantalising cup run followed by another Wembley defeat. Gullit resigned after little more than a year following the very unsexy experience of losing a local derby against Sunderland on a rain-sodden Tyneside evening. The following weekend Newcastle went to Old Trafford and lost 5-1, with Andy Cole scoring four goals for the opposition. The Hall-Keegan era of blue star effervescence, when a shiny new shopping centre had sought to replace the misery of mine closures, when high quality

Cole had been imported to Newcastle and multiple goals had seemed achievable, now seemed an elusive memory as the team languished near the bottom of the league.

1999–2004 SIR BOBBY AND THE BLING

By the turn of the millennium, football was heading ever faster towards a transformational era of huge new TV revenues and massive player wages. For Newcastle United, however, 1999 brought one last episode of old-style hope for revival based on what fans liked to think of as their club's traditional virtues. The appointment of Bobby Robson as manager seemed in many ways to take the club back deep into its past.

Robson had certainly kept pace with many changes in football in his English, European and international career. But as an individual he had remained moulded by his North East English upbringing. Few understood the black and white stripes of Newcastle United's historic identity better than he did. He came from a County Durham mining community. His father, who missed just one shift in five decades working down a pit, had introduced him to supporting the Toon within a family that 'bleeds black and white'. Robson had experienced the vivid chiaroscuro of mining life as a young trainee electrician; his working life 'began in darkness … I served my apprenticeship deep below the fields and football pitches of my beloved North East' before he 'left that blackened world behind' to become a professional footballer. Now he was 'coming home' to Tyneside from the Continent as he believed he could 'pull Newcastle back from the edge of darkness'.

So when it came to the shirt, Robson could identify all too readily with the old-style stripes, preferably as traditional as possible. He once commented on a picture of famous 1950s Newcastle players that 'without badges, the names of kit sponsors or advertising, those long-sleeved shirts look so clean and pure'. But there was no room for such sentiment as the club joined in the millennial rush to ever more intensive global marketing. The Brown Ale era was now over; Robson would even be invited later to press the plunger as the Scottish and Newcastle brewery building next to St James' Park was demolished. The new shirt sponsor from 2000 was NTL, a cable TV company to which the Hall family had sold part of their shareholding. Dwarfing the club crest on the shirts' front, and superimposed on the black and white stripes, was its company logo in thick-set green and purple.

Robson's tactical abilities brought a swift rise up the table and qualification for European competition. But off the field the manager, habitually clad in blazer with club crest and black and white tie, seemed increasingly mystified by the antics of a new generation of millionaire footballers lounging around in expensive leisurewear. The man who had travelled to play in England internationals in the 1950s by public transport had to deal with such incidents as one of his young players, Kieron Dyer, crashing his Ferrari on a bridge across the Tyne after speeding recklessly around the city centre. On another occasion Dyer reportedly asked for the team bus to be turned round after a game to return to the dressing room as he had left behind a diamond earring.

In August 2004, although Newcastle had again qualified for Europe, Robson was sacked by Freddie Shepherd, leaving him 'angry and bitter' and expressing conflicting emotions that many of the club's supporters would find familiar: 'I would always be a fan of the club. Inside, I felt convulsions of shock, indignation, and loss'. He remained in the region, however, facing the return of the cancer which had first afflicted him in the early 1990s, and would become a great inspiration for us when we came to face Ewan's diagnosis.

The sacking of Robson the great Geordie patriot seemed to symbolise a period of increasing angst in the region as the implications of globalisation emerged and the economic and social future seemed more uncertain than ever. Samsung's factory at Wynyard, opened with such fanfare a decade earlier, was now closed. The nihilistic mood was mobilised in a referendum on regional devolution when a campaign organised by a young County Durham activist called Dominic Cummings led to an overwhelming No vote. Back at Newcastle United the indiscipline which had so troubled Robson erupted in the most embarrassing way in 2005 when two players were sent off at St James' Park for fighting each other. New manager Graeme Souness, with his own reputation as a football hard man, looked baffled at times by the scale of the challenge he faced.

The Newcastle shirt design, meanwhile, became caught up in another kind of volatility: that of local and global finance. In 2003 sponsorship by NTL had been replaced by the Newcastle-based former building society and now bank, Northern Rock. Its connotations of local solidity suited the Robson regime and it was in the middle of a period of rapid expansion, seen as challenging the financial giants of the south-east just as Newcastle United hoped to challenge for national football success. In 2007, however, Northern Rock suddenly crumbled, becoming a byword for the greatest of instability after it came close to collapse at the start of the global financial crisis having borrowed recklessly in international markets. Its mostly North Eastern based customers were pictured queueing anxiously to withdraw their cash in the first run on a bank in Britain for a century and a half. The government stepped in to rescue as much as possible, and the bank, as well its sponsorship of Newcastle, limped on.

The club, like Northern Rock, was by now under new ownership in the form of billionaire retailer Mike Ashley. And with what struck me as grimly appropriate timing Newcastle United engaged in their own version of chaotic crisis management in January 2008 when the latest slump in fortunes led to the sacking of manager Sam Allardyce and the appointment of Kevin Keegan for a catastrophic second spell as Newcastle manager. Yet again the Newcastle faithful prayed for miraculous deliverance under the rule of 'King Kev'.

'It can be strangely addictive, football', he commented ruefully in a chapter in his autobiography on his return, a chapter entitled simply 'My Big Mistake'. Before long he 'came up against a wall of incompetence, deceit and arrogance' as players were recruited in bizarre fashion as a result of glimpses in video clips or as favours to agents. The Northern Rock shirt branding remained until 2012, when the government sold what was left of the bank to Virgin Money; a few days later Newcastle appeared, as Gavin Haigh notes, in shirts with 'a temporary Virgin Money patch hastily fastened over the old Northern Rock logo'. The patch did not last long, however, as Ashley had plans to take Newcastle United, and its shirts, into another new financial era of payday lending and gambling.

THE ASHLEY ERA – DEALING IN DISTRESS

Mike Ashley would be a figure of perverse continuity at the club, shaping its fortunes for a turbulent 14 years. Previously, the club's owners had always had some kind of connection to the club and region; Ashley, a retail entrepreneur who had grown up near London, had no links with Newcastle or the North East. But he had become a billionaire by knowing how to seize a commercial opportunity, especially when it came to football shirts, and I became immersed in his story watching on as a fan, and through making two BBC documentaries.

He didn't exactly welcome publicity – 'Britain's answer to Howard Hughes' was one description. After a brief period of companionable boozing with Newcastle fans in a throwback to the Brown Ale era, Ashley seemed surprised when poor results on the pitch led to hostility off it. He retreated into virtual anonymity, and when I began to try to piece together his life story, those around him put up the shutters. But key themes emerged. A childhood friend revealed his early ambition to be a millionaire, and his first money-making exercise re-selling crochet shawls made by his gran for a 100 per cent mark-up. Once he had opened a sportswear shop he began to see the potential in football shirts and tried to enter the national market. A cartel in the north of the country summoned him indignantly to a meeting and informed him that 'there's a club, son, and you're not in it'. Ashley responded by reporting his rivals to the authorities for price-fixing.

His particular retail genius, on which the success of his Sports Direct chain would be based, was on selling customers not only profitable Premier League shirts but also large amounts of cut price 'distressed brands' he had bought up, such as Slazenger and Lonsdale. It was easy to imagine him seeing Newcastle United's footballing distress as an opportunity; and like Sir John Hall, he clearly felt retail and football, shirts and shopping, could be lucratively combined. Yet Ashley the shrewdest of retail entrepreneurs did not seem to have grasped just what club ownership would involve. Footfall into shops he could predict; football on a pitch seemed beyond his grasp. Newcastle managers continued to come and go and the club was relegated not once but twice during his ownership. Chris Hughton, the first black manager of a Premier League club, arrived after one relegation, won over the dressing room and much wider respect with his distinctive, non-confrontational style, and took the team back to mid-table in the Premier League before Ashley sacked him. Players publicly expressed their shock and years later Ashley admitted 'I don't think I gave him enough time'. But Ashley the retailer was constantly restless. He had built his fortune on selling with enthusiasm whenever he thought the price was right and had at times offered the club itself for sale before withdrawing indignantly when buyers failed to offer what he thought was enough. Top players were also for trading. New manager Alan Pardew lost his best striker when Ashley used his helicopter to whisk Andy Carroll to Liverpool after they offered £35 million.

Where did this relentless instability leave the fans' idea

of unbroken allegiance to club and sport? Keegan's highly acrimonious departure had, he said later, 'changed my feelings towards the game I loved' and many Newcastle fans felt the fabric of their loyalty increasingly stretched. And what of the next generation of fans, how would they be attracted? I began to wonder whether it was fair of me, as a father, to encourage my sons to be drawn into an allegiance that might cause them such frustration, even despair. Our family visits to Tyneside were often made during the summer holidays and involved a pilgrimage to St James' Park. The strangest visit I recall was a few weeks after Newcastle's 2009 relegation. Ewan and Alfie were keen on new shirts and we entered the club shop at the ground which was utterly deserted. Mike Ashley, specialist in distressed brands, was now selling off at huge discounts shirts still bearing the logo of Northern Rock, a recently failed bank.

The boys bought at bargain prices but Ewan opted too for what would become a favourite T shirt with a very different feel. It was old-style cotton not nylon, its basic colour was yellow, and in the middle was not an official club crest but the Tyne Bridge logo with blue background, simply encircled by the name 'Newcastle United'. A statement of support for a club, but very different from its latest commercial version. He said he liked the yellow as it looked Brazilian, and I told him my story of an eight-year-old mesmerised by the 1970 World Cup winning team. Newcastle had once had excellent South American players, the Chilean Robledo brothers, in their 1950s Cup-winning era. And in the mid-1980s a Brazilian striker, Mirandinha, had arrived in an excited Newcastle via a bizarre process recorded by former striker Malcolm Macdonald, who was attempting to act as his agent. During his second season, however, he was dropped as Newcastle faced relegation.

The club still seemed stuck in what seemed like a cycle of brief optimism followed by farcical failure as we emerged from that ghostly, bargain basement club shop in 2009. The idea that within a little over a decade Newcastle would be fielding regular

Brazilian internationals would have seemed preposterous. We did find one way of enjoying an altogether sunnier experience of Newcastle as a team in this period, however, though it did, I must confess, involve marital deception. The boys and I noticed that Newcastle were playing a pre-season tournament in the Portuguese Algarve and we lobbied my wife Jane to make that our holiday destination, praising landscape, cuisine and climate without revealing our ulterior motive. Our feigned surprise when we 'noticed', while there, that we could by wonderful co-incidence attend two matches was swiftly seen through with affectionate indignation, but attendance was graciously conceded and Jane agreed that she had enjoyed the games themselves. We were gratified to discover that hundreds of other supporters had seen the journey (and any associated family deception) as worthwhile when we entered the stadium and were able to mingle with players in a relaxed atmosphere. Newcastle even won the mini tournament in a penalty shoot-out, prompting much mirth about how much dust would be released when the St James' Park trophy cabinet was opened after many years of redundancy.

It was a moment, a long way from the cold reality of struggling Tyneside football, to express yearning for the warmth of success. And it is a memory and image I treasure now of Ewan, clad in his distinctive yellow version of Newcastle allegiance, posing confidently next to the striker Demba Ba, enjoying life with defiant enthusiasm shortly before the first indication that he was seriously ill. A few weeks later, back in Newcastle, we watched the Brazilian Olympic team strut their stuff in St James' Park and carried on dreaming.

LOADED WITH WONGA

Mike Ashley, meanwhile, however baffled he might have been by Newcastle's football performances, applied his expertise in sponsorship and marketing ever more intensely. Club shirts became billboards for yet another lurch in the country's financial direction, reflecting the austerity many fans were facing.

In 2013 it was announced that the new shirt sponsor would be a so-called payday loan company, Wonga, founded a few years earlier to provide short term loans at high rates of interest to customers who might struggle to obtain cash from other financial providers. I swiftly persuaded my bosses at Radio 4 that this high-profile endorsement would be an ideal opportunity to explore a controversial development in personal finance. In Newcastle city centre I found some fans relaxed about the deal: 'Me, I support the team, I'm not bothered about the sponsors.' For others all could be justified by football success: 'I'm not bothered what they wear, so long as they win something.' But a grandfather in a sports shop engaged in a local ritual – buying a first Toon kit for a new baby – was adamant that his grandson would not be advertising Wonga.

The club granted me an interview with a senior executive who was cagey on the question of whether they would approve hard-pressed fans using Wonga loans to buy ever more expensive season tickets. He did make the point, however, as did others in my programme, that Wonga was at least preferable to street lenders who preyed violently on desperate people. The most sensitive part of the interview was when I raised the question of the team's Muslim players, one of whom, Pappis Cisse, had expressed disquiet at the club endorsing lending at such high rates of interest. A press officer intervened to stop that line of questioning. I took it up in an intriguing encounter with Archbishop of Canterbury Justin Welby. He had discovered the power of local football identity during his brief time as Bishop of Durham and was championing credit unions as a preferable alternative to payday loans. But even he seemed doubtful as to whether football – or anything else – could resist this new monetary movement. As I entered his study in Lambeth Palace he was immersed in a copy of the *Financial Times*. When I asked him about the Wonga sponsorship he told me he was not 'relaxed' about it but 'it's a fact of life' and 'we're having to adjust to very sharp cultural changes'. His visible discomfort intensified a few weeks later when it was revealed that the Church Commissioners had now through a packaged set of investments acquired a stake in Wonga. The Commissioners, once major investors in John Hall's new Metrocentre, had apparently now moved with Newcastle United into the payday loan era.

In the Wonga era the club even experimented in a 'member's shirt' with replacing the famous stripes in favour of black and white quarters. It never took on. But variation in the stripes' width during the Ashley commercial era had prompted the cruelly apt nickname for Newcastle fans as 'the barcodes'. Everything at the club, it began to appear, had its price. And yet there were always exceptions, as individuals made their own mark on whatever commerce was providing. Ewan was mostly unimpressed by the requirement to become a walking billboard for whichever sponsor paid most, and preferred retro kit. Until, that is, his brain tumour was first diagnosed and the coach of the team he played for in Oxford organised a shirt signed by the then Newcastle United squad. It is now a treasured part of the collection we still have, a record of human sympathy, whatever its logo.

Despite all the off-field controversy there were, as usual with Newcastle, tantalising periods of footballing improvement. Under manager Alan Pardew the team had surged in one season to a fifth place Premier League finish. Pappis Cisse enjoyed a glorious scoring spell, including one extraordinary, sliced half volley from outside the penalty area at Stamford Bridge, home to another highly controversial owner, Russian oligarch Roman Abramovich. Pardew was promptly given an eight year contract but left within two. Mike Ashley, the man who had begun his Newcastle ownership boozing with fans on the terraces, was by now an increasingly remote figure, like the distant CEOs of many a national and international company who had allowed their North East branch operations to wither. He helicoptered in occasionally to the training ground and gave very rare interviews to favoured outlets.

The curse of the Newcastle shirt struck again in 2018 when Wonga, said a few years earlier to be the future of financial services, went bust. But Ashley the entrepreneur, a man who, I discovered, had once bet a large legal bill on a casual game of chance, had already anticipated the change. The new main club and shirt sponsors were a China-based online gambling company, Fun88, of which many fans – myself included – had never heard, and bearing a logo in a language which hardly anyone wearing the shirt locally would understand. We had come a long way from the instantly recognisable branding of Newcastle Brown Ale.

But the shirt – and the banks of electronic billboarding stationed around the St James' Park pitch – continued to reflect the great global trends sweeping across football: ever closer commercial focus on an international TV audience, increased use of technology, and the reinvention of gambling itself. There had long been links between football and gambling, though as the historian Peter Clarke points out, the establishment of the weekly football pools 'offered a relatively respectable way of having a flutter'. I remember being puzzled as a child as to why people seemed obsessed with score draws when wins seemed much more exciting. There were also spot the ball competitions in newspapers, with ribald comment among Newcastle fans as to the futility of studying where our defenders' eyes were looking as they rarely knew what was happening around them.

In the 2000s came a sense that gambling was moving from a murkier place in society to greater acceptance. The Labour government liberalised rules on the sector including, crucially, on its advertising. And the National Lottery had been established as the pools faded, though I was haunted by the comment of a woman I interviewed in Liverpool soon afterwards, who told me that she would spend money on it every week, however little she had, as it 'buys me a few hours of hope'. I discovered the lucrative scale of the change that had now been unleashed when making a profile of Denise Coates, moving force behind another gambling company, bet365. Like Ashley she disliked almost any kind of publicity. But we pieced together how she had begun work in her family's chain of old-fashioned betting shops in the Midlands and had then, as a talented mathematician, spotted the transformational opportunities technology, the online world and smartphones presented. Instead of betting slips submitted in daytime visits to bookmakers there were now algorithms tempting punters through their phones around the clock and during football matches, monetising the mood swings, the reckless euphoria or anxious desire to hedge against disappointment. Coates the pioneer quietly became one of the richest people in the country, one of the few comfortably to outearn Premier League players.

As a parent and supporter, I had increasingly valued the playing and watching of football as a welcome alternative to increasing immersion in the online world. The visual onslaught of gambling advertising around games was now to challenge that hope ever more intensely. No longer was addiction to boozing or smoking celebrated on shirts; other forms of addiction were, however, still present. As was our addiction to the hope of Newcastle United becoming a footballing success. In 2015 the club's potential was still sufficient to attract a manager with the international heft of Rafa Benitez. He expressed a growing love of the fans and the region and stayed to mastermind another recovery after a second relegation under Ashley's ownership. But he left in 2019, sensing that 'it was not a proper project because there was not any intention to invest, to improve things'. Steve Bruce arrived as manager. Whatever might now be the mystifying global images now on the club shirt, Bruce, born in Northumberland and bred in Newcastle, could speak reassuringly fluent Geordie. He steered the club through the difficulties of the COVID epidemic with much dignity, but results still seemed mired in mediocrity. However passionately he might articulate local identity the club itself was about to experience the culmination of the wave of global change that had been gathering force around British football for years. In October 2021 the club was bought by the sovereign wealth fund of Saudi Arabia, the PIF.

Saudi upon Tyne

When fans gathered outside St James' Park there were new images of Toon vulgarity to complement those of shirtless beer bellies. Most fans were clad in ordinary clothes or standard club kit; but media pictures focused on the few who put their version of white traditional Saudi dress on top of their black and white kit. This provided a perfect image of the sportswashing which the Saudi takeover was seen as furthering; and it was clear that this latest lurch into a further dimension of globalisation had taken the club into even more troubling territory. Fans who cheered the overthrow of what they called 'the Ashley regime' had little sense that they might now be subject to another kind of distant and troubling rule.

I remember talking to Ewan about the questions around Saudi Arabia's persecution of political opponents, journalists and minority groups such as gay men and women. It was hardly the kind of association we would have chosen for our club, though there was at least a hope that acquisition of Newcastle United was part of a movement towards reform in Saudi Arabia itself. But there was another dimension to the debate as it erupted: did a change of ownership within the volatile global marketplace of Premier League sports assets mean all the fans of a club more than a century old had to abandon their allegiance; were all its traditions to be forgotten? Would the amount of money required now to compete at the elite level leave the ordinary fan far behind? By now I was living back in the North East, and heard frustration too at the way in which this acquisition prompted such controversy in the national media, when there had been relatively little coverage about or hostility towards the PIF taking stakes in companies as varied as Disney, Uber, Facebook, Starbucks and the pharmaceutical company Pfizer. And I knew from my journalistic work that the British state, its arms industry and its royal family had long had profound ties with the Saudi ruling elite and their economy, seen as vital for the British 'national interest' as well as manufacturing jobs.

When it came to the club shirts, the new Saudi owners and their commercial advisers began to tread a wary path between the modernisation and new branding they desired, and a sense that tradition could not be jettisoned too rapidly. A green shirt echoing the Saudi national colour was introduced for away games, and Saudi companies appeared as shirt sponsors. An 'event management' company called Sela appeared on the shirts' front, a sign that football matches in general were now seen as not just ninety or so minutes of sport but as 'events' with much wider commercial potential. A new 'sleeve partner', Noon, was presented as 'the Middle East's leading online shopping destination'. The club shop – where we had previously bought our cut-price post relegation shirts – was expensively revamped and was now packed on match-days. Near to its entrance stood a statue of 1950s striker Jackie Milburn, who had grown up among lads who could not afford football boots, playing 'with just a piece of wood, shaped like a shoe, strapped to their feet with a piece of string'.

The club's new commercial masters were aware, however, of the power of ancient loyalties to the Milburns and Macdonalds of Tyneside folklore. Noticing how many fans chose to wear older shirts harking back to, say, the exhilaration of the 1990s Keegan era, they began to market their own 'retro' style shirts. Meanwhile the new 2025/6 shirt, the club's publicity stated, 'draws inspiration from a classic northern motif – the shepherd's check – blending it seamlessly with our historic vertical stripes to create something fresh, and undeniably

Newcastle ... A full-colour club crest sits proudly on the chest, with "Howay the Lads" on the back of the neck – a call to arms that means everything in the stands, the streets, and on the pitch'.

But the stands and the streets were far from happy when, around the same time, the club announced that it was proposing to change the historic crest itself. The club had originally used the city's crest, including images of its castle, seahorses to symbolise maritime tradition, and a Latin slogan, *Fortiter Defendit Triumphans,* dating from successful defence against Scots incursion. It was the crest players would point to in moments of triumph to indicate their commitment, just as fans felt it essential that their team would 'play for the shirt'.

There had been adaptations of the crest, such as the incorporation of the black and white stripes in the 1980s. But now the club informed its fans that 'as our club grows on the global stage, the symbol that represents us needs to be able to keep pace. It needs to show up clearly and confidently across everything – from kits to screens to merchandise'. Anticipating with visible nervousness what was a hostile supporter response, 'consultation' was promised and the statement added: 'This isn't about walking away from our past. It's about carrying it forward with pride. The crest is part of our story. It's on our shirts and inked in our skin'. That last point was literally true, but not in a way the club might have approved. As change to the crest was debated, I saw increasing numbers of fans with the old-style crest defiantly tattooed onto arms and legs. Even the bare-chested fan could now sport his own traditional Newcastle branding regardless of that season's commercial offer. All seemed to confirm the wisdom of the football historian Percy Young, who wrote in the 1960s: 'Football as an activity mirrors the present. Its rituals reflect the more or less immediate past; its symbols, which lie within the ritual, the distant, inaccessible past'.

The row over the crest powerfully illustrated, it seemed to

me, what had been happening to the club, and the shirt, in recent decades, and the dilemmas it now posed in reconciling the global with the local. The revolution unleashed by John Hall in the 1980s, his plan to combine retail revolution and shirt-led football promotion, had entered yet another, ever more international phase. The ghostly presences in the battle between club history and commercial modernity came ironically into view when a video promoting the new season's kit in 2025 had to be withdrawn after it briefly and accidentally displayed a version of the Japanese imperial flag – the flag that would have been flying at St James' Park in 1906 when Japanese sailors were welcomed there after their victories using Armstrong's Tyneside-made guns. The new shirts did however bear an image of the Tyne Bridge, still one of the most popular symbols of the region but currently undergoing prolonged restoration after much neglect and disputes between local and central government as to who should pay for repairs. The club might be on the up; but could it carry the region with it?

GLOBAL TOON

In comments after his ownership of the club, Sir John Hall had reflected on what he had learned about supporting Newcastle and what it meant for the region. 'The obsession for football is overwhelming and sometimes I used to get quite frightened of the responsibility for people's lives,' he told Joe Sharkey. 'It's a strength – the great passion for the club. But it's a weakness that we haven't moved beyond it intellectually. And it sums up the area in some ways. There has to be something more than the football club…there has to be a lot more, if we're going to progress forward.'

When it came to his decision to sell his stake in the club to Mike Ashley he reflected that 'he was globalising Newcastle which I could not do'. That globalisation had now been turbocharged by the Saudi takeover. I occasionally saw a now very frail Sir John arriving for matches at St James' Park in this new era. But his enthusiasm for the benefits of globalisation seemed to have waned. In 2024 the man who had imported a US-style retail revolution to the North East and championed Korean manufacture and a Spanish-style sporting club was reported to have endorsed the Reform party in the UK general election, stating that it was the 'only party who will protect and save my English culture'.

We, meanwhile, are left like all fans with our family collection of shirts, evoking so much about different eras, matches and attitudes towards what was happening to our club. And in our case they remind us about so much more. The crazy range of sponsors, the moment when millionaire players sent Ewan their sympathy on a shirt, and his personal combination of faith in the Toon with a yearning for a yellow dash of Brazilian verve to enhance, not undermine, the deepest value of the black and white.

6

THE SOUL OF A STADIUM

DURING THE MIKE ASHLEY shirt era, many seemed content to keep an underskin of black and white and endure, or ignore, whatever sponsorship the owner had negotiated on top. When it came to the rebranding of the Newcastle United stadium, however, Ashley suffered a monumental defeat. And that saga made me realise how a stadium like St James' Park contains not just a football pitch but a whole community culture. In fact, I want to argue, it can be seen as a place of culture as much as a theatre or a concert hall. I was able to rediscover that after moving back to the region, and we managed to get Ewan there on several occasions despite his illness advancing.

A stadium like St James' Park stands for the past as well as the present; it is also what the French call a *lieu de mémoire*, a site of memory, an idea I first came across when learning about the legacy of the First World War. And now football's historians have begun to show how that idea plays into everything from the links between mining and the game, to how particular matches marked turning points in Cold War events. No-one knows the strength of that idea better than a father who finds the memory of his lost son in a football stadium as vividly as anywhere.

But stadiums are restless places, restless for success on the pitch, and redevelopment off it; memory and history can get in the way. Looking back further to my visits since the 1970s, it seems to me that there has long been a contest within the stadium about who really owns and shapes its atmosphere and identity. Now that contest has entered a fascinating new phase, as fans find dramatic new ways of shaping its atmosphere in sound and vision, while the stadium's future has swiftly become one of the greatest challenges the club's new owners face.

ASHLEY: A REBRANDING TOO FAR

In 2009 the newly Mike Ashley-owned club began to moot the idea of adding a sponsor's name to that of St James' Park. Many expressed anger at any such dilution of the stadium's historic identity but in 2011 he went further, completely renaming the stadium the 'Sports Direct Arena'. Large signs to that effect were placed inside and outside the ground, making it hard to distinguish at first glance from one of his brash megastores.

The fusion of football and retail empires begun in the John Hall era seemed to be complete, though Freddy Shepherd, part of that previous regime, sought to distance himself. 'I don't think the fans will be very happy' he commented, putting it mildly. 'St James' goes back to when the monks used to work there, a convent used to be there, and St James' Park goes back hundreds of years.' His invocation of monastic tradition might have seemed somewhat surprising to those who had read in the *News of the World* of his mocking comments made in a Spanish brothel about Newcastle fans' alleged gullibility. He was however on stronger ground when pointing out that the name change and its supposed branding value would be undermined in the city by simple everyday rejection. 'Fans in Newcastle, like myself, will always call it St James' Park anyway so anyone claiming the rights, it's not going to do them much good'. There was political as well as popular resistance. The city council made it clear that none of the local street names nor the Metro station would be altered to acknowledge Ashley's change.

A war of attrition ensued around the ground, like a football version of hostile countries jockeying for territory and status near a disputed border. Ashley began to buy up parcels of land close to the stadium for his own commercial purposes, trying to bolster the visual assertion of his ownership. Reminders of his critics, like former striker Alan Shearer's name on a stadium bar, were removed. When a new statue of Shearer was created the club refused to allow it to be placed within the stadium's precincts but the Freemen of the Town Moor, prickly defenders of land rights and local identity over the centuries, provided a space just outside the ground for Shearer, arm raised, to signal defiance of the St James' Park usurpers.

CULTURED CLUB

The dispute focused minds on why the stadium, not just its name but its wider resonance, mattered so much to the club's supporters. Its location, high above the city centre yet within easy walking distance, and enhanced height after the 1990s expansion made it visible from many directions. The impression it now makes has had admirers stretching for superlatives. Bobby Robson praised its appeal with an especially engaging enthusiasm. 'Athens has the Parthenon, Newcastle has St James' Park', he declared. The stadium 'perches like a colossus in the centre of the city, where it occupies and entrances its citizens'. And the football ground, he believed, was integral to the city's wider distinction. 'Newcastle has a history, culture and location that makes it wonderfully, beguilingly different. It is a single-club city with a stadium at its heart'.

Mentioning 'culture' in the same passage as 'stadium' might strike some as incongruous; but never for me. In the late 1970s I would be at St James' Park one evening, and the city's Theatre Royal the next, relishing a sadly brief time when real commitment to national cultural provision meant the Royal Shakespeare Company brought its entire Stratford season annually and affordably to Tyneside. We paid a pound for standing tickets, like proper Shakespearean groundlings, and manoeuvred towards the best spaces and viewpoints we could find in the theatre just as we did on the football terraces.

I learned later I was following in the footsteps of Lawrie McMenemy, later a top football manager and early devotee of St James' Park. He grew up in some poverty in Gateshead but recalled how he would often meet his Mam in the centre of Newcastle 'and we'd head for a night of opera at the Theatre Royal ... She wanted me to love the opera she was so passionate about ... taking her child to a theatre where both of us could dream our dreams'.

Football stadiums sometimes became cultural venues in their own right. The most extraordinary one I went to with my sister Rachel was Ayresome Park in Middlesbrough in 1976, where the entire line-up of the Newport Jazz Festival including Ella Fitzgerald, Dizzy Gillespie and Oscar Peterson came across the Atlantic to Teesside. In the 1980s St James' Park hosted the Rolling Stones, Bob Dylan and Bruce Springsteen, who wrote a $20,000 cheque for a striking miners' support group.

That kind of activity, cultural and political, would have come naturally to one of Newcastle United's first stars in its Edwardian championship-winning team, Colin Veitch. He was not only a great player but also an enthusiastic trade unionist, amateur actor, choirmaster and friend of George Bernard Shaw. In 1911 the football correspondent of *The Times*, still wedded to the Corinthian ideals of amateur football, was struggling to admire the Newcastle United professional team that had recently become a national powerhouse. They were, he said 'the most scientific eleven in the country' and grudgingly acknowledged that: 'For all that they are paid for their services and for the most part imported players, the Newcastle men have a fine *esprit de corps* and an acquired sense of local patriotism which puts them on a higher plane than, say, a troupe of music-hall performers'. When it came to their captain Veitch, however, the *Times* man was far more fulsome. He was 'not only one of the cleverest and most versatile players the game has ever produced, but also a sportsman of very best type – one who has a strong claim to our respect and regard as any of those professional cricketers, for example, who play the game for the game's sake and teach us their art by precept and practice. Veitch's personality is the soul of his team'. When I sent Ewan material on Veitch he replied: 'What a life – they don't make them like this anymore! He is my new hero.'

Yet some always insisted on seeing football in the North East not as part of the cultural scene, but as a preferred local alternative. While I was joining sell-out Newcastle audiences at the RSC in the 1970s, local grandee Lord Ridley was opining: 'Northern Arts is trying to ram culture down people's throats when they prefer football.' Kevin Keegan declared of the St James' Park crowd: 'they come here to be entertained. It's like the people down south going to the theatre'. As a manager, however, Keegan had said endearingly that he hoped Newcastle would 'win the league with beauty'. So could football really be cultural? That idea was always likely to appeal to a region with a strong tradition of craft skills and individuals combining muscular strength with delicate working ability; I was always especially impressed with shipyard workers who operated in the most hazardous places using hot metal with a skill and courage that was, in every sense, riveting. I thought Keegan's goalkeeper Pavel Srniček, who relished the *Zeitgeist* on Tyneside as 'the Entertainers' came so close to winning the Premier League, would have liked this statement by his compatriot the great Czech writer Karel Čapek: 'Culture comprises a kitchen as well as a university, football as well as poetry, a home bathroom as well as a comprehensive school. It depends on how every single thing is used... If we decide to consider man as a cultural creature, everything that emanates from his hands and that he uses to live well is a cultural fact'.

In the 1970s a Labour council leader in Newcastle had told author John Ardagh: 'We spend thousands on parks and sport – who needs art? ... It's high-falooting (sic) to think culture just means Mozart. We have one of England's best footballers and he's a great artist too'. And there have been plenty of fans who reach instinctively for the language of the arts to describe the best of what they see on the pitch. One of Bobby Robson's favourite players at Newcastle had, he said, 'a paintbrush of a left foot'. I once heard it said that a pass by Newcastle winger Terry Hibbitt had been so good 'you could hang it in the Louvre'. And that could apply, even if with regret, to admiring the brilliance of opposition players. One of the greatest, if not *the* greatest, Premier League goals was scored by Arsenal striker Dennis Bergkamp in 2002 at St James' Park. Like much great art it remains mysterious; few could ever work out just how he had done it. He received the ball at pace backing into a defender, Greek international Nikos Dabizas. With the outside of his foot he spun the ball one way round Dabizas, ran past him the other, held him off and then calmly side footed the ball past the goalkeeper.

It was, conceded Dabizas, 'like a perfectly-written script, an act of genius, a work of art'. 'They should slow that goal down with some classical music' marvelled Bergkamp's Arsenal team-mate, Ian Wright, 'and put it into a museum'. Like many others, no doubt, Ewan and I went down to our local football field to attempt ruefully to recreate the goal after seeing it on TV; after twisting awkwardly in the role of Dabizas I then had lower back discomfort to accompany the psychic pain of another loss to the Gunners. But Ewan, who spent many years with a wonderful Oxford youth dance group, suffered no such after-effects and loved the idea of a good striker pirouetting around a defender.

A Chorus of Despair

If the players were capable of art on the pitch, what about the role of the crowd? Were they merely passive spectators like those in a theatre or opera house; or an essential part of the culture too? There were some who detected a change towards greater passivity in the stands as the club modernised, ticket prices went up and the composition of the crowd changed.

When I made my profile of Sir John Hall for BBC radio in the mid-1990s, I was given a tour of the modernised St James' Park by a veteran employee, Eric Jobson, who had had blissfully little training in the dark arts of PR. Speaking from the heart as a fan, he showed me what he called 'millionaire's row' in the directors' box, noting that this was the only stadium in country with carpets on the terrace as 'if you're a millionaire, you can't get your feet cold'. While a new economic elite was now attending Newcastle games he said he felt 'sorry for the people who supported us in the bad times' as many could afford neither match tickets nor the satellite TV now broadcasting games.

Hall had told me that 'soccer's been on the cheap for too long'. Under his control there was a 'vast' increase in corporate facilities with high-end restaurants and hospitality suites named after Northumberland castles. Newcastle's New Football Castle was taking the region's old aristocratic bastions under its rebranded wing. What that also meant in practice was that fans wanting to keep their season tickets had not only to pay higher prices, but also take out a ten year bond to secure their seats, some of which were moved to make way for corporate entertainment. A bitter dispute ensued. The inability to pay for either tickets or bonds became a topic of constant anguish on Tyneside, captured in a novel *The Season Ticket* (later made into a film) by author and local teacher Jonathan Tulloch. A Newcastle season ticket, says one of the main characters, Gerry, 'means we watch every game. We never miss a game. It means we belong'. Failure to buy a bond, he is warned, means staying on an ever-longer waiting list 'until kingdom come'. But the dream, however financially impossible, cannot be abandoned as without a season ticket 'we're nowt'. Football meant identity, but for many, like culture, it became increasingly unaffordable as the old, assumed bond between club and supporters was steadily superseded by a very different kind of bond-driven financial ambition.

There was a period towards the end of the Ashley regime

when the football was so disappointing, and the ownership so unpopular, that tickets for St James' Park had to be given away to prevent the embarrassment of many empty seats; the Newcastle barcodes had, so to speak, become the Premier League bogofs. The remaining crowd during this period had meanwhile shifted from their customary role of irrepressible cheerleaders to a kind of tragic Greek chorus, punctuating long periods of stoic silence with horribly resonant lamentations.

The stadium's role as a training ground for trainee or veteran comics was another of its cultural functions, providing a rich vein of dark humour. Ewan loved this aspect as a consolation when footballing times were hard. And he would later write about the value of humour in every kind of circumstance. I remember watching one game with Ewan and Alfie early in a season near the end of the Ashley era when West Ham's Declan Rice waltzed through the Newcastle team and a voice rasped through the silence at our end of the ground with the simple prophecy: 'it's gannin' to be a laaaang, hard winter'. On another occasion the Brazilian Joelinton, signed expensively as a striker but dismally unsuccessful in his first seasons, completed a trademark move in which he ran into a promising position near the penalty area before losing his balance at the crucial moment. 'It's aaaalways the same' wailed a lone voice resounding like the sentinel in a Greek tragedy across our section of the ground. 'He runs, he gets clooose and then he aaalways, he aaaaaaalways faaaals aawer'. Characteristically articulate Geordie vowel sounds became ever more elongated as despair deepened, and a thousand heads nearby shook in mournful agreement, while others grinned painfully in recognition of tragi-comic truth.

The idea, at that moment, that within a couple of years the same player would be a Brazilian international and part of a Champions League Newcastle team, that he would be worshipped from the stands and would rush to the crowd to celebrate not only goals but tackles like a rock star, sending a jolt of energy right across the ground: that would have seemed a work of the most outrageously improbable fiction. But within that stadium a new era, with all kinds of exhilarating new achievements, but also fascinating new tensions, was about to be staged.

GLAD TO BE GLOBALISED?

We happened to have tickets for the first match after the takeover of Newcastle United by a consortium mostly funded by the Saudi Arabian Public Investment Fund (the PIF). The atmosphere of anticipation was, not surprisingly, intense. As far as much of the crowd was concerned, renewed hope for the football future was fuelled by the strength of the Newcastle tradition, the idea of revival. A powerful display was organised by Wor Flags, a fans' group which had been formed a few years previously, centred on celebration of black and white imagery but also expression of many fans' frustration at what they felt had been lost. (The 'wor' in the name was the local word of belonging, meaning 'our', applied to everything from closest family to pressure on referees as impassioned cries of 'wor ball' resounded in claiming a corner or throw-in.)

As well as flags there were banners displayed ahead of games, making trenchant statements to players and owners. 'We don't demand a team that wins', said one, 'we demand a club that tries'. One of the players in the late Mike Ashley era, Matt Ritchie, gave a fascinating account later of how constraining the atmosphere around stadium and city had become. 'We were dead and buried. It was suppressing the city. I'd been there a long time and it was, "Are we stagnating?". Even if we won at the weekend, it was, "What are we winning for?".' Under new ownership, the same players were released from their cage'.

After the Saudi takeover, the hope was now not only for a title-winning team but also for regeneration of the whole area, an end to that 'suppressing (of) the city' Ritchie had identified. A song by Jimmy Nail, 'Big River', was played ahead of the first game of the new era; he was a local actor who had come to fame in the TV series *Auf Wiedersehen, Pet* as one of the Geordies forced to work abroad in the 1970s when local jobs disappeared. The song's main lyric was displayed on a massive Wor Flags banner: 'This is a Mighty Town, Built Upon a Solid Ground. And Everything They've Tried to Kill, We Will Rebuild.'

But the singing of 'Big River' and the emotion around it was suddenly interrupted by the stadium announcer calling for a 'great Geordie' welcome for the club's new chairman, head of the Saudi Investment Fund (as well as chair of the Saudi oil company, Aramco) Yasir Al-Rumayyan. He was the man now really in charge, despite shrewd use of Amanda Staveley, a minority shareholder in the takeover, to front much of the PR. At first euphoria was sustained as Newcastle scored soon after the kick off but before long normal service was resumed. Visiting Spurs looked better in every department and should have won by more than 3-2. Al-Rumayyan may have begun to realise then that he had taken on quite a challenge, a sentiment reinforced a few weeks later when he returned for what had doubtless been promised as an easy home win in an FA Cup tie against Cambridge United. Some of us, veterans of the curse of Cambridge from the early 1980s, could have warned him against such hubris where Newcastle were concerned and sure enough the visitors won 1-0 with a goal by a player called Ironside from Middlesbrough.

The Saudis were said to be 'patient' investors and now realised perhaps why they might need to be. But before long a new manager, Eddie Howe, and some excellent recruits began to organise a march up the table. The ability and reputation of Wor Flags also grew as they created ever more formidable pre-match fusions of the black and white belonging, passion, supporters' art, song, poetry – a full panorama of popular culture created after consultation through their own fans' democracy. We loved the hugely impressive atmosphere and the way it seemed to energise the Newcastle players before one game near the end of the season when Arsenal, needing points for a Champions League place, arrived, faced the wall of black and white intensity and noise before kick-off, and looked utterly cowed in a 2-0 defeat. Their combative midfielder Granit Xhaka lamented afterwards: 'if someone is not ready for this pressure, stay at home. You can't come here and play like this.' Kevin Keegan recalled from his time as a player that 'at Liverpool all the noise seemed to come from the Kop. With Newcastle, it was from all four sides, like speakers on a surround-sounds system'.

After such victories there were more celebrations with songs, flags and player parades. One of the last videos preserved on Ewan's phone was a recording of ecstatic post-match supporters singing 'na, na na na na na naah, Geordies'. It might not have been the kind of singing in which he'd been so superbly coached as a choirboy, but there could be no doubting its passion. It would be easy to be carried away by the choreographed emotion, however, and assume that the fans always made the difference. While the management and players made all the right public noises of approval, there was a sense that, particularly at Newcastle, sometimes it was important for the team to avoid being too influenced by emotion. Riding what Keegan had once called 'the black and white tiger' had its hazards and some believed manager Eddie Howe's success was down to his ability to remain detached and level-headed amidst all the hype. The traditional stadium contest continued, and the crowd-chorus could inspire confidence or powerfully articulate anxiety and persistent pessimism.

THE DIGITAL DAMPENER

Whatever was happening between fans, players and managers, there were also more profound changes, affecting football generally, that the takeover would accelerate. In order to afford the gigantic wages of top-level players much more money had to be made. And technology was changing football too as it became even more of a global 'product'.

Near to St James' Park, on a site where previously there had been a brewery and a coal mine, Newcastle University had opened a data mining centre. It symbolised powerfully how the local economy was shifting. And the spread of the digital now extended into every fan's life via a new ticketing system, replacing paper tickets with passes on smartphones. For older fans like me, who had grown up in the pre-computer age, it was another sharp adjustment, and many of us assembled anxiously outside what the club called its 'box office' for advice. In conversation as we waited, I learned how the new system was playing havoc with long-established traditions of families and friends sharing season tickets, passing around the old paper documents in a kind of communal economy. It reminded me mischievously of when I travelled behind the Iron Curtain during communism where the queues – for everything from sausages to books to car parts – were the places where you really learned what people thought about the powers that be. In the St James' Park queue I heard stories too about the misery of missing out on a season ticket, such as the man who had had to give his up a few years previously when made redundant and who could now see no way back to that state of belonging. He had to join the rest of us sitting on our computers entering ballots for games or chasing frantically small numbers of one-off sales.

In some ways going to the game had seemed a blessed escape from digital domination as mobile signals did not work well inside the crowded stadium. There was something refreshing about seeing 50,000 plus humans all focused on a flesh-and-blood experience rather than staring at their screens. But the digital revolution was not to be denied inside the stadium too. Data monitors lurked by the side of the pitch and players wore strange-looking garments under their shirts so their ever more important stats could be monitored. Before long, we joked, fans might be wired up to ensure acceptable levels of enthusiasm were sustained, or players might be replaced

Croydon family, early 1970s, initial allegiance to Crystal Palace

2022: Jane, Alfie, Ewan, Laura and Chris

DELAY HAS A SILVER LINING

WHEN his enthronement as Bishop of Newcastle was postponed from January 20 to February 13, Canon Ronald Bowlby accepted the fact with the resignation that befits a Christian gentleman.

The little cloud, however, had a silver lining, for the postponement means that the football-loving bishop will be free to see the Newcastle United-Crystal Palace match that day and cheer on his new team against his old one.

The Bishop-elect, who is being consecrated in Durham Cathedral tomorrow, has come from Croydon, where his home team is Crystal Palace, but he has told his 11-year-old son, Christopher, to put away his Crystal Palace scarf for good.

Canon Bowlby, who is 46, enjoys walking and swimming as well as football. He is no stranger to the North-East, having been curate at St. Luke's, Pallion, Sunderland, for four years and vicar of St. Aidan's, Billingham, for 10.

He said today: "The Newcastle area, with its great unemployment problem, presents a very different scene to the one I have just left. My basic task will be to find out the problems of the community and decide how the Church can help with them.

"This is an area with a strong tradition of church life. It is good to come back to the North-East, and I am looking forward immensely to living here."

Speaking of the ecumenical movement, he said

Early 1973. The new Bishop of Newcastle makes clear his future football loyalty
(from the *Newcastle Evening Chronicle*)

1970s Newcastle – a club and its stadium writ large across local identity
(Copyright © Newcastle City Libraries)

Late 1970s: Chris in action on his beloved Town Moor

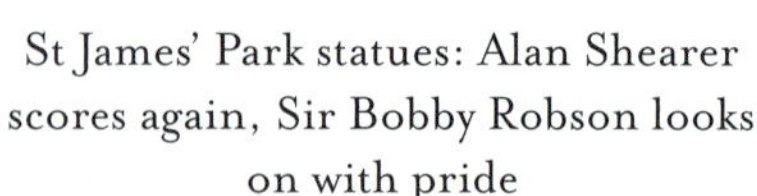

Emma Hicks, star of Morpeth Post Office Girls FC in 1917, one of the many 'lost lasses'

St James' Park statues: Alan Shearer scores again, Sir Bobby Robson looks on with pride

Fans' group Wor Flags
salutes Kevin Keegan,
Newcastle's Messiah,
as he faces cancer

St James' Park walkway
– a place of memory

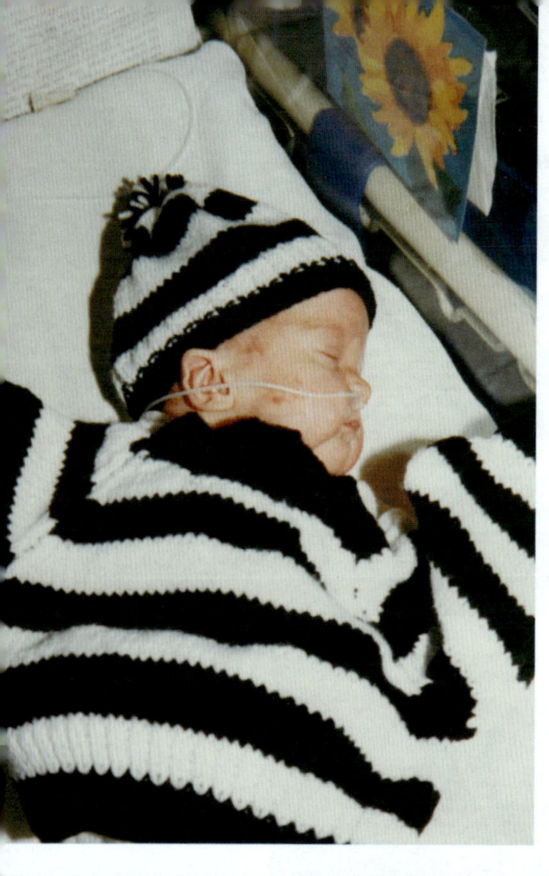

Alfie in a special care
baby unit, kitted out for the
1998 FA Cup final

Alfie and his Dad as the Toon
finally win a trophy,
the 2025 Carabao Cup

Ewan, in his favourite Newcastle shirt, and his schoolfriend Charlie
with the striker Demba Ba

Proudest of family finishers in the 2022 Great North Run

St James' Park, first game after the Carabao Cup win,
remembers those not there 'who didn't make the night'

in a football dystopia by totally wired robots. The pitch itself meanwhile was now surrounded by digital advertising displays that might be something recognisable or might be entirely for the consumption of TV audiences thousands of miles away, with adverts in unfamiliar languages.

By far the most visible – and controversial – digital intervention came with the introduction of VAR, the video assistant referee. In the past, the scoring of a goal or dismissal of a player happened in dramatic synchronicity with the crowd's loud emotion; I remembered how as a youngster I would monitor anxiously from afar as crowd roars or groans broadcast across the city seemed to transmit reliable news of events. But now the spontaneity of huge surges of emotion was regularly followed by a sudden, bewildering hiatus as a cold, distant intervention from afar brought events into question. The raw immediacy of drama and adjudication in the thick of the stadium's atmosphere was replaced by detached screen analysis from far away.

These infuriating pauses revived the kind of caustic commentary from fans that I remembered from the desperate days of the Ashley era. Yes, VAR might sometimes provide a favourable judgement for the Newcastle team but somehow it seemed to many against the spirit of the game, and the place. VAR seemed somehow symptomatic of the kind of arbitrary, distant computer-based and apparently unaccountable authority that made many aspects of people's lives more miserable and incomprehensible as organisations of all kinds retreated from human contact. A VAR official ruling a glorious goal offside because of a stray toenail became an unpleasant reminder of the compliance officer whose algorithmic lack of imagination meant your application for, say, a vital piece of health assistance had been rejected. Such was the mood I sometimes detected during prolonged waits for the verdict from the all-powerful judges, inevitably located far away in London.

A Bowl-Shaped Future?

One of the ways of killing time while waiting for VAR decisions was to play the game of spotting the new club elite sitting in the directors' box. The millionaires with warm feet had come in under John Hall; what kind of alliances would the Saudis be striking? It was perhaps not surprising that a Gulf elite steeped in hereditary family status would gravitate towards the North East's ancient landowners. The new Newcastle club hierarchy was soon to be found holding meetings at Alnwick Castle, home of the Percies, the Dukes of Northumberland, though they did so with a modern PR twist, allowing some of their encounters to be filmed for an Amazon documentary.

The Percies had an intriguing relationship with the history of football, presiding over an ancient version of the game played in Alnwick each Shrove Tuesday. They had moved it in the nineteenth century from their town centre after it allegedly became too rough. The game now commenced with the Duke throwing a ball down from his castle battlements. Football historian David Goldblatt believed this had been part of the deliberate suppression of a popular attempt to use football to 'reassert the people's control of common land and byways'. The Percies had always been shrewd commercial operators too, whether as landowners, property developers, mine owners or, in most recent times, enjoyers of a tourism boom based on the local filming of Harry Potter and the development of a 'destination' garden. The new Saudi-Northumbrian alliance had been sealed in marital form too when the Saudi Ambassador to Britain married the Duke's niece, Lucy Caroline Cuthbert. Following the announcement of the Saudi takeover of Newcastle United the ambassador strove gamely to suggest that the two places had much in common. Saudi Arabia, he claimed, is 'very similar to Northumberland in some ways, just one is brown and hot, the other green and cold'. He hoped Newcastle fans would now visit his country 'but they won't be able to drink, so it might be a bit of a shock'.

The PIF takeover not only created the expectation for a much more successful team; it was also assumed that the new owners' huge wealth would soon be directed towards plans for a new stadium. As the Saudis will have sensed in the magnificent surroundings of Alnwick Castle, all of the North East's powers-that-be have wanted to leave their monuments. The Normans built the first New Castle as an assertion of power. But perhaps the most resonant builder of local infrastructure was the Roman Emperor Hadrian. The route of his famous Wall ran through the city and he remains a popular brand name today. The only city centre structure to rival St James' Park for height is the recently constructed Hadrian Tower. In my home town of Hexham the Hadrian brand is, somewhat bizarrely, used to promote everything from pet care and oven cleaning to renewable energy. Perhaps, in a world where much seems to have stopped working, Hadrian is admired simply as someone who got things done.

Hadrian had his Wall; the Saudis, in their own country at least, are building The Line, a futuristic linear city stretching for more than 100 miles through the desert. It is due to include a football stadium 350 metres above ground to host matches during the 2034 World Cup. A new stadium for Newcastle ought, by comparison, to be trivially easy. But as any Newcastle fan with a sense of history could tell them, transforming this stadium might not be so straightforward. Part of the challenge, as Paul Joannou explains in his history of *Fortress St James*, is that the club does not own its ground and the land on it, still ultimately in the hands of the city authorities and governed too by the ancient rights of the Town Moor freemen and women. As the Duke of Northumberland could advise, outright land ownership does enhance the power to act.

The Milburn stand where the club's management now operate carries on some of its walls a mini-museum of previous failed attempts to secure a new stadium. The ground on the edge of a Moor, its pitch long known for dodgy drainage, had become stuck in what club historian Joannou aptly called a 'political quagmire'. As property developer John Hall began to wrestle for control of the club from the late 1980s he collaborated with the city authorities in devising a new plan for an entirely new stadium to be built on another part of the Town Moor. Plans embraced the idea of the stadium as a cultural venue by having 'a huge, hydraulic, sliding screen' which 'would separate the core football arena from a multi-purpose stage and theatre'. Another scheme in the 1990s foundered on opposition by those objecting to its effect on green parkland and local architectural harmony. As so often, redevelopment plans ended in tiers. Rather than engage in a prolonged public enquiry the club opted instead to expand part of the current stadium upwards. Development was now lopsided and vertiginous, a good representation of the club's on-field inconsistencies. The yearning for a completed, coherent, modernised structure remained as unfulfilled as the yearning for trophies.

The stadium's capacity, a little over 50,000, is currently far from sufficient to satisfy the demand for tickets. More than that, the last few years have shown watching fans that the demands of elite football competition now require clubs to see them and their stadia very differently, as sources of much more than ticket revenue. Although the Saudis may now be the ultimate owners at Newcastle, it is global, and especially American, commercial sports culture that is setting the tone.

When I was a graduate student in the US for a year in the mid-1980s, it was the almost complete absence of interest in 'soccer' that was striking. And that stood for US sports investors too, baffled no doubt by a sport that went for 45 minute periods without commercial breaks and was stubbornly attached to the geography of local allegiance rather than allowing franchises to be traded and moved around a country. But such has been the global popularity of the Premier League and the allure of TV revenue that US investors have felt they could not miss the opportunity, moving more and more into football ownership. And they have brought with them the belief that much more revenue can be extracted from fans everywhere.

The key figures at Newcastle United recruited after the Saudi takeover were a far cry from the local businessmen, solicitors and regional grandees who had previously run the club. CEO was Darren Eales, British-born but who had made his name as president of Atlanta United in US Major League Soccer. The job of Chief Commercial Officer, meanwhile, was taken by Peter Silverstone, who had worked earlier in his career liaising with Netflix over a documentary about Arsenal, and had built and led the 'Brasil Global Tour', described as 'responsible for the organisation and commercialisation of the Brazil national football team's global friendly schedule'. Newcastle might be the HQ; the target market was now the world.

But there was, of course, an inheritance of passionate local support, one which, handled well, could give the club globally appealing character. Silverstone hinted at the delicate balancing act he and the club now faced, stating 'I am committed to immersing myself in the heritage and culture of this giant club, and the vibrant city of Newcastle' while building a commercial operation 'that will deliver the commercial success vital to power the fans' and the club's ambitious growth plans'.

For many fans, the heritage of St James' Park was not just something physical or structural, but the time-honoured ritual of many thousands of locals who bought perhaps one replica shirt a year (or wore a treasured older one) and arrived at the ground just in time for kick off having had food and drink in the city on the way. Those planning the club's future, however, wanted more of a new kind of football-consumer, a change in approach from what Michael Walker called the 'milking of devotion' of the traditional fan. Since the 1990s company boxes and hospitality areas had been there; now there was a marked expansion in areas devoted to special match day packages. It was noticeable that crowds began to include more one-off or first-time visitors from abroad, often clad in brand-new club shop purchases.

When football crowds seemed in sharp decline in the 1960s, it was believed that the mobile consumer-fan would steadily replace the diehard local supporter. Percy Young, in his *History of British Football*, published in 1969, wrote: 'the old style spectator supported his team through thick and thin. A few of this type survive, but the connoisseur will only watch attractive football while the materialist will patronise only a winning side'. There are plenty of connoisseurs and materialists today, but the supposedly disappearing diehard has remained stubbornly, loudly, visibly present, even at a club like Newcastle which has known so little success.

The idea of a new stadium, mooted so often in previous decades, has now been revived for the 2020s, though detailed proposals remain elusive. The word 'bowl' has been widely used, with images of an all-encompassing design. No longer would some of the stadium be open to dramatic views of the city and its environs behind, but would enclose the pitch, and its extensive hospitality facilities, in a world designed to entice the fans in early to spend their money there rather than within the city economy.

LEAVING HALLOWED GROUND

If a new stadium is approved, if the present St James' Park is demolished, there is one aspect unlikely to feature in the prospectuses or plans or media coverage, but which I, and many fans, will feel keenly: that this is a place of community culture, and memory. For me, it is now forever the place where I revelled in that culture with Ewan. The club has in the past made some acknowledgement of this role. For those whose minds are fading with conditions like dementia the club holds Memory Cafes where ex-players meet fans. Fans, and some prominent players such as Jackie Milburn, had their ashes scattered around the pitch. When that area was controversially covered over in 2013 facilities manager Eddie Rutherford consoled the relatives of those whose remains were there: 'In laying the tarmac we feel we are 'sealing in' the ashes which are already there to protect them for eternity and people will still be able to lay flowers on anniversaries if they so wish'.

Elsewhere at St James' Park, there is a memorial garden in front of the Milburn Stand, and set in the walkway in front of the turnstiles are hundreds of plaques dedicated by families to former fans, with inscriptions like 'The Hush family, Past, Present and Future'; 'Land of Hope and Dreams' and simply 'For My Girls'. They are dedications that articulate the desire to remember a place where, perhaps, the departed were happiest, or at least felt they really belonged though times good and bad. Some are now worn away by the thousands of passing feet and nearly illegible. Their future, if the stadium were to be demolished as part of a relocation or expansion, is uncertain.

So this can rightly be called be called hallowed ground; as the Oxford English Dictionary reminds us, to 'hallow' means both to consecrate and also to 'urge on with shouts'. How far the sense of hallowed memory can survive the demands of a hyper-modern, commercially successful, future-focused new stadium is hard to know. The fear for many fans is that frustration at possible planning restrictions and the desire to detach fans from the temptations of the city around them will lead to a decision to move the stadium far away from its historic, longstanding location, and sweep away its tradition. Wor Flags, who have done so much to revive and celebrate the stadium's culture in recent years, warned in a statement that 'our home of 132 years, smack bang in the city centre, where generations have fallen in love with this club … isn't something we should give up lightly'. 'We would not be supportive', they added, of 'another soulless bowl, where increased revenue has been of greater importance than creating an environment conducive to supporting the players.'

After Sir Bobby Robson's death was announced in 2009,

journalist George Caulkin described how many families came simply to stand at the ground 'talking about place and time and perspective, personalities and meaning. St James' Park felt like a grand old stadium again, suffused with history'. Robson, whose statue now stands a little down from the fans' memorial plaques at St James' Park, had once captured what the place meant in what has become a justly famous statement, which I find myself reading after Ewan's death with newly painful appreciation.

> 'What is a club in any case? Not the buildings or the directors or the people who are paid to represent it. It's not the television contracts, get-out clauses, marketing departments or executive boxes. It's the noise, the passion, the feeling of belonging, the pride in your city. It's a small boy clambering up stadium steps for the very first time, gripping his father's hand, gawping at that hallowed stretch of turf beneath him and, without being able to do a thing about it, falling in love.'

The man who had managed at some of Europe's most dynamic clubs and knew the way global football was going also sensed acutely just why that kind of passion posed such a dilemma for today's stadium developers. 'Sometimes', he said, 'clubs need to break from the past, but the danger is they lose an element of their soul.'

7

KEEPING THE FAITH

IF A STADIUM CAN HAVE A SOUL, does that make it a place where we share a kind of religious belief? The most popular description for St James' Park might remain 'fortress', in keeping with the city's founding identity as castle location and the region's martial tradition. Recently another kind of association for the stadium has become popular, suggesting it is also seen as a place of pilgrimage and worship.

Ewan, theologian by training, football fan by passion, was endlessly curious about our cultures and their wider resonance, what shapes our psychology and beliefs, how formal religion has faded but its spirit lives on. And he thought a lot about why football had such a hold on us and the way we looked on wider life – why, as he teased, my influence in persuading him to support Newcastle United had 'taught me everything I need to know about existential despair'. At least, I tried to console myself, the despair would make made any victory all the sweeter.

So can there really be much of a link between the religious instinct and football in what I have seen at Newcastle United? I believe there is, and in one way I am uniquely qualified to say why.

THE MAGPIE PRELATES

Being the son of a bishop burdens you with a lot of assumptions. One is that you will be prissy or annoyingly well-behaved; another, I found, is that you will somehow be dedicated to more rarified pursuits than the rougher world of sport. After I had performed well during a game of football in a Yorkshire Dales field during a school camp in the mid-1970s (having to circumnavigate cow pats certainly encourages good ball control) a fellow pupil came up to me and said: 'When I heard you were a bishop's son thought you would be a total wimp, but you're actually okay.'

Not exactly overwhelming praise, but still welcome. And the idea that episcopacy and football were fully compatible was encouraged by my Dad himself, who maintained the interest he had first developed as a clergyman in the 1950s North East, keen to understand a place so far socially and geographically from what he had known in his youth. When I came to understand more of the history of football itself, I discovered that he was simply following in a great regional tradition of clerics supporting the game and hoping it would encourage a better approach to life.

Believers had not always been so keen. In what is now my home town of Hexham in Northumberland, seventeenth-century Puritans fined locals two shillings for playing football on the Sabbath; potentially lucrative in a place like this, but desperately bad PR given local football fanaticism. As a broad-church Anglican my Dad was always wary of the zealotry of some religious enthusiasts and would have realised such punitive taxation was a futile enterprise. Much more congenial to him would have been the tradition of the 'sporting parson'. Take George Ferebe, like Ewan a former chorister at Magdalen College, Oxford, who was much exercised in improving his Wiltshire congregation's singing and bellringing. When King James I visited in the early-seventeenth century, Ferebe entertained him not only with music but also a football match. In a combination that would have made perfect sense to Ewan, his parish, it was said, 'would have challenged all England for musique, football and ringing'.

By the nineteenth century, clerics were in the forefront

of encouraging modern football in the name of muscular Christianity. 'The curate, and often the vicar, inspired by his own early education' wrote football historian Percy Young, 'frequently set out to claim souls with a Bible in one hand and a football in the other'. This approach was especially evident in North East England. Bishop Auckland was the ancient HQ of the Prince Bishops of Durham who in their time had run virtually everything in their region in an extraordinary form of divine devolution; and football was initially no different. The local team lived up to its name in the 1880s, with no fewer than three future prelates starring as they won the Durham Senior Cup. But North-Eastern football swiftly cast off such leadership as it grew in mass popularity and came to challenge as vigorously as anywhere the attempt by the old public-school elites, including future bishops, to dominate the game. My Dad would have been amused by a report I found of a victory at Headingley in the 1895 Amateur Cup final by Middlesbrough over the Old Carthusians. It was 'a poor day for football' sniffed the *Times* correspondent. 'No doubt' he added, the 'severe strain of the excessive play of late in the cup ties and the long railway journeys affected the game of this fine race of footballers, the Carthusians'.

In the early history of Newcastle United, moreover, footballing clerics did not have happy associations. The club became a national powerhouse in the Edwardian era, winning its first top division title in 1905. But in what would become a familiar tale to Toon fans, its early attempts to win the FA Cup were accompanied by repeated last-ditch failure. In the 1908 final against Wolverhampton Wanderers they were clear favourites but after forty minutes had failed to score. Then a Wolves player from an amateur background, the Reverend Kenneth Hunt, received the ball some forty yards away from the Newcastle goal and, as one account puts it, 'calmly and thoughtfully' struck the ball 'with such ferocity that the Magpies goalkeeper could do nothing but embarrassingly palm the ball into his own net'. Wolves went on to win 3-1.

So a lifetime before Ronnie Radford of Hereford had famously hit a long-distance shot (now endlessly replayed on TV) to shock Newcastle in the FA Cup in the early 1970s, Revd Hunt had done it first. I looked further into the life of Hunt, intriguingly described by Arthur Appleton as a 'hefty, fearless, shoulder-charging clergyman and teacher', and discovered that he had once played for Oxford City reserves, as had Ewan. It turned out that he was not only a player but an enthusiastic evangelist for the game, how he believed it should be played and its beneficial effects on society. My favourite library, The Literary and Philosophical Society of Newcastle upon Tyne, even had a copy of book he wrote in the 1920s entitled *First Steps to Association Football* (published by Mills and Boon, no less).

There was stern moral advice on how to play the game properly, especially for goalkeepers: 'a goalkeeper who every now and again misses a "sitter"', he wrote, 'has a very bad moral effect on the rest of the side'. Most eye-catching for me however was the Revd Hunt's criticism of schools that were abandoning football in favour of rugby. 'Sport, and particularly football', he argued, 'affords a common meeting ground for men of all creeds, all colours, all nations. If Rugby is to become the game of the Public Schools, and Soccer is to be left entirely to the working classes, we are deliberately severing one of the chains which still serve to hold the classes and the masses together ... For any further schools to abandon Soccer will be detrimental, not only to the game itself, but to the country as a whole'. Amen to that. If only my Newcastle grammar school had listened.

The influence of clergy as players swiftly faded, but their role as supporters could remain strong; and, I was delighted to discover, Newcastle has long had a special episcopal fan club. Basil Hume, who later became Catholic Archbishop of Westminster, had first gone to St James' Park as a boy in the 1930s and remained faithful ever after. As he approached retirement he told the then Pope, John Paul II (himself a noted former goalkeeper) that he was looking forward to spending more time watching his favourite team. One of his proudest achievements, Hume said, was to have got Newcastle striker Jackie Milburn's autograph when, many years after he retired from playing, he was made a freeman of the City of Newcastle. There was, he said 'a quality of goodness in him which inspired others'. When Milburn died his funeral was held in Newcastle's Anglican cathedral, and his ashes were scattered at the Gallowgate end of St James' Park.

The Church of England also had its episcopal football fans. To this day one of the top producers of footballs is called Mitre International because its Huddersfield founder was friends with a bishop. My Dad, who worked in the early 1950s for a Coventry engineering firm in preparation for industrial mission, was an admirer of the city's bishop, Cuthbert Bardsley. Bardsley was asked to become president of Coventry City FC which made him, he claimed, 'as pleased as if they had asked me to be Archbishop of Canterbury'. The Coventry crowd was said to have regarded Bardsley as a source of 'rather more than human strength', but in moments of stress during matches he found himself calling out 'Oh, folly! Folly!'. That amused Prime Minister Harold Wilson, attending one game, who had 'always wanted to know what a bishop said in moments of crisis!'. My Dad to my knowledge never uttered the Bardsley F-word but would respond to footballing and other crises with 'Blast!' – applied occasionally to Newcastle United and generally to players who passed backwards rather than forwards.

Anglican episcopal interest in Newcastle would be reinforced when the first female bishop was appointed there in 2015. Christine Hardman became a season ticket holder and described in her maiden speech to the House of Lords her region's 'places of pilgrimage such as Holy Island—or St James' Park'. She came to my Dad's funeral in 2020 and I enjoyed discussing with her the strength of the Newcastle episcopal-football connection. She told me that she had even been influential in persuading Rafa Benitez to stay at the club in

2016 after one of its disastrous relegations in the Mike Ashley era. She and her assistant bishop wrote privately to Benitez asking him to stay in Newcastle 'as he had already brought back hope to the city and saying that the flourishing of the city was so dependent on hope triumphing over despair'. When Benitez gave an interview explaining why he had stayed to manage the club in the Championship, he mentioned the influence of Bishop Christine alongside that of his daughters, and Alan Shearer and Ant and Dec.

Bishop Christine has now retired but the tradition has been maintained by the Bishop of Sheffield, Pete Wilcox, discussed as a possible choice for Archbishop for Canterbury in 2025. who happily calls himself a 'Newcastle United nut'. This episcopal link is also pleasingly embodied in the club's best-known nickname, the Magpies. The bird has had very negative connotations in religious belief and is best known in popular mythology as bringer of bad luck or obsessive pursuer of elusive shiny things (such as football trophies). But look further in your folklore and you will find another use for the word: as a nickname for prelates because of their traditional dress. So the black and white bishop-Magpies have now become a firm part of my Newcastle-supporting identity. United even had a famous fan, Alan Hutchinson, nicknamed the 'Toon Pope', who would preach uplifting sermons to fans ahead of games clad in his own version of cassock and mitre.

Yearning for the Messiah

Bishops aside, there is a much broader way in which the language and customs of religion have become so prominent in the way Newcastle supporters and players speak and act. For longsuffering fans, the temptation to borrow from religious language to express their yearning for deliverance has been hard to resist. That fervour reached its height in the Kevin Keegan era. He had been for many years a Liverpool, Hamburg and England star and was twice voted European player of the year. But when he arrived to play for Newcastle in 1982, he said he had 'never experienced that kind of deification before'. The club did little to dampen such hyperbole. Keegan's last appearance as a player at St James' Park concluded with the staging of his ascension from the pitch by white helicopter. 'I went down on bended knees to bow and genuflect in front of the Gallowgate End' he recalled, 'and made a dash for the helicopter door, turning to wave one last goodbye ... I was off, still in my muddy kit, peering down at all those people, with their necks craned and their arms raised'.

Keegan's return to Newcastle as manager in 1992, with the club perilously close to relegation to the third division, was inevitably christened a Second Coming. Keegan 'the Messiah' was uneasily aware that it was in fact an 'incredible gamble ... a leap of faith'. When he departed suddenly in 1997 new levels of hype were audible among some fans. One, aged 16, was quoted as saying: 'football and Newcastle United are my life. How can Kevin Keegan leave us? He is god, he is even bigger than god. He is the life of Newcastle.'

Faith in Keegan's omnipotence was finally and cruelly punctured when he returned again for his disastrous spell as manager under Mike Ashley's ownership. As Ewan pointed out later in his theological wisdom, we should have known that a Third Coming was not going to end well. But the yearning was still there 'Whoever wins one trophy' prophesied striker Les Ferdinand 'will be the god of Newcastle. For ever'.

FAITHFUL PLAYERS

There has also been another strand in the intertwining of faith and football; the believing player. For some time after the Edwardian era of Revd Hunt, open professions of faith were rare among football stars, and often seen as incompatible with continuing to play. In 1969 Peter Knowles, a skilful 23-year-old Wolves forward with rangy good looks, stylish clothes and a Beatles-style haircut astonished the football world by retiring to become a Jehovah's Witness preacher. He fretted that fans were, as he put it, worshipping and idolising him. 'Five days in a week I am a Christian, but when Saturday comes and I put on a football shirt I am not a Christian.'

Bobby Robson knew all about idolising, once declaring that 'footballers in Newcastle are like matadors in Spain – sporting gods'. He struggled with millionaire players' lifestyles when he was Newcastle manager, but sensed he had to balance his concerns with acceptance of at least some of the hedonism for which the city was famous. One of my favourite email exchanges with Ewan came when I sent him this classically baffling Robsonian statement about attracting players to Newcastle: 'If we invite any player up to our Quayside to see the girls and then up to our magnificent stadium, we will persuade any player to sign,' he claimed. 'They can't be monks — we don't want them to be monks. We want them to be football players because a monk doesn't play football at this level.' 'That is glorious!', Ewan responded, but added generously: 'I don't see why a monk couldn't play at that level.'

Newcastle United never had monks, but they did have one of the first players to combine being on the pitch with openly professing belief. Striker Gavin Peacock played for the club between 1990 and 1993 and is now a full-time pastor for a Baptist church. For him, unlike Knowles, there was no contradiction between football and faith. 'When I scored, and the crowd roared', he asserted, 'I felt God's pleasure.' Looking back in his autobiography on his time at Newcastle and the fans who supported him he sensed a deeper meaning: 'It's about a city, their team, a sense of dignity and belonging and the persevering hope of glory.' 'In all of us', he went on, 'there is a desire for identity, a desire to belong and be accepted, and a desire to praise something glorious. Through their team, supporters can participate in something that takes them beyond the ordinary to a sense of victory in lives filled with many hardships and defeats.'

Another Newcastle striker, Shola Ameobi, known to fans following his derby match exploits against Sunderland by the somewhat un-Christian title of 'Mackem Slayer', was the son of a pastor who began to appear in local churches speaking of his Christianity. Christian Atsu, a talented Ghanaian who joined the club in 2017, described his faith as 'the most important thing in my life' and did hugely impressive charity work before his tragic death in a Turkish earthquake in 2023. And when Newcastle began to sign Muslim players, footballing faith appeared in another guise. More and more, faith was seen not as a distraction from footballing performance, but potentially a helpful grounding.

Eddie Howe, the manager who has masterminded Newcastle United's recent revival, is not known for professions of religious faith. But one of the key texts said to have influenced him most is a book by John Wooden entitled *Pyramids of Success*, praising virtues such as industriousness, loyalty and team-work. Wooden was a basketball coach in the US and a devout Christian. It was claimed that 'the gyms he coached in became chapels, the court a pulpit where he preached a different kind of success approach'.

MATCH RITUALS

It would, of course, be wrong to suggest that football managers, players and supporters were somehow defying the trend towards less formal religious belief and a more secular society. But as someone who grew up with a lot of churchgoing, I know that it is in football grounds where I am now most often reminded of the communal rituals of that experience. There is mass lamentation at sin (when a referee turns down a penalty), exaggerated penitence (when a player attempts to avoid a second booking) and ecstatic praise. Admittedly much of the singing and chanting may be a long way from any kind of spiritual content but there can still be echoes of old belief. 'You'll Never Walk Alone', now a great football anthem, began life as a musical showstopper but has taken on a religious aura, immensely popular at funerals, and its huge commemorative power was evident following the death of Liverpool fans in the Hillsborough disaster. Indeed the memory of the departed is as powerfully marked now in football as anywhere else. Black armbands are worn by players and there are hugely impressive shifts from a cacophony of noise to the most disciplined of silence when pre-match commemorations take place. The liveliest, noisiest venues in our cities have also become places where death is marked communally like nowhere else.

Liverpool had a renewed confrontation with tragic death in the summer of 2025 when their forward, Diogo Jota, was killed in a car crash soon after his marriage. His former manager Jürgen Klopp spoke of wrestling with his doubt afterwards. 'This is a moment where I struggle!' he wrote. 'There must be a bigger purpose! But I can't see it!' Klopp was another of the open believers to have reached a prominent position in football. When I was making a BBC documentary about the 500th anniversary of the Reformation in Germany, I discovered that he was one of three patrons of the celebration organised by the German Evangelical Church. My request to interview him about this sadly did not manage to overcome the defences of the Liverpool FC press office, who must have assumed that this was a ruse to evade normal media controls and that I was really interested in Mo Salah not Martin Luther.

Most fascinating of all to me is players on the pitch making gestures of faith that I previously only ever saw in church – such as crossing themselves, pointing heavenwards when they score, or dedicating their achievement publicly and emotionally to the departed. Newcastle's captain Bruno Guimaraes does so regularly; he comes from a tough Brazilian background, refers regularly to God in interviews and plays with a passion that reminds me of a compelling line from a Brazilian commentator quoted in Alex Bellos's book *Futebol*: 'Football is the shout that comes from the depths of those who hardly live, of people who aren't sure where their next meal will come from. The jubilation of scoring a goal renews the soul.' Sometimes the gestures are made in private. At the end of one successful Newcastle United season, Guimaraes fulfilled a promise, away from the cameras, to walk the length of the St James' Park pitch on his knees, like a grateful pilgrim approaching a shrine. If the 'True Faith' celebrated in the name of a famous Newcastle fanzine and podcast needs a liturgy, Bruno will be the man to write it. He ended one tweet in 2025 about scoring a late winner against Fulham with the words: 'Until the end. Glória a Deus. Howay the lads.'

For players and fans who may not be religious believers there are the rituals of superstition. Waiting outside St James' Park before a game I have seen numerous fans come to the statue of Alan Shearer to touch his right boot reverently before entering the ground. In our supposedly hyper-rational age there is probably no fan in the land who does not have some kind of superstitious ritual they dare not abandon. For Ewan and me it was refusing to turn on live radio commentary when Newcastle were playing, as we were convinced that always led to the opposition scoring. Utterly ludicrous and unscientific but at least, Ewan joked, our continued adherence to this rule helped him understand for his studies the religious philosophy of Pascal's wager (that you might as well, in short, hedge your bets).

We Need to Believe

'Football', Ewan once wrote, 'deals with the natural undulations of human life: the fluctuations between joy and agony, expectation and despair which shape all our experiences.' He was far from blind to aspects of the game that seemed a long way from the spiritual, but believed football and religion could benefit each other. 'Problems with venality, corruption and hypocrisy are hardly unknown within the ranks of believers, so these tests of faith could also be approached as a problem in common. The architecture, art and rituals of religious traditions offer football models for embodying and communicating powerful shared convictions, just as the commitment and passion of the football fan might be able to teach the believer something about the trials of holding to unconditional faith and irrational hope.'

That kind of thinking has sustained me in the last few troubled years, as has the memory of the Magpie-prelates. Football may not have evolved in the way their nineteenth-century ancestors hoped, as a force that complemented rather than superseded the life of the church. As historian Peter Clarke put it, 'in twentieth-century Britain organized mass sport may have filled some of the psychic space which was being vacated by organized mass Christianity'. Yet even if old-style religion is in decline, the old language of belief is still potent. After Newcastle had succumbed to a shock home defeat in a match we were at in 2025, my son Alfie shrugged, looked across at me, and said simply: 'keep the faith'. How his brother Ewan would have been proud of him. Yet at the same time we all knew, and know, that such faith in football, and in happiness, can still be hard to sustain, especially for those who face the toughest of life conditions. But there can still be hope and inspiration there too. We can move on now to find that story close to but in many ways a world away from the St James' Park football cathedral.

8

MEN AND THEIR MOODS

THERE HAS BEEN MUCH TO WORSHIP for Newcastle fans in recent years. But for other football supporters within the region, it has been exceptionally hard to keep believing. Another team and place nearby, which also came to play a big role in our lives, has offered a very different perspective on what the game can mean.

STUBBORN SURVIVAL

When we arrive in the city of Newcastle for football, instead of heading up the hill from the Central Station towards St James' Park, we sometimes go east. First, down towards the Quayside, scene today of ebullient social life, and once at the heart of the area's maritime economy. There is the Custom House where shipping wealth was assessed and smugglers resisted, nearby is the ingenious Swing Bridge through which Armstrong's huge battleships emerged for worldwide export; we also pass a poignant board on a building listing all the destinations to which you could once voyage from this place. After crossing a modern engineering marvel, the Blinking Eye bridge, we head left past the Baltic art gallery, a former flour warehouse.

If there's time, we sometimes pause to visit one of the Baltic's exhibitions. My favourite in recent times was by the Lebanese-born artist Ali Cherri, with sculptures, films and installations reflecting on themes such as creation and borders. For one extraordinary installation, entitled 'Of Men, Gods and Mud', he had filmed Sudanese brickmakers who work

149

semi-immersed in mud shaping and baking bricks, earning a pittance. They were wearing cast-off football shirts bearing the names of millionaire players such as Neymar, Kompany, and Götze.

We have now crossed a milder yet still pronounced kind of Tyneside economic border. So far, the walk has highlighted much economic 'heritage' successfully repurposed for culture and commerce. Once past the Baltic gallery, though, on the south bank of the Tyne in the borough of Gateshead, the road eastwards suddenly becomes much quieter, scruffier, with far less evidence of new development. There are entrances to businesses whose names evoke past prosperity, such as one offering 'boats, engines, chandlery''; it supplies the few remaining vessels on this river in a North East region that once built a large proportion of the world's shipping. There have been some spectacular success stories in this transition, such as the family firm of Barbour further downriver which began by making seafaring kit and has now become an international fashion brand. But others based here are trying to coax a modern living from services and supplies, ranging from lorryloads of asphalt to office furniture or 'fancy goods and hardware'; some premises are boarded up, the padlocks on their gates protecting only rusting skips and encroaching weeds.

There is more attractive greenery further on, next to a special nesting structure for the kittiwakes who noisily frequent the riverbank. But the sense of natural relief from urban activity is rudely interrupted by 'Keep Out' signs warning that soil around here is contaminated. So much of the industry around the Tyne is long gone but its harmful legacy lurks in the stagnant land where chemical waste was poured, the fires that burn in abandoned mineshafts, and the elderly workforce with its fragile health.

Regeneration has been tried along this riverbank, to match that in Newcastle city centre. In 1990, to the west, there was the Gateshead Garden Festival, reclaiming the site of former cokeworks and gasworks, championed by national government and enthusiastic politicians like Michael Heseltine. It was modelled on a German idea, the *Bundesgartenschau*, used to revive bombed out post-war sites. I remember reading about its promised benefits for Tyneside while visiting Germany that year as it celebrated reunification and Chancellor Kohl promised 'blooming landscapes' in the former communist East. Within two decades, that German region had overtaken Northern England's economy while places like Gateshead still struggled to find their decontaminated future.

Just as in the 1930s Slump and often since, this place remains what officialdom termed a 'depressed area'. In J. B. Priestley's famous *English Journey* travelogue, first published in 1934, he was hardly complimentary about Tyneside as a whole, but when he came here his prose reached a level of damnation found nowhere else on his journey. 'A great deal of Gateshead', he wrote, 'appeared to have been carefully planned by an enemy of the human race ... insects can do better than this.' 'If anybody ever made money in Gateshead', he added, 'they must have taken great care not to spend any of it in the town.' 'Every future historian of modern England', Priestley advised, 'should be compelled to take a good long slow walk round Gateshead.'

At the same time, however, he did admire the spirit of some of those he met facing such appalling conditions. He praised cultural life in one district, concluding that while 'conditions are probably worse ... than anywhere else in the country ... it is only fair to say that in no other districts are more determined efforts being made, by these settlements and their activities, to help the unemployed.' Side by side with massive challenges, in other words, was resilience, a community spirit despite everything.

Yet Priestley's much-quoted words of damnation have added to a kind of psychogeographic contamination – both in the perception of the region from outside but also in a kind of permanent pessimism that seems rooted in the local culture. Here is author Jonathan Tulloch, formerly a local teacher, now a noted nature writer, describing its long winters:

> 'In Gateshead, when October drips into November, the nights grow desperately long and often the days never seem to even begin. The sun peaks, if at all, just above the horizon. The rain is ceaseless ... the tower blocks rise like icebergs in a frozen sea.'

It is in fact not nearly as wet here as many assume, nor as unremittingly gloomy in winter; Gateshead also has areas with leafy suburbs, pleasant parks and new-build housing. But I recognise the mood which can feel hard to shift in some parts of the town and its psyche. On our football trips to Gateshead we walk on from the Quayside uphill past a pub once called the Ship Inn, celebrated in a 1960s documentary for its folk singers, then renamed the Schooner in honour of the ships that sailed from here to the world; now, under new management, it bears the less expansive, more melancholy identity of 'The Fog on the Tyne'. And we begin to spot fellow fans, for a short walk further on is Gateshead International Stadium, home to Gateshead's football club, four divisions below Newcastle in league rankings, but on another planet as far as finances and fan numbers are concerned. Yet football globalisation still affects this club too, as the club tries to find its way of anchoring local loyalty while sustaining a team that can compete.

The stadium seemed, in its time, a bold attempt to outrun the past. It was built in the 1950s on the site of an old chemical works spoil heap and in the 1970s lived up to its international name when athlete Brendan Foster, then working for Gateshead Council, broke a world record there and held major athletics events. Steve Cram was another locally born global running star. Top competitors were, as Foster put it, 'lured to a town they had to look up on a map'; and Gateshead fans still sing ironically of being 'just a stop on the Metro'.

Foster who as a boy 'had wanted to be a professional footballer because it was like a religion in these parts' attributed his achievements to his environment – not that of permanent subterranean depression but defiant aspiration instead. 'We have been reared on sport', he said, 'since the days when it was one of the few escapes from the drudgery of work. Our society has a steeliness in it which tends to give northern people a head start as competitors.' The huge Great North Run he co-founded, in which sixty thousand or so surge past the stadium every September, still expresses that spirit brilliantly. Athletics failed, however, to attract sustained global broadcasting revenues; a few pop concerts came and went, and the stadium's prestige faded. Most of its seating is rarely used as its football occupants, Gateshead FC (known as 'the Heed') has always struggled to attract support.

In his 1960s book about regional football, *Hotbed of Soccer*, Arthur Appleton mused that Gateshead's 'poor support from the public in the midst of football-conscious Tyneside does not seem to make sense. The club is a happy one, the players play with spirit.' In the early 1950s the team came close to reaching the FA Cup semi-final. Any happiness and spirit, however, was always tempered with anxiety: the club has been buffeted, sometimes nearly capsized, by constant tempests blown in from the wider football world. In 1960 Gateshead finished third from bottom of the old Fourth Division of the Football League. The rules then stipulated that the bottom four had to apply for 're-election' and Gateshead were voted out, to be replaced by Peterborough, while teams that had finished below them stayed up. Some put it down to southerners not wanting to make the long journey north; others including, shamefully, Newcastle United, failed to support them. Gateshead have languished outside the top leagues ever since.

Still they played on, defying economic gravity, with fans

small in number but whose loyalty is movingly impressive. There have been liquidations and bail-outs, and periods as the plaything of the bizarre international intrigues of modern football investors. A few years ago they were owned by a naval architect based in Hong Kong who subcontracted much of the running of the club to one Joseph Cala, a man who had worked his way through a number of football clubs in Britain and Europe leaving a chaotic trail of mismanagement and unpaid bills. Among his many business ventures had been a plan for underwater casinos in the US and he was rumoured to have asked one Gateshead official to ring the local council to ask whether he could lease a stretch of the Tyne for a similar venture.

At one point the club was put up for sale for a humiliating price of £1. Yet the team found new talent and defied the odds. Twice the final of the FA Trophy at Wembley was reached. The first time in 2023 we witnessed defeat to a scrappy goal, then torment on the return journey as we were stuck for hours with hundreds of Heed fans at King's Cross station due to a fault on the main line at – where else? – Peterborough. Then in 2024, after another journey south on a train renamed for the day the 'Heed Army Express', came victory after a penalty shoot-out. The club now had silverware, but still no guarantee of survival, nor even a stable home. The Gateshead local authority, stadium owners, have faced huge financial challenges paying for their obligations in care for the local community as central government austerity has bitten. Leisure facilities and libraries have been closed and the authority sought to offload ownership of the stadium to cut its losses. Confusion over that meant that even when the team played well enough to reach the 2024 National League play-offs the club had to withdraw, unable to satisfy requirements for a possible promotion.

Despite on-field success attendance at home games, measured in the hundreds rather than thousands, has never been sufficient for running costs. Meanwhile fans do their best to boost revenue through voluntary effort, and wealthier supporters have donated larger sums to keep the club going. It is all highly precarious, but for now the club, like many others in the country's lower leagues, stands for extraordinary resilience, pride and community spirit. The main bar at the ground is not named after some major corporate sponsor but rather a former fan of the club, Mick Thornton, a milkman who devoted many hours of his spare time to helping the club in any way he could. Fans gather there before games to discuss football but also to swap news on life, and sometimes death. When I arrived there before one game a fan told me his mother had died the day before. He had not known what to do that day but said her last words to him had been 'gan' to the match, son'; and that was where he instinctively now sought solace.

It was my younger son, Alfie, who discovered all this for us. Football grew more slowly into an interest for him than it did for his brother Ewan. But as a teenager Alfie decided he was going to take more of an interest in his own distinctive way. On a memorable day while visiting his sister in Maidstone in Kent he decided to head for the local football ground and stand in the away end amidst a handful of diehard Heed supporters who had made the long journey south. He (and I, when I began to join him at Gateshead matches) were unusual additions to the travelling Heed Army. Yet we were welcomed in simple acknowledgement of our willingness to travel great distances, never knowing whether we would experience joy or crushing disappointment. It is the risk all fans take with every match. And when you are a Gateshead fan, not only is there the added cost and inconvenience of travelling so far; there is also a very long time on the return journey afterwards to reflect on a bad result.

Arthur Appleton had already witnessed this in the 1960s. 'If anyone wants to observe how humans behave in deep and sore disappointment,' he wrote, 'he should be with North East supporters who have travelled to see their team play in an "away" cup tie, and who are waiting for train time, far away from home, with the taste of defeat fresh in their mouths. Supporters in the North East really have their hearts in the game, or in their teams, I should say. The detached enjoyment of a game is foreign to them. They want to have good ground for giving respect to their teams, a respect they are always ready to give'. At the end of away games Gateshead players make a point of coming to greet the hardy handful of travelling fans, whatever the result, often embracing in shared happiness or consoling sympathy. It is the very opposite of Premiership millionaires living mostly in a carefully PR-controlled personal bubble.

So we adopted the Heed as a kind of second team just as they adopted us. For some of their fans allegiance to any other team is anathema, and those with knowledge of 1960 still loathe their powerful Newcastle neighbours. I would hope however that putting desperately-needed money though the Gateshead turnstiles could be seen as a minor act of contrition for that past, as well as a statement of support for the region's football as a whole. Some of the most bitter regional rivalries, such as that between Newcastle and Sunderland, are in fact fairly recent inventions, and did not exist when my Dad started watching and supporting both teams from the 1950s.

More significantly for me, the warmth and spirit of the Gateshead fans we have come to know have deepened my discovery of how football's emotions can help deal with a weight of grief and despair. These Gateshead fans, with often insecure employment in, say, warehousing or retail or catering, know all too well how much of the world has become more transactional and provisional in the way it deals with people. But the support in every sense of those who may travel hundreds of miles on a winter's evening to follow their team is a demonstration of unconditional loyalty, a version of the kind of unquestioning backing from family, friends or club that sometimes seems like the last line of defence against an overwhelming world.

The unpredictability of each match's result may make the

attraction seem baffling to those more used to a calculated approach to work and leisure. But especially for those with monotonous jobs life can seem all too predictable. During the working week, there may be little scope for a moment of individual skill or bravery or imagination to change the whole direction of events. In his 1950s history of football Morris Marples asserted, if a bit loftily, that the game had always 'appealed strongly to those who, by reason of their occupations or the place they live, find few other thrills in life – the industrial populations of our big cities'. One can well believe, he went on, 'that some of them never really live, except when they are watching a football match'. The tone is patronising, but you do sense especially in a crowd like Gateshead's the craving for unexpected joy, a new story to tell, the humdrum muttering of hundreds suddenly transformed into communal ecstasy. And for me, facing years of anxiety about my son's health and the relentless stress that went with it, moments of sudden enjoyment and distraction had added appeal.

Conversely, this explains too the depth of fans' frustration when the football they pay to watch *does* seem to become utterly predictable, as teams nullify each other, and anxious players seem more concerned with avoiding mistakes than taking risks; it's as if the character of the sport has been corroded by a modern culture of anxious compliance. Perhaps it's those electronic monitors worn under players' shirts, logging every bit of movement and passing, which can seem more like punitive risk-averse straitjackets than liberating recorders of individual achievement?

Mind you, there was one occasion when a match involving Gateshead turned just a bit too unpredictable for everyone's liking. We were at a pre-season friendly at Dunston further west along the Tyne, a relaxed summer evening. At half-time queues formed for burgers and ice cream while children played around the pitch. Suddenly the metal doors behind one of the goals leading into a car park burst open and two vehicles drove onto the pitch at high speed; one of them was, of all things, an undertaker's hearse. Nonplussed fans initially thought this was some kind of bizarre interval entertainment but the vehicles then stopped, young men got out, faces partially covered, and one appeared at first to be carrying a gun. An instinct from my experience working in Northern Ireland during the Troubles prompted me to pull Alfie down behind a wall.

Within minutes however all was over as the vehicles drove off rapidly, pursued now by a police helicopter. The pitch was left gouged, the match was abandoned, and we headed home, as all kinds of rumours spread as to what had happened, most involving some kind of gangland rivalry and a brazen show of strength. Even friendly football, we now knew, was not immune from the intrusive and occasionally explosive pressures of society around. And yet the incident also prompted instant expression of football's community resilience too, with mutual concern among rival supporters, swift offers of help with the financing of pitch repairs, and a determination that football would swiftly resume, whatever. There was also much spontaneous expression of the kind of dark but essential humour with which anxiety and shock in football or life can be faced. For months afterwards, players feigning excessive injury at Gateshead games were warned that, if they didn't get up, a hearse might have to be summoned.

Ewan loved football jokes, just as he liked almost any kind of joke (even, generously, some of his Dad's jokes). Laughter was good in itself, but he came to understand more than most that it could also play a deeper human role for those, like him, facing the toughest of circumstances. In his book about facing cancer he wrote about 'a failure to take comedy seriously'. He knew that football jokes, or jokes made at football, could often reflect the desire for relief from what was happening elsewhere in life. That is captured perfectly in a story told by Harry Pearson, brilliant chronicler of northern sporting humour, about what he overheard on the bus to a game:

A chap in a replica shirt who was already seated greeted the scarf man warmly. 'What fettle, nowadays?' he asked. The scarf man smiled. 'Much better, much better', he said. 'I had the six month check and I got the all clear.' The other man expressed happiness at the good news. 'Aye', the scarf man said and fingered the coloured band of wool around his neck. 'Mind, I've still got the pitiful agony of watching these bastards.'

I remember Ewan laughing out loud at that one, as someone who had (as we all had) lived for years with the stress of six or four or two monthly check-ups that constantly threatened disastrous news.

And yet the idea of humour always offering consolation and relief did not always work. It ought to have meant we could cope easily with the disappointment of, say, losing a game; after all, if you could joke about cancer, surely a football match was an utterly trivial concern by comparison? But there was a puzzle, which we often experienced and discussed. Why, in the end, did results, not of check-ups but of matches involving our teams, matter so much to us? Why could they affect our mood, for a while, more than anything? And how much could that sometimes lead into unhealthy territory?

Losing It

At college in Scotland Ewan had a wonderful group of friends who played sport with him and supported him through his illness. They knew him to be, despite all he went through, a generally mild-mannered, restrained kind of character, not given to dramatic emotional outbursts. Which made it all the more shocking, his flat-mate James recalled, when one day he saw Ewan pound his fists on the kitchen table in frustration at news that Newcastle United had thrown away another lead. Our superstitious message of 'no complacency' had, once again, proved cruelly apt. He, like I, would now experience the great irrationality yet irresistible power of a period of frustration at THE RESULT. It reflected what was, in essence, a distant arbitrary event over which we could have had no influence, yet was disturbingly empowered to transform our mood.

'The football fan', wrote Arthur Hopcraft in his study of *Football Man*, 'is not just a watcher. His sweat and his nerves work on football, and his spirit can be made rich or destitute by it.' A former GP I know remembers being asked by a patient for tranquillizers before a Newcastle appearance at Wembley. And in the North East, a region with a proud footballing history but a record of little recent success, the harmful effects of reaction to disappointing results have been especially visible. This is not just a matter of anecdote. Medical researchers published in 2003 a study focused on the region (as well as Leeds) with the title: 'A Matter of Life and Death: Population Mortality and Football Results'. They found a correlation between the results of local teams and deaths from circulatory disease among local males. 'Those with personal experience of the passion generated among fans devoted to a particular team may not be surprised by these results', the researchers wrote, 'having seen at first hand the effects of defeat. Others may question why disappointed fans do not simply switch to a more successful side. Although some do so, to the true supporter this would be unthinkable.' For a population in a place like Gateshead, where underlying health has historically been poor, the price of such loyalty may have been especially high.

It is however the effects on mental health that may, for the most vulnerable minority of fans, be most harmful. Bobby Robson wrote of the extremes he had witnessed in local football: 'when victory beckons, there is a feeling of invincibility, like riding a wave of elation, but lose and the despair is subterranean. The contrast can be very, very severe.' One of my Northumberland neighbours recalls a friend who, after a Newcastle cup final defeat, simply 'disappeared for three weeks'.

I have seen fans rail throughout a match at referees and

players in a way that suggests they see the game not as escape from routine or pressure but rather the place when all of life's frustrations can be vented. Players on the pitch are sometimes affected too by such conspicuous anger as skill or control disappears, confidence visibly wanes and movement becomes sluggish and evasive rather than imaginative and incisive. And when I'm heading out of the Newcastle or Gateshead stadium after a game, I see the result expressed so clearly in fans' body language too. After a win, animated movement, heads up and alert competing to offer comments about the game and optimism about the next one. After defeat, the trudge towards home or maybe alcoholic consolation, muted conversation, comments often addressed darkly to the ground below; a sense of the inescapable hardness of life as if returning resentfully from an ill-paid shift.

At its most extreme, the consequences of poor mental health can be truly terrible. The North East's male suicide rate stands shockingly at twice that of London. There is a long history of such desperation, dating back at least to the height of the industrial revolution when work could be so insecure and poverty so crushing. Set against such problems, football may of course seem utterly trivial and irrelevant. These are the deeply frustrated words of a miners' leader speaking in 1910, berating crowds in Newcastle for celebrating their team's FA Cup triumph:

> 'Thousands of people were there talking about the football match, and yet that very day a father of three children had gone out onto the moor and cut his throat because he had been out of work for 18 months and could not obtain bread for his family. He could stand the thing no longer, and ended his life; yet the thousands were more interested in the football match than they were in one human soul who wanted their help and aid so much. In conclusion, he would urge them to keep their heads right, and remember that a

crust of bread to a starving being was of more value than all the Cups and Leagues in the country.'

And yet football too – supporters and players – is far from immune from the challenge of poor, sometimes catastrophically poor, mental health and the effect it can have on all those around an individual.

Hughie's Tragedy

The story that most haunts me in considering all this is that of Hughie Gallacher, who played for both Newcastle and Gateshead. He was born in the Scottish village of Belshill, a place with twenty pits nearby but famous for producing great footballers. Gallacher was diminutive but ferociously talented and resilient: 'that wee fellow was not born. He was quarried', said one defender. His goals were crucial in Newcastle United securing their last top division championship a century ago. Eminent sports writer John Arlott called him 'the deadliest and most adroit forward I ever saw ... out of an apparently inconsequential phase of play he would suddenly materialize with the ball and, coldly, quickly – almost disdainfully – score some little masterpiece of a goal'. He was dubbed locally 'the Gallowgate God' and said he believed 'a footballer should be paid like all artists, according to his drawing power'.

Not only did he play memorably; his presence around town, in tailored suits and white spats, wearing a white hat or a bowler, and carrying a tightly-rolled umbrella marked him out, said Bobby Robson, for 'a special slot in Tyneside folklore'. He was, wrote poet Keith Armstrong:

> ... a man
> with poetry in his feet,
> a bottle of Brown in his pocket
> and a Championship medal
> around his neck.

After a big-money transfer to Chelsea in 1930 Gallacher made his mark on London too, though he claimed media stories about his lifestyle and relationship were highly exaggerated. The North East was where he felt most at home, and in 1938 he returned north to play for Gateshead.

After his playing career was over, however, Gallacher faced financial difficulty, working at one point sweeping floors in a factory, and succumbed increasingly to the temptations of alcohol; he also suffered depression following the death of his wife. After an incident at home in 1957, in which he had thrown an ash tray, his son Hughie Junior was removed from his care and he was summoned to appear before Gateshead magistrates. On the day of his hearing he was seen pacing back and forth near the main rail line south from Newcastle, before he stepped in front of a train. 'I literally wept the day I learned he had walked on to the railway crossing', said another great Newcastle striker Jackie Milburn, '… how a man so loved and so idolized could feel so alone I'll never know.' 'People built him up as a hero figure' commented his son later. 'Then they crucified him, as though he was a criminal.'

For some in the game, his death cast an especially long shadow. As a child I used to see on TV the great striker Jimmy Greaves, who had also played for Chelsea. He seemed an affable, sunny figure, endlessly joshing with his co-presenter Ian St John about how football was a 'funny old game'. But Greaves admitted in his autobiography that he had been haunted by the way he was often compared as a player to Gallacher. As he descended into alcoholism Greaves knew how Gallacher had a 'drinker's reputation' and had died, apparently 'forgotten and friendless'. Fearing he was 'going to follow in his path' he stood at the back of railway stations away from the tracks 'in case I got the sudden urge to end it all under a train'.

Gallacher and his reputation is now left in an extraordinary kind of limbo. He was inducted into the National Football

Museum in 2014 in the presence of Alan Shearer, who said his own father had told him, 'no matter how many you score, you'll never be as good as Gallacher'. His goalscoring achievements and personality would ordinarily have had him on a plinth outside St James' Park alongside Shearer and Jackie Milburn. But there is no statue, nor even a proper grave, due to the circumstances of his death.

The only Tyneside memorial is in the Redheugh district of Gateshead where the team once played, its creation furthered not by any conventional fan club but by the particular efforts of a remarkable amateur historian and writer, Kal Singh Dhindsa. He is from Derby (another place where Gallacher played) and has devoted himself to stories like Gallacher's as part of his own attempts to come to terms with the death of his father, who also took his own life. He sees Gallacher with instinctive sympathy as 'a man who struggled, under terrible pressure, and at one moment he lost it'. And he has befriended Gallacher's surviving family, including his son, feeling 'so respectful of Junior, he carried that weight for sixty years'.

Dhindsa looks for stories in football and elsewhere that help him comprehend what has happened in his own life, and which feel worthwhile in themselves; his approach resonated for me as I grappled with football's place in my life after Ewan's death. Dhindsa's stories embrace heroism – one is a forgotten Derby goalkeeper who refused to join teammates saluting the Nazi regime on a 1930s tour of Germany – but also frailty and failure. They are a counter to the one-dimensional way in which football and its people are often portrayed in a world of careful 'reputation management', for players at least. Gallacher – his brilliance on the pitch, the adulation he enjoyed, the behaviour he was driven to, the fate he endured – stands for the messier world of football's extremes which can prove truly destructive.

Gazza's Fears

There is another, far more famous character deeply rooted in Gateshead, whose life has also embraced the extremes which those drawn into football may face. As I explained in chapter 3, I was aware of him first as a seemingly ultra-confident player and extrovert, but these days I find myself more and more aware of his lifelong vulnerability. Near Gallacher's only memorial, near the Dunston where we witnessed the bizarre Gateshead match with the hearse, are the streets where a boy called Paul Gascoigne grew up in the 1960s and 70s.

It was another area south of the Tyne facing great economic hardship and social disruption. Gascoigne's father when unemployed would scavenge coal from local tips so the family could make beans on toast; he was also violent towards Gascoigne's mother. Gascoigne himself grew up with a morbid imagination, thinking constantly about death, especially after he witnessed a fatal road accident involving a young boy he was meant to be looking after. 'It didn't make sense. Why had God let him die? For weeks and weeks I'd wake in the night, reliving the scene. I suppose I should have had grief counselling, if they had such a thing in those days.' His talent at football, which brought him a contract at Newcastle United as a teenager, 'saved me from a far worse fate than I've experienced'.

The boy became notorious as 'Gazza', England star and subject of a million tabloid stories about drinking, drug-taking and generally crazy behaviour. For some of the many national media commentators who took aim, he confirmed everything they had chosen to believe about his home region. 'He's a fat, ill-mannered Geordie who has urinated a God-given talent against numerous walls', wrote one. Yet Gascoigne himself, when not playing the fool for the cameras, often talked of playing football as a kind of refuge from the threat of life – or death. At times he came close to following the tragic example of Gallacher, once seriously considering throwing himself in front of a train and confessing in his autobiography that,

'I've often wished I was dead, but I just haven't got the balls to commit suicide … I'd like it all to be over, to be in heaven, or hell. I'd like to be cremated and have my ashes scattered on St James' Park.'

He now makes personal appearances at small venues, switching between emotional fragility and comic bravado. Yet 'for all the precariousness of Gascoigne's existence', wrote one observer of such events, noting his 'fragile soul', tears and constant mood changes, 'one certainty is that wherever he turns up, he encounters a reaction of near-universal love.' And that, for me, stands for the way in which all those associated with football in a place like Gateshead can experience immense convulsions in their moods and experiences, yet also a solidarity that sometimes seems like the only thing preventing a precarious situation from ending in catastrophe.

REFLECTIONS THROUGH A TRAIN WINDOW

Whenever I begin the journey south from Newcastle by rail, as we head across the Tyne into Gateshead, I now think of Gallacher's final day of despair and Gazza's craving for safety and security. The economic insecurity that they also knew so well is still visible. The train runs on alongside the Team Valley industrial estate, one of the many initiatives built to bring jobs to the area since the 1930s but always vulnerable to bewildering change. The factory once run by De La Rue is one of its most conspicuous recent casualties. It used to print the nation's cash (most of which, like locally mined coal, headed south) and also its passports, but that was outsourced, ironically enough, to a Franco-Dutch company after Brexit: 170 precious Gateshead jobs disappeared.

Then as the train towards London gathers speed, the one which many from the North East have taken to escape unemployment, we pass on the left the Angel of the North. Antony Gormley's great steel creation has become emblematic for the region, appears on Gateshead FC's shirts (and has occasionally been adorned mischievously with a black and white shirt by Newcastle United fans). That hints at all the different identities that have been and are projected onto its 54 metre wingspan. Gormley himself neatly summarised the ambiguities in the Angel's functions:

> Firstly a historic one to remind us that below this site coal miners worked in the dark for two hundred years, secondly to grasp hold of the future, expressing our transition from the industrial to the information age, and lastly to be a focus for our hopes and fears.

The desire to emerge from the darker past, the search for a brighter economic future, the expression of hopes and fears. The angel embodies a yearning for security and solidarity, prompting moving memories in one of Jonathan Tulloch's football-obsessed characters of a father's relationship with his son:

> 'What ah remember best is me auld man's coat. He used to always wear it when he took me to the Toon ... We always used to get a cup of tea at half time. Ah was too small to get to the hatch, but me dad, why, he lifted wor reet up ... He looked oot for us. Made sure neeone pushed wor, or owt. He stood over wor, Miss, looking after wor, like, well like the statue.'
> 'The statue?'
> 'Y'kna. The Angel. The way its arms are oot.

That makes me think too of my son Ewan, who when he faced the fear of early death studied angels in culture going back to Dante's poetry, expressing the hope of flying high, of levity, 'light-heartedness as an escape from the gravity of weighty anxieties', something that could take us 'out of the density of despair'. The Angel of the North spreads its wings over Gateshead; the local team and its fans wear it as a symbol on their shirts; all are hoping, I like to think, for a light-hearted escape through football from the weight of a place's past and present problems and the despair that can cause.

Taking Heed

But for all that to continue can the club inspired by its angelic emblem really rise above the challenges of modern globalised football? There is one more journey through this part of Tyneside that gives me hope. It was early July 2025, and a new season was soon to begin, traditionally a time for all football fans of new starts and revived optimism. Yet Gateshead fans were still bruised by the calamitous end to the previous season, when an apparently secure place in the National League play-offs was lost after a disastrous run of defeats, and constant corrosive uncertainty over talk of a mysterious take-over weakened the club. Players had left in despair, a new management team was in place and they had agreed to meet the fans at a social club.

I headed for the meeting reminded constantly of how this place, which may superficially seem introverted and isolated, has its global history as much as anywhere. After getting off at Gateshead's main Metro stop the depressed town centre reflected at first how tough life has been, with very little spare money for upmarket retail. Nearby was the fenced off local flyover, a key transport artery, suddenly closed in 2024 as its concrete was failing. Impoverished local government scrambled to find millions to demolish and replace this essential route.

So far, so predictable, in terms of the perception of Gateshead from afar as a place permanently blighted by poverty and decay. But within minutes, variation is visible, for those who choose to look. On one side, a multilingual library, an impressive initiative by the Kittiwake Trust for the area's increasingly diverse population. Further up, playing on the streets, I passed many children in Orthodox Jewish dress as this is home to the Gateshead yeshiva, one of the largest and most prestigious Talmudical colleges in Europe, described as 'the Oxbridge of the UK Jewish community'. Much of life here is lived in a degree of seclusion but football is, appropriately for this part of the world, among its pupils' extra-curricular activities.

Then I turned right past the Shipley Art Gallery, home to a Tintoretto, a fine collection of Dutch and Flemish art, and, completing the proper cultural spread, a pictorial representation of the folk song adopted as Newcastle United anthem, 'The Blaydon Races'. And now via a few more streets I arrived at the fans' meeting, another passionate football tribe in a packed room, with the mood poised uncertainly between simmering resentment at how last season ended, anxiety about where the club now was, and yet hope that something more stable could now emerge.

The new chair Bernard McWilliams was in confessional mood, describing the bizarre events of a few months before, when a consortium including a former Everton and Sunderland player had expressed interest in a takeover and was allowed to enter the club and talk to its players, unsettling many of them, without making any commitment. After weeks of disruption an email arrived announcing they were no longer interested. 'We chased a dream, now we've got to chase it in a different direction', was the chair's rueful conclusion. The dream was of sudden financial liberation after decades of scrambling to keep the club afloat (the club's previous co-chairman had been, of all things, a Royal Navy submariner). Could Gateshead fashion a Hollywood-fuelled happy ending, perhaps, to match that enjoyed in recent years by the Netflix stars of Wrexham? I had been to a Gateshead fixture at Wrexham a few years before and it was sobering to think of how far their trajectories had since diverged.

From now on, said Gateshead's new hierarchy, they would be operating under tight financial constraints, with far less for everything from player contracts to kit to people to answer the phones. Yet still they had to live within the framework set by the global football authorities. We were told of a difficulty with a Gateshead player registration which had triggered an international ban on transfers to the club; it could only be lifted by the new chair grappling with a baffling FIFA portal run by the distant powers in Zürich. While FIFA officials sat well insulated in their multi-million funded Swiss HQ, Gateshead sought to make urgent contact through the chair fiddling with his smartphone.

Following McWilliams' candid explanation of the challenges, fans at the meeting seemed reassured, even cheered by news that the club had stopped chasing impossible dreams and was determined to set itself on a more realistic footing. There might not be promotion or cup finals for a while at least, but survival was more likely. And the fans would be crucial. The group which had arranged the meeting was also holding a fascinating debate about what they should call themselves, and what their future symbol should be, to attract as many new members as possible.

'Gateshead Soul' had played a crucial role in saving the club in 2019 when foreign ownership had brought it to the brink of collapse, and longstanding employees were sacked by anonymous electronic messages. And 'soul' seemed to many fans the perfect expression of how its members viewed their commitment to the club, transcending the short-term material mentality of investors now hovering around so many clubs. But more members, and their contributions, were now urgently needed. Was 'soul' too limiting a word in its appeal? In the end a compromise was reached and it became the 'Gateshead Soul Supporters' Society'. As for its symbols, some favoured a feisty goat, old emblem of Gateshead itself, representing the earthier enthusiasms of many Heed fans. But the Angel of the North, pictured presiding like a giant goalkeeper over a football below, also won favour. How I wished Ewan could have been there to hear a roomful of passionate football fans discussing the relative artistic merits of souls, angels and goats as symbols of football's significance.

The meeting ended with a feeling that, however bad the news had been, however frustrating was further buffeting by sharply manoeuvring international investors and global football authorities, the club at its most basic level, with fans alongside, was again surviving; its soul was undergoing modernisation but remained intact. And there was simple confirmation too that this club matters. Much more than just on match days, it is a group that offers a sense of belonging and achievement and continuity when so much else seems as fragile and unreliable as a 1960s flyover built with dodgy concrete which the powers-that-be have failed to maintain.

THIS ROUNDE ROLLING FOOTBALL

J. B. Priestley did not visit Gateshead's football club for his 1930s *English Journey*; perhaps just as well given what he had to say about other aspects of the town. But he did go to a professional game in Nottingham which prompted reflections on football's effect. Those in the crowd, he said, were not 'mere spectators', but 'are driven into despair, are raised to triumph; and there is thrust into their lives of monotonous tasks and grey streets an epic hour of colour and strife that is no more a mere matter of other men's boots and a leather ball than a violin concerto is a mere matter of some other man's catgut and rosin'. He disliked what he called the crowd's 'cat-calling idiocy' but found it 'still good, when the right side has scored a goal, to see that wave of happiness break over their ranked faces, to see that quick comradeship engendered by the game's sudden disasters and triumphs'. At the same time, however, he wished for what he saw as higher culture: 'I know that religion, art, politics would give them something infinitely truer and more enduring.'

I thought about football and art – not as alternatives but as companions – as I walked back from the Gateshead fans' meeting, and saw white goalposts painted on one wall, glowing in the dusk. They stand for the way in which football is imprinted on the landscape, and the ambitions of many of those born there, right among where they live. Such ghostly outlines were often included in paintings by Charlie Rogers, a Gateshead artist who 'had two passions in life: art and football'. He once had a trial for Sunderland and had discovered painting while recovering from a football injury. He had also brought his talents to bear on Gateshead and Dunston's stadiums and had captured moments such as the mood in Newcastle city centre after Kevin Keegan's first resignation as manager. Rogers continued playing, as well as painting, into his sixties, and remembered a cheeky young Paul Gascoigne trying to join in his local park team's games.

Then I was heading back down towards the centre of the town and looking not at buildings and goalposts but at distant views across the Tyne to where, just a few miles away at Newcastle United, multi-millions of pounds were swirling around on spreadsheets, hundreds of staff were employed, and fan numbers are measured in the many tens of thousands, or maybe international millions, rather than Gateshead's hardy few.

Yet in a way both clubs are facing a different version of the same challenge: how can local passion and pride be preserved in a global football marketplace? As Kevin Keegan rightly put it, 'football in this big vibrant city is about self-esteem'. And when that self-esteem has been most diminished, the consequences have sometimes been truly catastrophic, for fans but also, sometimes, for football stars too. But when football and its people can sustain that esteem, it can sustain much more too, as I have found when dealing with catastrophe in my own life. And I have found that not only in the St James' Park world I grew into, but more recently in the great embrace of Gateshead, home and away, in its stories, its spirit, its extraordinary will to survive and laugh at adversity.

Football finding its place in the world's troubles, in people's troubles, in the way they think about the world; it is an ancient story. On the train back into Northumberland, I opened one of the old books about the game I have become somewhat addicted to researching this book and the deep roots of my sport's identity. And there, in Morris Marples' *History of Football*, was no lesser a thinker than Sir Thomas More writing as far back as 1532, calling the world 'this rounde rolling football that men walke upon and shippes sayle upon'.

The world as a rolling football, on land and storm-tossed sea: maritime Tyneside would understand that image especially well. When you set off on a voyage, or to a match, or to play a game on a patch of grass with your son, anything can happen to you and your mood; and then you will understand something else about your life. It is how you manage your mood, what kind of effect you have on others, what kind of support you can rely on, that will really matter.

9

LOST LASSES

WHERE MEN AND THEIR FOOTBALL moods have led into the most harmful territory of anger, alcoholism and domestic violence, it is the women around them who have suffered, who do suffer, most. That has led, understandably, to some women seeing the sport in its traditional, male-dominated form as a blight on society. But there was always another, hidden or forgotten story – that women had been, and could again be, football stars, inspirational players, coaches and fans, showing the game's enthusiastic potential for all kinds of beneficial change in sport and society. And what has especially impressed me is that this change has included a more open conversation about coping with grief and loss.

The idea of loss and memory is central to the history of women's football. Its recent growth and success have been central to my sons' experience. But the fact that it happened so long after I first became attached to the game prompted me to discover more about what had happened before. It is a shocking story that I am ashamed I did not know more about earlier, a story of prejudice and lost opportunities that needs to be commemorated constantly while we celebrate what women's football has finally been allowed to become. My home region of North East England has been at the forefront of new generations of accomplished female footballers; it is also the place where the story of the lost lasses of twentieth-century football, the ones who were cruelly denied the game, is especially poignant.

American Pioneers

One of our best holidays with Ewan was spent in summer 2019 in the French city of Le Havre. It was a visit full of his favourite things. There was a characterful place to explore, a port city with markets and modern art, and a concrete church, St Joseph's, glowing with stunning stained glass; 'an explosion of light and colour', Ewan called it, 'framed by the concrete'. There was also delicious Normandy food, which Ewan, an enthusiastic cook, relished. And to complete the menu there was football, as we had tickets for England's women's team versus Argentina in the 2019 World Cup, played at Le Havre's Stade Océane. The team, including three key players from the North East, Lucy Bronze, captain Steph Houghton, and Jill Scott, won 1-0.

But the tournament's deserved winners, who beat England in the semi-finals, were the USA. And their star player and captain, Megan Rapinoe, made an impact well beyond the football field in her activism for racial equality and gay rights, as well as her willingness to criticise the football authorities. As women's football began to grow in popularity and media exposure, it took the game into territory where men's football had long failed, or refused, to tread.

I had first come across the potential strength of US women's football decades earlier. In 1983 and 1984 I spent a year as a graduate student in Boston, studying everything from art history (with a charismatic young lecturer called Simon Schama) to German cabaret to Latin American film. It was a wonderfully international environment but football seemed, initially at least, to be absent. While the game, largely invented in Britain, had spread across much of the globe from the nineteenth century onwards, the US was one place where that had not apparently happened.

I discussed such anomalies, and much else besides, with my best new friend in the US, a brilliant economics student called Abhijit Banerjee. He was from Kolkata and had grown up a keen footballer. But India too was a place where the professional game had never taken off. The team he supported, Mohun Bagan, had long ago seemed all-conquering when in 1911 they had generated immense local pride by defeating a British Army eleven to win the Indian Football Association cup. A crowd of many thousands massed in the centre of the city had reportedly been kept up to date during the game through kites flown from the ground trailing the changing score. Yet Indian football had never been able to rival the popularity of cricket and other sports subsequently, as we lamented when I stayed with Abhijit back in his home city later.

I was delighted though to see, when Abhijit was awarded the Nobel Prize for Economics in 2019, that some of his superb work on poverty reduction was attributed to the fact that he had grown up playing football with children from slum communities. A former schoolfriend recalled a scholarly boy who was 'passionate about football' and 'would invariably share his exploits on the field with us'.

I could have done with transatlantic kites trailing English football results back in the mid-1980s US. In that now almost unimaginable pre-Internet age, finding news about Britain was tough. The only time that year I saw anything on US TV news about my home country was footage of the police on horseback charging striking miners at Orgreave, which made Britain momentarily look like some kind of chaotic reconstruction of a medieval battleground. When it came to the football results, information was even more elusive. Every Sunday I sat anxiously in a café with a British friend Adam, a keen Arsenal fan, as we worked our way through the reams of advertising supplements in US newspapers hoping that that week they had found room, amidst the lawn-mower ads and baseball trivia, to print the all-important scores.

Whereas these days US investors are piling into the globally lucrative opportunities of the English Premier League, in 1984 men's (association) football was seen locally as a very foreign eccentricity. Some of the regular American guys did attempt a bit of cultural appropriation. When a 'soccer match' was advertised at my college I turned up and started playing, but as soon as the opposition were awarded a free kick I and half of my team were immediately substituted. Our coach, steeped in American football, said he was bringing on his 'deee-fensive team'. A few minutes later, when our new team had won a corner, back on I came as part of the 'offensive' effort. And so it went on. I was enjoying a year's scholarship designed to cement Anglo-American relations but at times like this, hovering bewildered on the touchline, I sensed more profoundly than ever my grassroots European identity.

Yet one day I did find a much more recognisable form of the game, being played by the college's women; plenty of skill on display, impressive tactical nous, no sign of sudden formation changes at the whim of confused quasi-quarterbacks. While the movers and shakers of male American sport, amateur and professional, were mostly baffled by or ignorant of 'soccer', many US women were in the 1980s making it their own. In subsequent decades the women's game in the US developed well ahead of most of the world; by the year 2000, notes David Goldblatt, the US had seven million registered women players, compared with around 300,000 in Germany, and the foundations were laid for success such as that 2019 World Cup win.

So if women's football could be so advanced in the US, where, I should have asked myself, were all the British women players? Still stuck, it seemed, in the category of amusing anomaly. While living in the US I went to see the film *Gregory's Girl*, a romantic comedy about adolescent love in Scotland with its stars including a lovesick young man and a girl, Dorothy, who displaces him on the school football team. The confusion caused by her skill to the team's players and managers had its comic effect but that, in the end, was what it was seen as by most of the film's audience: a fictional moment of outlandish comedy.

Few, including me, seem to have wondered whether, film scripts aside, there really were Scottish women like Dorothy who wanted to play but were being rejected. Only recently have I discovered that her character was at least partly based on the story of Rose Reilly. She was an excellent footballer from Stewarton in Ayrshire who in the 1970s as a girl had to cut her hair to disguise herself so that she could star in boys' teams. A Celtic scout wanted to sign her until he was told she was female. Gradually she realised how little opportunity she would have in Scotland: a BBC documentary about her life uses TV coverage from the time where the most patronising of male reporters describe women's football as 'a bit of a joke' and obsessively ask players whether their husbands approve of their participation.

With hugely impressive resilience and determination Reilly moved to Italy to join AC Milan, taught herself the language, took out Italian citizenship and became national team captain and a formidable box-to-box midfielder. In 1984 she was voted the best female player in the world but it is fair to say that hardly anyone in Britain would have heard of her. In Scotland, she told an Italian interviewer at the time, a female footballer was 'a nobody'. 'I played when there wasn't much visibility', she reflected later with rueful pride, 'but I know what I've done'; and she is now a valued role model for Scottish and other women players who finally have more opportunity to fulfil their potential.

Rose Reilly's story is one of hundreds that could be told of twentieth century women who should have had great football careers in Britain, but were denied by a combination of blatant male prejudice, ruthless administrative power, and the indifference and ignorance of most of the population. What makes the story all the more shocking is that the women's game had been well on the way to becoming truly popular much earlier in the century before it was suppressed, just when society was supposed to have found the political will to improve women's rights.

Explosive Stars

After returning to Britain I spent some months beginning work on what was meant to become a PhD in history. Bedazzled by the range of subjects I had enjoyed in the US I vexed my Cambridge academic supervisors by constantly changing focus. 'Have you ever considered journalism, young man?', remarked one exasperated but prescient don. The subject I had spent most time on was a planned comparison of the great armaments producer on Tyneside, Armstrong's, with its German rival, Krupp. I still have some of the notes I made from my first forays into the Armstrong archives where I researched the way women had begun working as munitions producers when the men left to fight during the First World War. I had one index card marked Football where I had noted simply: 'women playing'.

Before long my academic research was abandoned as I began to make my way towards journalism via parliamentary work; those research notes gathered dust but the memory of that initial discovery returned years later when I came across a copy of Patrick Brennan's book *The Munitionettes: A History of Women's Football in North East England during the Great War*. On its cover was a striking photo of Emma Hicks, a 1917 player from Morpeth in Northumberland, foot on ball, nonchalantly ready for the next game. Now I could begin to discover how women's football in the region had once prospered before its ruthless suppression.

Not only had these women replaced the men in vital jobs; they had also provided popular football for thousands to watch in wartime while the men's leagues were suspended. Munitions workers led the way but there were also women's teams for everyone from Post Office staff to, down south, the employees of Lyons Corner House cafes and Harrods. But this was not just a wartime invention; it built on the pre-war popularity of women's football. In 1895 a crowd of 8000 had watched Nettie Honeyball's British Ladies Football Club play a game at St James' Park in Newcastle. And after the war was over in 1919 another 10,000 turned up at the same ground in the snow to watch the final of the Munitionettes' Cup.

Yet all that had happened against a background of relentless hostility from many men, and some women too, towards the idea that women could play at all; and that fed off broader cultural hostility in the 1920s towards female emancipation. Women over 30 may have been given the vote, but once the men returned from fighting, they wanted their factory jobs back, and women back into subservience. Brennan quotes a Labour party official's cynical claim that 'the majority of women would prefer domestic service to factory if the conditions were reasonably improved'.

Many also wanted women's enforced return to the service or domestic sphere to include their removal from football pitches; prejudice was dressed up as defence of femininity. A letter allegedly written by a North Eastern woman appeared in a local paper in which she criticised her sister for taking up the sport: 'what mental aberration has prompted you to become a "lady" footballer?'. Meanwhile the Dean of Durham James Welldon, old Etonian and keen footballer, preached that sporting prowess was key to British imperial growth: 'The pluck, the energy, the perseverance, the good temper, the self-control, the discipline, the co-operation, the esprit de corps, which merits success in cricket or football, are the very qualities which win the day in peace or war.' When it came to females playing his favourite sport, however, he worried that 'if women play football in the spirit in which men play it, they will lose something of the refinement which is womanhood's peculiar grace, and hopes that they will, in their own interests, choose other games of a less rough and exhausting nature'. Dean Welldon could have had an interesting debate with Oscar Wilde, who once quipped: 'Football is all very well a good game for rough girls but is quite unsuitable for delicate boys.'

The captain of one of the most successful women's teams, Alice Kell of the Dick, Kerr Ladies, did her best to argue that the war years had proved the wider value of women's football: 'We are told that sport laid the foundation of the spirit and constitution that won the war', she wrote, 'that being so, the nation of the future should also enjoy the advantages of a fully developed and healthy womanhood.' The debate was also evident in the pages of the football comics, then enjoying huge circulations. In early 1921 *Boy's Pictorial* published an article entitled 'Should Girls Play Footer?: What the Mere Man Thinks About It'. The anonymous 'mere man' complained of 'the girls wanting to copy the men' and compared women's football to a pantomime: 'instead of the spectators watching tactics, they watch antics'. Another publication sensed what was looming as opposition to women playing ominously intensified, publishing 'Nell O'Newcastle – a Thrilling Story of Girl's Footer Team' featuring Nell Harmer, described by the male author as 'a very pretty girl and clever footballer'. Nell, working at a Tyneside engineering firm, faced a plot to undermine her team and force her to leave the city.

Such fiction became brutal fact at the end of 1921. A Football Association committee passed a resolution stating that: 'complaints having been made as to football being played by women, the Council feel impelled to express their strong opinion that the game of football is quite unsuitable for females and ought not to be encouraged'. In practice the decision will have had much more to do with stifling an increasingly financially and publicly successful rival than any spurious concern as to its suitability. Alice Kell responded eloquently but in vain, hinting at how in some ways women's football was creating what was a superior version of the game: 'We girls play football in a proper spirit. We do not retaliate if we are bowled over, and we show no fits of temper. We are all simply amazed at the action of the authorities in placing a ban upon the sport we love with all our heart.'

Women were banned from FA facilities for the next fifty years in what was, says historian Jean Williams, part of 'a peculiarly English expression of contempt for women who play football'. It was sobering to realise that during the first decade of my life, when I discovered the joy of playing, the FA ban had still been in place.

SIDELINED STARS

There were some women's teams who valiantly tried to keep playing, using parks and public spaces. But much of the women's game fell away and the idea was reinforced that football belonged exclusively to the male world. Matt Busby, famous Manchester United manager, said of the Belshill district of Scotland where he came from that, 'the inhabitants were interested in having babies and looking after their menfolk if they were females; coal-mining and football if they were male'.

Some women came to see football not as a sphere in which they should pursue equality and liberation, but rather a part of oppressive male cultural domination. In her famous 1929 work *A Room of One's Own*, Virginia Woolf wrote that 'it is the masculine values that prevail ... Football and sport are "important"; the worship of fashion, the buying of clothes "trivial".' No room there for the fashion-conscious modern female footballer, apparently, though Woolf was keen to distance herself from the idea that she should be preoccupied with shopping. And in *Three Guineas* in 1938 she explored how men seemed to have felt threatened by the football women had created, and its potential for challenging 'current values', quoting 'official football circles' who 'regard with anxiety the growing popularity of girls' football' at a time when many men's clubs were 'in a parlous state through lack of support'.

Whatever the motivation behind the men and their committees, pioneers of women's football in places like the North East now had to face the immense frustration of seeing their careers and fame stifled. Bella Reay, star of Blyth Spartans, ended up playing the occasional game for pub teams and otherwise expended her energy working on local farms into her seventies. Lillian Ritchie, a teenager who had scored 45 goals for Barrington Colliery in one season 'was reduced to kicking a turnip across the floor of the Co-op'. The immensely sad story of another brilliant teenager, Mary Lyons, has only recently come to light. A shipyard worker in Jarrow, in 1918, at the age of just 15, she scored on her England debut against Scotland in front of a crowd of 20,000 at St James' Park. After the FA ban she was said to have become embittered, 'robbed of her main passion in life'. Her town would soon become synonymous with catastrophic economic and social decline in the 1930s, the era of the Jarrow March. In her 1939 book *The Town That Was Murdered* Jarrow MP Ellen Wilkinson wrote about attempts to provide activities for young people: 'a football league has been organized ... and attempts have been made to get a netball league for the girls. It is generally admitted that the girls have far less chance of healthy exercise than the boys.'

Mary Lyons died in obscurity in a care home in 1979, and was buried in an unmarked grave until she was given a headstone in Jarrow cemetery by admirers in 2025 after her story featured in a new play, *Wor Bella*, about the region's women footballers. One of the many consequences of the 1921 ban, Jean Williams has noted, 'is that there are no fixed or discrete local or national sites to place the memory of women's football'. In a small way sites like Mary's new grave are beginning to put that right.

Some women continued to be as close to the game as they could, even if they could never play. Elizabeth Milburn was born in the Northumberland mining town of Ashington in 1912, and grew up disdaining 'girls' toys or girls' games': 'Lads' games played on lads' terms and lads' territory – that was what I wanted. And why shouldn't I? I could kick a pig's bladder football just as far and as straight as any boy.' After the First World War was over 'normal life could begin again, and for us Milburns, normal life meant football'.

But not for her as a player. While four of her brothers

became professionals, and her cousin Jackie went on to become Newcastle United's centre forward, she was set to work washing the clothes of local miners. 'It does upset me now', she reflected later, 'that women in those days were regarded as little more than slaves with no right to expect any other life.' Then, like many other young women from her impoverished area, she was sent to the south of England to enter domestic service and face class and regional prejudice: 'I never got over the shock of discovering the class system ... it horrified me to discover people who regarded me as being beneath them.'

Returning to Ashington she followed the conventional path, marrying a miner called Charlton; and among their sons were two, Jackie and Bobby, who would become English footballing superstars. It was Elizabeth, known to all as Cissie, who was their early coach and mentor. 'Football was in my blood' she said, 'and it would not be denied'. She wanted their talents to save her boys from 'having to go down that terrible black hole in the ground' as their miner father did, and 'most Ashington men had to do every working day'. Women could not escape their own black hole of endless laundry or domestic service through professional sport, but Cissie did find a highly consequential outlet for her acute footballing brain. 'Cissie Charlton knew her football and, what's more, she practiced it' wrote Jack in his autobiography. 'Other parents might shriek and shout while watching their boys play, but she just stood there, watching and analysing'. At home she would endlessly discuss tactics, 'jabbing with the teapot'.

She took Bobby sprinting to enhance his pace, and when he won a place at a rugby-playing grammar school had him transferred to one that played football, ensuring his talent was not lost to the game. When he had to recover from the trauma of the Munich air crash, where many of his Manchester United team-mates perished, it was to Ashington and Cissie that he returned, saying initially that he wanted to give up football before he was persuaded to change his mind. 'I suspect, deep down, it was something of a regret for her that she wasn't born to play the game herself', said Bobby. Cissie herself was 'sure that I could have been a top-class athlete'. She had to settle, instead, for playing a key role in nurturing the talent and temperament of two of England's 1966 men's World Cup winners, much celebrated by the Football Association, whose ban on women using its pitches was at the time still firmly in place.

Other women who could not play were dedicated spectators, though they were a tiny minority in men's professional grounds; Arthur Appleton records matter-of-factly that at the first game played at St James' Park in Newcastle in the 1880 'Mrs Watson was the only lady present'. In his account of how *Newcastle United Stole My Heart* author Michael Chaplin discovered Margaret Petrie, then in her early eighties, who had been going to St James' Park since the 1920s, and also travelled to many away matches. 'I savour the game quietly, fascinated by the flow of games' she told him, 'the different kinds of players. The selflessness of some, the genius of others'. Among those she had seen play were Hughie Gallacher, 'kicked black and blue' and she had once met Colin Veitch, accomplished midfielder in Newcastle's glorious Edwardian era and amateur actor: 'the most beautiful man. He looked like a god.'

Margaret had taught at my wife Jane's school in Newcastle, Central High, where the pupils were full of sporting enthusiasm but – just as in my school across the road – football was never remotely considered as a playing option for young people supposedly aspiring to the finer things in life. Yet football enthusiasm has always been there among women of every background if only people knew where to look. As an archaeologist Jane was amused to join once at a conference on Viking Age Europe two eminent Oxford women professors in a coffee break arguing intensely about whether Middlesbrough or Norwich City had that season's best promotion prospects.

When it came to covering football in the media, female

expertise was until recent decades also entirely unused. I knew one of my first bosses at the BBC World Service, Mary Raine, as a specialist on global politics. Only much later I was astonished to discover that she had been, briefly, the first woman allowed to report on BBC radio on a football match. Mary had grown up in a Northumberland village, daughter of a doctor, devouring every bit of information she could find on football and taken to matches in Newcastle and Sunderland. Her father used to amuse his waiting patients by asking them to quiz her on, say, who was Huddersfield's centre half. When it came to playing, however, 'there was nobody to play with as the boys weren't going to play football with a girl, for God's sake'; she was put in goal and used by the boys 'as target practice', later using the experience to become an accomplished hockey 'keeper.

At boarding school in Scotland Mary was given special dispensation to listen to Newcastle United's 1950s cup finals on the radio, though a teacher ordered her to take down pictures of famous players. After joining the BBC she enjoyed swapping football gossip with her male colleagues and in 1969 was asked by one to go and report on Chelsea versus Sunderland. The tabloids responded with horrified fascination to her broadcast. 'Meet the BBC's soccer shocker!' was one headline. 'Mary Raine, the girl who silenced a million males' ran another. The experiment did not last. When she went to the 1970 FA Cup final and submitted her report a Scottish editor insisted that a male reporter voice it for broadcast as 'I simply cannae put a woman's voice on air'.

Change in attitudes, and actions, was by the 1970s beginning patchily to happen. In 1971 the FA finally rescinded its ban on women using its facilities in England, though a rearguard action was fought when it came to achieving full football gender equality. One of the most influential legal minds of the period, Lord Denning, ruled that the 1975 Sex Discrimination Act had rightly exempted women's football as women 'have not got the strength or stamina to run, to kick or tackle, and so forth'.

And the English women – now known as the 'Lost Lionesses' – who took part in the brilliantly successful but unofficial women's World Cup in Mexico in 1971 faced a demoralising response when they returned. Carol Wilson, team captain, had been enthralled by football when she first heard the crowd roaring at St James' Park. She went with her father to a dinner at Newcastle United after returning from Mexico and was invited onto the stage with the words 'we've got a superstar in the audience'. However, as she told a BBC documentary, the compere 'then did nothing but rip women's football apart. Everyone was laughing and I was humiliated. I came off the stage and my first words to my Dad were: "I'm finished with football".'

But the women who had kept playing despite all the institutional and personal hostility were slowly laying the foundations of modern revival. The names of Scottish workplace teams from the time – such as the Cambuslang Hooverettes, Johnny Walker and Fife Dynamites, and Aberdeen Prima Donnas – reflected their sassy defiance. Playing wherever they could, 'the challenge of facing the winter cold and mud' had, argued Jean Williams, 'led to feelings of being in control, identification with the body and pride in its achievements'.

Women footballers reported that it was often a father or older brother who had first encouraged them into the game with a kickabout in garden or park. I found myself wondering whether I had not tried hard enough to encourage my daughter Laura to take up the game alongside her brothers. The moment I sensed that might never work however was at a summer party held by her primary school in which she was meant to be playing in a mixed game of football, standing on the left wing. Before long she had demonstrated goal-scoring skills, but sadly at the wrong end of the pitch. Indignant at the dismay rather than appreciation this prompted, she became fatefully tempted by the alternative attractions of a line-dancing demonstration nearby. Gradually she was lured towards the music and when the ball arrived again in her part of the pitch she was nowhere to be seen. Music, to be fair, was her great talent and enthusiasm and the football enthusiast (father Chris reminds himself) needs to accept that some will never understand nor share a love of the sport. More recently her attitude towards the game has also been coloured by her experiences as a police officer faced, sadly, with instances where the male game's old curses of alcohol-fuelled violence have resurfaced.

However there have been promising signs that the women's game can help to win her over. She went to a Lionesses England international with our younger son Alfie. And it was the enterprising Alfie, discoverer of the delights of supporting Gateshead FC, who also first encouraged us to go more regularly to watch women's football. He found the atmosphere at these games more appealing and inclusive in many ways than the harder edged experience of male matches. Yet we sensed too the precarious nature of the reviving women's game. Our local team when we first started going, Oxford United women, were playing at a small ground in Abingdon some distance from Oxford itself. There together with a few hundred others we saw them play local rivals including Reading. That team would sadly be hugely undermined a few years later when the club's then owner drastically reduced funding in order to support the men's team, leaving them suddenly demoted to the fifth tier and a ground in Slough.

We, meanwhile, had moved to the North East and were now watching the Newcastle United women's team rise after the club's takeover by the Saudi Public Investment Authority. I heard the club's head of football, Su Cumming, speak with a bittersweet pride of being part of the 'banned generation' of women in football who were now working to give new generations of female players the opportunities they had never had. But the Saudi takeover posed challenging questions about how far Newcastle, like other women's teams, could champion the rights of women in general, and also oppose homophobia in a way that men's football has markedly failed to do. For some, the tensions are blatant and insupportable. But perhaps, just perhaps, hope the optimists, a successful Newcastle women's team might be given the chance to further a conversation about such matters in a Saudi Arabia tip-toeing towards reform?

Grief and the Game

In the first women's games we watched, there was no doubting who was the best player: teenager Fran Kirby of Reading would later go on to be an England star. What we had no idea of at the time was that she had previously given up football due to depression. This had followed the death of her mother after a brain haemorrhage. 'I needed to get back on track and make sure I could be the best player I could be,' she told the BBC later, 'which is ultimately what my mum wanted me to do. That's what drives me.'

Football is endlessly, exhaustively, sometimes excessively talked about by friends, family, workmates and total strangers; grief is by contrast one of the least popular subjects for anyone. Most prefer to pretend that, like death, it doesn't really exist, and that if we don't talk about it at all it will somehow lose its power. As I have come to know, talking about grief is exceptionally difficult and exposing yet can be immensely valuable. That there could be a link between the worlds and agendas of football and grief may strike most on first hearing as improbable or even offensive. But, take it from me, it is an area which has seen some remarkable creativity. And the place I have discovered it most directly is in my 'other' football home in Germany.

There is one conversation and initiative led by a football woman that has especially moved me: a project called *Trauer und Fussball*, Grief and Football. It was founded by Carmen Mayer following the stillbirths of her son and daughter. She is a keen supporter of, among others, the women's team Turbine Potsdam; football, she told me, became for her a 'really important resource', partly as it enabled her to switch off and focus for 90 minutes on something different. But then she also noticed how, through football, 'many friends gathered and grieved with me'. Football was the arena in which every kind of emotion, including grief, could be experienced: 'failure, sorrow, suffering … but also pleasure and joy'.

She also began to study how 'there are so many grief cultures in football' ranging from the more familiar moments of silence and applause but also carefully choreographed community commemorations organised by fans, And there have been memorable gestures she noticed by players on the pitch, such as when Andres Iniesta scored the winner in the 2010 World Cup final and lifted his shirt to reveal underneath a tribute to Dani Jarque, a former Spanish international team-mate who had died the previous year from a heart-attack but was *siempre con nosotros* (always with us). For Iniesta, a moment of new ecstatic joy, the greatest a player could imagine experiencing in a World Cup final, could still be celebrated alongside an expression of grief.

Carmen's personal experience and research are now being spread among many supporters and clubs in Germany. The Hamburg team HSV, for example, have rooms at their stadium devoted to the commemoration of fans and players. I saw too where fans can sit and reflect around a huge sculpture of the foot of one of their greatest players, Uwe Seeler, captain of the West German team that lost to England in 1966. And there is a section of the local Altona cemetery I visited where fans can be buried, it is explained, 'a close as possible to the club of their hearts after their death'. It has incorporated a memorial paid for by past supporters to commemorate HSV fans killed during the two world wars, though as so often in Germany such commemoration is controversial given that some of those listed may have served in the SS. That is faced openly, however.

As part of their work on grief and memory, many German fans have been in the forefront of researching and revealing every aspect of their clubs' history.

Carmen and her colleagues' work has also lent itself naturally to promoting international cooperation. I met her handing out material about her project at a friendly match in Hamburg between local club Altona 93 and Dulwich Hamlet from London. Much in evidence was a whole subculture of football networks embracing supporters' groups, fanzines, civic initiatives. 'Society can learn a lot about this from fans' she says, when it comes to facing grief more openly and creatively. 'You feel powerless, but then there is the community, you'll never walk alone.' And alongside her, appropriately after that mention of their great anthem, is a Liverpool fan, Chris Law, who is working with the project to help bring it into Britain. He began going to games as a young boy with his Dad who died in 2016 as the result of a brain tumour. Chris recalled he had previously been 'falling out of love with football' but after his Dad's death it became 'a kind of binding thing in a way'; he felt 'a spontaneous, bigger connection to football' even if there were also moments when he had felt guilty about continuing to go.

MATCHES AND MEMORIES

When I watch women's football now, there are always people missing, friendly ghosts at the game. There is also no Ewan, so I must console myself with memories of a summer's day in France when we wandered in Le Havre, ate wonderful food and then watched the Lionesses win. And when I see Newcastle United women now, I find myself thinking: I wish I could have seen an earlier version of the team, starring Lilian Ritchie, Mary Lyons and Cissie Charlton. Cissie was still coaching in her seventies in Ashington, encouraging girls who were, as she had been, 'besotted with the game' and now reminded her of 'someone I used to know'. And it would have been good to see the reaction of, say, Dean Welldon of Durham or Virginia Woolf to the young female fans at Newcastle United women's games, who wear proudly their black and white tops but mix them with all kinds of sparkling accessories; who happily combine, in other words, all kinds of enthusiasms including football and fashion without anyone trying to tell them which is appropriately feminine or feminist.

And the spirit in which these games are played, the sense of benevolent community among the fans, the willingness of the players to be open about their feelings or mental health: all helps restore a faith in football, a feeling that the women's game can contribute not only to sport but to society beyond and to individuals, people like me, who have suffered such sorrow and loss. A decade ago, I would never have understood that grief could belong with football in a sentence, in a single experience; in the last few years I have been so grateful to discover why.

10

FLOODLIT MEMORY

THE SPIRIT OF WOMEN'S FOOTBALL surged across the country in summer 2022 when England's Lionesses won the European Championships, beating Germany with such steel and grace. It was one of the most positive football moments I remember sharing with Ewan. The joy following that final and what it meant to football as a whole was in such stark contrast to depressing events at Wembley a year earlier. Then England had not only lost the final of the men's Euros, but fans storming the stadium and racist abuse of England players afterwards seemed to be dragging the game back towards the worst of its past.

The Lionesses' success matched the mood of our summer after we had enjoyed in May a great family celebration of Ewan's wedding to a fellow student from his time at St Andrews, Karlee. But that day's delight was in defiance of a troubling time as his cancer had again become threatening. At the start of the year he had had another round of brain surgery to try and remove as much of the growing tumour tissue as possible. We were now all based in Northumberland and I dropped him off at the Royal Victoria Infirmary in Newcastle, a few hundred yards from St James' Park and the hospital which, many years before, had saved Jane's life after a major childhood road accident. Due to COVID restrictions we could not accompany him; seeing him trudge into the hospital alone and anxious I felt especially bereft. He endured not only the operation but days afterwards on his own as he recovered from surgery: 'I was a solitary soul' he wrote later 'stripped of the support that I have always relied on.'

We hoped that brilliant surgeons had once again stemmed the cancer's growth, and Ewan recovered so much during the first part of the year that he decided to take on the Great North Run in September, a half marathon from the centre of Newcastle to the coast. The local paper, the *Evening Chronicle*, covered his story and helped with his fundraising for the Maggie's Cancer Care centres that meant so much to him and his research. But he winced at the standard headline for such stories: 'Heroic Northumberland 27-year-old doing Great North Run despite battling cancer'. So many seemed to want to talk about facing cancer as a kind of battle that the only the strongest or bravest win. Ewan often showed immense courage but knew that was not how he or other patients sometimes felt; and he wrote about the psychological effect on patients of the way in which a disturbing language of combat has come to prevail as 'the medical treatment of cancer is often characterised as a violent assault against death and disease'.

The start of the run in September was on the urban motorway, closed for the day, which cuts through my old Sunday football home on the Newcastle Town Moor. Alfie and I lined up alongside Ewan with some trepidation, knowing well his innate determination but wondering whether, at some point, we might have to support him physically to complete the distance. But this was our Ewan who, maybe sensing he might not have a lot more running in him, was going to relish what he could still do. He had once insisted on entering the 100m sprint at his school sports day shortly after a previous brain operation. As he won the race I had stood speechless at the finish line, torn between anxiety at how hard he was pushing himself and awestruck admiration at his refusal to let illness slow his ambition.

Now, as we set off and approached the Tyne Bridge, it was clear he would have no need for support. I was in awe again as Ewan strode ahead, weaving between runners, some dressed in local football kit, some raising money to research cures for cancer. Others were supporting special care units for premature babies, the sort of units that had helped Alfie survive birth at little more than 23 weeks' gestation, weighing around 600 grams, the Alfie who was now also striding among the mass of runners, cheered on by thousands of locals. This is what makes the Great North Run so special not only for individuals but also for the region, as I wrote later for a publication about images of health: 'In a place still facing some of Britain's greatest health challenges, this is a day of joyful defiance, an annual running rebuke to the image of regional depression and hopeless decline'. On we went, a mere twenty or so kilometres seemingly trivial in comparison with what my boys had been through, and I enjoyed immensely their smiles of triumph at the finish on the South Shields beachfront.

Exhilaration, joy at Ewan's defiance, all intense and real enough; but we could never enjoy complete respite from the awareness, long engrained in our minds, of underlying fragility, of temporarily outrunning but never wholly escaping what he still faced. Soon afterwards came the devastating moment that would turn the rest of the year into the most heartbreaking yet utterly moving weeks we had known. Throughout Ewan's decade of living with a brain tumour our lives had acquired a kind of brutal punctuation: scans of his brain every few months, and then the wait for the results. One of us would always be there with him for the appointments. But at times when I was elsewhere, at work, my mind could never escape. I remember once having to leave my office in London in complete mental paralysis, unable to speak or think of anything else, and pace the streets until I received the call with news of the latest clinical verdict.

For some years in the middle of the decade the news was elating as all seemed stable and the consultants extended the period between scans. But we always knew that every scan and analysis had the potential for disastrous news if the tumour, and then the cancer, had spread and another operation followed by radiotherapy and chemotherapy would be needed. Beyond that was the awareness, which we tried not to think too hard about, that conditions such as Ewan's could suddenly become lethal.

His treatment was now based at the Freeman hospital in Newcastle, also home to the cancer research centre set up in Sir Bobby Robson's name and funded by money raised by him and many supporters, including Great North Runners. Sir Bobby had managed Newcastle United and England while enduring many years of cancer treatment. 'I'm desperately proud', he wrote shortly before he died, 'that a facility in Newcastle, my city, my father's city, the city where football burrowed deeper into my body than any disease ever could, will bear my name … Yes, I was born into a black-and-white world. But as my last great challenge draws to a close, I am more convinced than ever that we are surrounded by light, not darkness.'

There were black and white images of the Newcastle team on the walls of the Freeman, and I found myself thinking that these waits for consultants' verdicts were the most extreme version imaginable of the anxiety with which we would go to a match, wondering whether we were about to experience ecstasy or despair. And then we went in, and the consultant told us what the latest brain scan had showed: that Ewan's cancer, now a glioblastoma, was spreading rapidly, and he had at most a few months to live.

Words begin to fail, or seem cruelly inadequate, when attempting to recall or convey how it felt to hear such news. Sudden death prompts one kind of shock for those affected; to be told death is coming inescapably soon for your loved one is another, different, drawn-out kind of torture. As any parent will know, the strongest instinct that emerges after having a child is to protect that individual from harm; and while my head knew there was nothing that could have been done to prevent this most horrible blow, still the heart felt a sense of bleak failure and impotent rage. As so often, however, Ewan's response prompted agonising pride and a determination to make the best even of this calamity. He was of course visibly shocked but still felt capable of taking the immensely courageous and dignified decision to say no to more treatment. It might briefly have delayed his death but left him with debilitating side-effects, further harming what was now his precious final phase of life. We live so much of our lives in denial of death's inevitability, clinging to the belief that everything can be fixed, that medicine and technology will somehow enable us to escape what no one has before. Ewan, who had throughout his decade of illness thought so profoundly about such things, knew better.

There was time for him to make a final visit to St James' Park when we managed to get Ewan and Alfie tickets for a match against Everton. They sat in the East Stand looking across to a banner which declared the stadium to be 'the cathedral on the hill'. Newcastle, now becoming a force in the Premier League, were expected to win but for a long period failed to score. Then the ball came to Miguel Almiron, a talented but often frustratingly ineffective forward, who whipped a wonderful shot into the top corner. It was one of those moments of sudden skill, executed with a kind of geometric beauty, that all fans crave as they endure a messy defensive stalemate. Ewan, who had a clear view from directly behind of the shot's parabolic perfection, texted me a single word to describe the moment, 'sublime'. That message made me think of an extract I had once sent him from the autobiography of the great Arsenal manager Arsène Wenger, who imagined a conversation with God justifying the meaning of his life after his death and concluded that, in the end what mattered were 'those moments of grace that football offers to those who love it and who give it their all'.

And so we entered the final phase of Ewan's life which had its own moments of great grace, aided by a wonderful palliative care team, seeking to do what seemed most important in the cruelly short time left. We helped him see the family and friends who came to say farewell, held conversations to try to say the things that we and he wanted most to say, yet attempted also to enjoy lighter moments to prevent despair overwhelming us all. The death of Queen Elizabeth that autumn was a strange backdrop, as we felt the inward intensity of our impending grief while much public performance of mourning dominated the news. But there was humour here too, the kind of humour Ewan wrote about whereby 'spiritual insights and liberating perspectives could seem more appealing when conveyed in the language of laughter'. As part of his challenge to our denial of death he had noticed how increasingly unwilling people were to use the word 'death' at all, assuming it was somehow kinder if it was carefully avoided by all kinds of euphemism. We were in our kitchen one day soon after news of the Queen's death when we heard on the radio a famous football manager expressing his 'regret at the Queen's passing'. Ewan looked at me with a mischievous grin and instantly quipped: 'But what about her heading or ball control?'

Before long he was largely confined to bed, facing the onslaught of symptoms, and we watched with despair as his extraordinary brain was overcome. He was often weak and drowsy but there were still moments of delightful lucidity. Our daughter Laura brought her cello to fill his room with glorious sound and remind us of how much all kinds of music had enriched his and our lives. His university, St Andrews, rapidly organised the virtual award of his doctorate which he could watch from a laptop as he lay in bed.

Towards the end he could no longer speak but still sometimes registered his reactions through what had always been wonderfully eloquent eyebrows. I brought him reports of another strange phenomenon of that time, World Cup finals played in winter to avoid Qatar's summer heat. Taking turns with others in my family, I sat for hours just talking and holding his hand, the same hand I had held when first guiding him down to the park as a toddler as we had begun our football adventure together. The page in my diary for the week he died in late December had at either end, as so often, a note put in months earlier of possible Gateshead and Newcastle United games to attend. They were crossed out; none of that now mattered. The only entries I added was one for an appointment to go to our Register Office to record his death; the other was the day of his burial.

NO MORE FOOTBALL?

The New Year began days later, a time during which people are usually preoccupied with new plans and resolutions. We had some immediate things to do to break what would otherwise have been the paralysis of shock. Most important was the organisation of a service of thanksgiving for Ewan's life, with hundreds there who had been touched in so many ways by all he packed in to his 27 or so years.

And then, at the end of that first month, a sense of growing football-emotional confusion. Alfie and I had tickets for Newcastle's biggest game for a long time: a Carabao Cap semi-final against Southampton which they won, taking them to their first Wembley final for a long time. We streamed out of the ground afterwards surrounded by deliriously happy supporters; but all I could feel was flat indifference. Here were the moments when, in the past, I would have been messaging Ewan and our contact would have been the most satisfying coda to a winning performance. I could talk about the game with Alfie but he too seemed, not surprisingly, still subdued.

As the cup final approached that sense of being profoundly out of step with the mood only grew. Much was said in media coverage about the decades-long yearning among fans for Newcastle to win a domestic trophy, what it would mean to club, city and region. But to my inner astonishment I felt more and more that I did not want my team to win. So soon after Ewan's death I dreaded how I would feel amidst what I knew would have been an explosion of local happiness. On the day of the game

I was not even sure I wanted to watch but in the end felt I had to. My mood was confirmed as the first Manchester United goal went in and I felt not the familiar dejection but profound relief. It was easier to hide my own feelings amidst the disappointment and gloom expressed by fans after a 2-0 defeat.

As the season progressed however I felt my mood beginning to shift. The heartache was still huge and I missed Ewan acutely around football's timetable – anticipation as Newcastle kicked off, the moment we would have messaged about the result, the noticing of a quirky story about a player I could no longer pass on. Yet I remembered too how Ewan had said with such characteristic generosity that he wanted us to continue to enjoy our football without him, but in the spirit we had shared. Ever since childhood I had had a kind of imaginary conversation or commentary in my head about football as I walked about or lay in bed, sometimes involving, say, dreams of stardom or team success. Now there was a running conversation with Ewan, about what he would have noticed or enjoyed or lamented in the latest football news.

I sensed how much he would have appreciated moments like Alexander Isak's extraordinary dribble around multiple Everton defenders that April to set up a goal for Newcastle, a demonstration of the kind of sustained mesmerising skill I had first seen from those brilliant 1970 Brazilians, but had never expected from one of our players. By the end of the season Newcastle had reached the Premier League's top four and a place in Champions League. When the next season began, it was harder than ever to get tickets. But there was one match that would become the moment when I finally felt I could bring the memory of Ewan, the grief of losing him, into my football future.

Bright Sadness

As autumn days shorten, floodlit evening games are, for the football fan, a welcome dose of intense additional light. In autumn 2023, as the first anniversary of Ewan's death loomed,

I think Alfie and I were craving that kind of boost, a counter to the gathering gloom. We were still searching for a way to embrace his memory without feeling only bitter and depressive regret.

On a Tuesday in late September we were back in Oxford for the first time since his death, the place where we had lived for many years and Alfie and Ewan had grown up. Gateshead were playing at Oxford City FC where Ewan had been a junior player. Within sight of its stadium was the John Radcliffe hospital where his first brain operations had taken place. And so there were darker memories prompted by that place but also much that could cheer me. The thought of Ewan's dancing runs through opposition defences as a rapid young player; the kindness of his team's coach and players who had organised a shirt signed by the Newcastle United squad after his first brain tumour diagnosis; and gratitude towards friends who had been so supportive during his illness, some of whom arrived at the game to express their sympathy and share their memories.

Among them was my former BBC colleague Chris Morris with whom I had made many programmes about Brexit and its aftermath. Our shared love of football had helped preserve our sanity as we grappled with such toxic and complex territory and attempted to present it in an engaging way. One of our best ruses had been to call in Charlotte Green to liven up a programme about trade policy by reading a list of tariff levels in the style of the classified football results she had once read on the radio every week. I joked now with Chris about how Newcastle qualifying for the Champions League meant the city was now en route to 'return to Europe' whatever Brexit might have done to our continental connections.

Gateshead further brightened our mood with a decisive win and 24 hours later Alfie and I were beginning to feel disconcerting football optimism after returning to Newcastle and watching United beat Manchester City in the Carabao Cup. I wondered how worried Ewan would have been about the curse of growing complacency as the most exciting of the club's autumn fixtures approached: the first home Champions League tie against the glamour of Paris St Germain, for which we had also been able to get tickets.

On the evening of the game Alfie was working beforehand so I had time to spare before meeting him at the ground. My mind was still racing with the experiences of the previous couple of weeks and a residual feeling of guilt about beginning again to enjoy football. So I sought initial calm and reassurance at the cathedral in Newcastle where I lit a candle of remembrance for Ewan (as we have done in many churches). I nodded to the carved list on a wall of previous bishops here, including my father, who had helped me understand what football meant to this region, and one of his successors, Christine Hardman, who had been a regular at Newcastle United. The cathedral choir started to rehearse Evensong which took me back to the times when Ewan sang anthems and psalms so movingly after playing football immediately before. I found myself musing on the memory of fleeting musical and sporting talent reflected in glorious yet fragile candlelight.

Then out into the bracing darkness of the October evening, with the white stripes of gathering Toon shirts glowing along the pavements. I passed the Literary and Philosophical Society where the world's first lightbulb was demonstrated in the 1870s. The Parisians visiting us tonight might think they came from the 'city of light', but Newcastle knows better. On I went past the packed Milecastle pub whose interior includes a panel about the great French revolutionary Jean-Paul Marat who spent years here in the 1770s while writing *Chains of Slavery*; I suspect he would have enjoyed the phalanx of chanting PSG fans who marched from the main station up through Newcastle with flares and flamboyance, clearly confident of victory.

And then I was next to the city walls, a memory in stone of how the city acquired its slogan of *Fortiter Defendit* for resolute defence against invading Scots, a slogan later preserved on

Newcastle football shirts but increasingly worn, as the club prospered, by Scots defenders who had been recruited rather than repulsed. All kinds of historical craziness, in other words, is bouncing around in my pre-match head, and I pause to smile as I think how Ewan would have enjoyed telling me I'm basically bonkers. Now, finally, looming ahead is another burst of illumination as St James' Park comes into view, its vast stands and roofs crouched in anticipation above the city centre. But it is also on the edge of the Town Moor, my moor, the people's space where I played so much football, then came here to watch it, experiencing decades of occasional delight, but much more regular disappointment. What would tonight hold?

On finally past the statue of Alan Shearer outside the ground, arm raised, superstitious fans touching his boot. And there too memorialised is Sir Bobby Robson, suited and nonchalant, foot on a ball, a great European manager yet with a simple love of the game, someone like Ewan who was stricken by cancer while he tried to keep the football faith. Then, having met Alfie, up into the Milburn stand, through a gloomier interior of subdued concrete and corporate catering, before emerging into the bedazzling arena of a stadium electrifying in its atmosphere, raucous in its noise. A potent display of flags and slogans completed the sense of irresistible theatrical excitement.

The players emerged. Yes, World Cup star Kylian Mbappé really was there, playing at St James' Park. Newcastle were clad, unusually, in white shorts – an extra dose of light for a super-optimistic evening? We had been assuming those Newcastle shorts and shirts would be up against it, backs against the wall, *fortiter defendit* all game long. But then something strange started to happen, our team kept insolently pressing forward, attacking confidently or stealing possession. Suddenly Isak shot, the goalkeeper could only parry and Miggy Almiron, the forward Ewan had blessed as sublime, provided another moment of beatific joy as he guided in the rebound.

We hardly dared believe this could continue. But PSG were

about to face another Newcastle Nemesis by the name of Dan Burn. TV adverts had been running with the catchline 'Born In Blyth, Made in the Royal Navy'. Burn is from Blyth and now transformed himself into a kind of English *force de frappe* as he launched his giant frame towards a chipped cross and headed the ball too powerfully for the despairing 'keeper. VAR checks were made for the ball crossing the line and offside to prolong our agony but tonight, for once, all was well; there was to be no thwarting of joy by distant officialdom.

It was 2-0 at half-time and Ewan was saying in my head: 'wonderful but please can we not sit back like we so often have after taking the lead and give the opposition more and more time to recover'. Confirmation that this night would be different came a few minutes into the second half. Another local lad, Sean Longstaff, raced into the area, swept the ball across the six yard line and in it went off the hapless goalkeeper's outstretched arm. A large man in full length coat returning from half-time refreshment promptly picked up Alfie, gave him a spontaneous bear hug and appeared, at first, to be carrying him off as a kind of trophy. He had, appropriately enough, just passed a club sign encouraging all fans to 'elevate your matchday experience'.

A few minutes later, in the spirit of Ewan's non-complacency, PSG did score one in response; some Newcastle fans were perhaps reassured by their familiar feeling of brief anxiety, so bafflingly novel had been the experience of dominating and scoring three against such illustrious opposition. But as we approached the end there was not the expected further PSG goal to make the last few minutes miserably uncertain. Instead the Parisians were on the receiving end of a final Newcastle moment of glorious panache. Defender Fabian Schär, who generally plays with an unruffled air to match his film-star looks and well-coiffed hair, won the ball in midfield, played a casual one-two with a team-mate and then curled the ball elegantly, unstoppably into the top corner.

Fab all round; noise intensified yet further as did incredulity. Kylian Mbappé waited forlornly to kick off yet again, puffing out his cheeks and looking utterly bemused in the Tyneside drizzle, whose drops glistened in the floodlights. I knew now this would become a potent memory for everyone there, a story to be told in the future, an echo of the memories of famous past victories that have been passed on. And all the more precious because so rare and unexpected, a confirmation that one of the things we love about sport is its glorious unpredictability.

Final whistle and prolonged, uncomplicated delight? Yes, for the vast majority of those Newcastle fans in the stadium, but not for me. As we left the stadium we were carried on a torrent, down the corridor behind the Milburn stand, stepping across the hundreds of memorial stones to past fans embedded in the pavement, fans who had craved the success we had witnessed. 'I have spread my dreams under your feet': the lines from Yeats which I first saw on a Cumbrian gravestone for some reason sprang to mind. 'Tread softly because you tread on my dreams.' And no one in the beaming, chanting crowd noticed in the darkness of the corridor that while they were deliriously happy, I was in tears.

On we swept down the hill past the statue of Bobby Robson, foot on ball but ready, I thought now, to dance a jig of happiness like he famously did after a late England winner against Belgium in the 1990 World Cup. And he would have understood my mixed emotions better than most, coming from his mining background. Historian Dan Jackson, describing an inherited North Eastern ability to mix mourning and celebration, quotes one observer of the Durham Miners' Gala who stated: 'Miners rub shoulders with death. They know how to face death. Last Saturday I saw, too, that they will not let death spoil life.'

As we emerged into the light of the city centre I could begin to smile and appreciate the crowds through stinging eyes and talk happily with Alfie, imagining how much Ewan would have approved. The night's enjoyment had not come through blocking out his memory; the tears had proved that. But there had been progress, carrying the memory with us, finding new light beyond. Carmen Mayer and her colleagues in Germany had called one of their projects about football and grief *Trauer unterm Flutlicht*, 'Sorrow under the Floodlights'. 'Why floodlights?' I asked her. 'Because', she replied, 'in any stadium where people are gathered there will somewhere be grief, but the floodlights can also be seen to illuminate the memory of all those fans who have died in a way many find helpful, even heavenly.'

'Continuing to try to find a way of walking with Ewan', I wrote in my diary soon afterwards, 'of not being paralysed or simply enraged by grief but incorporating his memory into current motivation. Far from always successful; the ambushes of raw emotion still occur. But the hugely moving support of the best family and friends do help.' And I found too the perfect motto to encapsulate how I had felt after this extraordinary game, and how I was now feeling more broadly. Sorting through some of Ewan's theology material I noticed his interest in an old Russian idea of 'bright sadness': somehow holding together joy and grief, accepting and appreciating both. It had special resonance on dark nights lit by brilliant light, and in places full of black and white everywhere you looked. That would be how I would now approach football too: with bright sadness, never the same as it had been, but still open to new joy as well as rich memory, and appreciated more deeply than ever.

11
WINNING REDEMPTION

THE WIN AGAINST PSG was a wonderful one-off; the rest of Newcastle's European adventure was less thrilling. There were losses in the two other games at St James' Park and the club did not progress. An increasingly injury-affected squad failed to reach the European places in that season's Premier League. So the start of the 2024-25 season hardly seemed to promise glory; perhaps Newcastle were returning frustratingly to type?

But there was something about the Carabao Cup and Newcastle United that still stirred as that season's competition began. Nottingham Forest, enjoying a brilliant season, were overcome in an early round; then Chelsea and Brentford were among those defeated before an impressive 2-0 win at Arsenal in the first leg of the semi-final. Back at St James' Park for the second leg we marvelled at how the visitors were softened up by a strident pre-match saxophone solo played by one of local music star Sam Fender's musicians like a medieval bugler emboldening troops into battle. Another 2-0 victory, another Wembley appearance, prompting familiar national speculation as to just why Newcastle had failed to win a trophy for so long. I realised I was a member of the generation most acutely affected, born at the start of the decade, the 1960s, which the great chronicler of North East football Arthur Appleton described as 'our doldrums'. There had been moments of brilliance and hope since, even a European trophy in 1969, but the domestic doldrums had continued to leave us stranded without success.

Unlike the last time they had reached the Carabao final

two years previously, too close to Ewan's death, this time I was ready. Whereas then I had been disconcerted by not wanting Newcastle to win, now I was taken aback by unprecedented optimism. I dared tell a few friends and family members that I had a funny feeling this might be our year, even though our opponents were the Premier League's runaway leaders, Liverpool. I wondered whether Ewan would have permitted such a shocking break with our no-complacency pact but decided he might have allowed it in the name of defiant new beginnings.

BRAVE NEW NEWCASTLE

In the week leading up to the final, part of the club's ownership decided boldly to project their ambition into the nation's capital. Property developers the Reuben brothers had attracted far less attention during the takeover of Newcastle United than the Saudi Public Investment Fund which took much the biggest stake. There had also been another minority shareholder, Amanda Staveley and her husband Mehrdad Ghodoussi. Staveley initially became the public face of the club as the PIF was not exactly used to answering to the media. After they moved on the other minority shareholder, the Reubens, increased their stake to 15 per cent and now listed Newcastle United as a 'great English institution' on their website alongside various international luxury hotels and London landmarks.

The Reubens were another fascinating example of how football was attracting the most dynamic of globalisers. They were from a family of Jews originally from Iraq who had spent time in India, then made money through British textiles, metals and property, invested in the lucrative minerals privatisation of 1990s Russia and spent the proceeds acquiring mostly high-end property in places including New York and London. The Reuben family like the PIF did not seem fond of publicity; in fact it often appeared to me that the more the Premier League heaped media obligations on managers and players the less owners, and those who actually took key club decisions, felt obliged to face public accountability.

The Reubens' interest in the North East of England and Newcastle United was an intriguing addition to their portfolio as they asserted via their website that: 'Newcastle United represents more than just a club – it is a pillar of identity and pride for millions. Reuben Brothers are proud to support its evolution into a globally recognised, values-driven institution'. Quite what were the 'values' driving them was a fascinating question. They added that they were simultaneously 'deeply committed to the socio-economic revitalisation of Newcastle and the wider region'. Now one of the Reubens' most visible properties in London, Millbank Tower, was used audaciously by Newcastle United's new shirt sponsors Sela to project giant images of the club and its players.

There were ghostly presences in the shadows of these striking images. For this was a new version of an old North East story: global enterprises promising to sustain regional growth. Millbank Tower had originally been built in the 1960s as HQ of Vickers, the company that had inherited what was left of Armstrong's, Tyneside's great engineering and armaments company. A short distance along the Thames still stood, right next to the Houses of Parliament, what was once the grand base of Imperial Chemical Industries, the international concern that dominated Teesside when I was born there but had virtually disappeared within a few decades. I had noticed previously on the building's outer walls carved tributes to great figures from ICI like its founder Alfred Mond, said to have been the inspiration behind Mustapha Mond, one of the ten World Controllers in Aldous Huxley's novel *Brave New World*. On the ornate doors were images of human striving throughout the ages, and great inventions representing economic progress. Few of the Londoners hurrying by, or indeed the building's modern users, will have had any recognition of such symbolism, nor of its links with the industrial North East.

So could Newcastle United's footballers with their own striving and invention make London sit up and take notice, putting Newcastle back on the map of national success? Alfie and I decided we would strive to make this our ultimate football weekend by watching all three of our teams within around 24 hours. Early omens on the Saturday were not good. In a foretaste of the catastrophic loss of form that would blight the end of their season while a phantom international takeover failed to happen, Gateshead played dismally in a 2-0 home defeat to Maidenhead. On the Sunday morning, the day of the Carabao final, we went first to watch Newcastle United's women's team play against Durham. They scored early, cheered on by an especially vocal supporter clad in a full black and white striped suit topped with a clown hat. Sadly some of the Newcastle defending then became comically inept as they lapsed to a 3-1 defeat.

I was beginning to doubt ruefully my Carabao optimism as we now drove back north towards Newcastle, though the sight of the Angel of the North draped for the day in a black and white shirt boosted morale. Our attempts to secure Wembley tickets had, like those of many thousands of Newcastle, fans, stood little chance. Wembley may have 90,000 seats, but by the time all its corporate guests have been catered for only around a third remain for each of the clubs actually playing.

BIG DAN DELIVERS AGAIN

We had decided however that this match demanded more than another couple of hours on the sofa at home. So we were joining a friend at an evocative Tyneside venue: the former Federation brewery in Dunston, near John Hall's Metrocentre. It was once the home of Newcastle Brown Ale and is now an events centre equipped with several large screens and many Newcastle fans exhibiting every emotion from bravado to intense anxiety. Smaller children danced around impatiently; older fans drew chairs up in front of the screens, reminisced about past finals and disappointments and tried to laugh off any apprehension. Among the guests on stage was Keith Gillespie, former Newcastle winger who knew all about disappointment, having been part of Kevin Keegan's 1996 team that had squandered a 12 point Premier League lead. But he too expressed the feeling that today might be different.

I still dared to agree, imagining a game in which Liverpool attacked relentlessly, but failed at key moments or were blocked by heroic Newcastle defending before a scruffy late goal brought us guilty glory. It was nothing like that. Liverpool seemed flat; Newcastle played with verve and conviction. The score remained 0-0 for most of the half but then Liverpool made the same mistake PSG had made eighteen months earlier: they failed to understand that Dan Burn was one of the most potent weapons to emerge from the North East since the guns on Lord Armstrong's battleships. He stood at a corner a long way out, was marked only by a player who looked about three feet shorter, and powered the ball in. The Liverpool manager Arne Slot still looked bemused after the game when he admitted that: 'I have never seen in my life a player from that far away heading a ball with so much force into the far corner'.

All of us watching were a bit bemused too, not by Dan Burn's power which we had all seen pulse across the pitch for the previous few seasons but the way we seemed to be winning with some ease. A second goal ruled out for offside early in the second half looked like an ominous setback but then another move ended in a smart Isak finish. I saw delight on some faces but more signs of uneasy incredulity on others. This could surely not be happening like this, without all the usual agony? Finally there was some Liverpool response but our 'keeper Nick Pope initially held firm. Fifteen minutes to go and in the absence of what would once have been multiple messages to and from Ewan outbidding each other in superstitious pessimism I was instead conducting a bizarre conversation in my head with him about the theology of today's football. Arne Slot the Dutch Calvinist must have thought he was predestined to win with his opening line-up? But now he had converted, bringing on an Italian called church (Chiesa) who put one past the no longer infallible Pope. Surely he was offside? VAR drew its lines as if in a prolonged medieval disputation and then ruled against us. Aaargh! 2-1, still minutes to survive. Around me there was the kind of fervent Geordie communal prayer which might once have delighted my clergyman Dad but when a Newcastle player carelessly gave up possession this was followed by mass utterance of what he used to call 'the kind of words you may not have heard before'.

And then the final whistle, and a range of emotions all around us impossible to summarise but spanning the spectrum from wild delight to head-shaking disbelief. Dancing feet lurched across a floor lubricated with spilt beer and tears, many tears. What immediately struck me then and would continue to impress in the hours and days that followed was that celebration was accompanied instinctively with regret for those who had never known this joy. Two years previously I had worried that a Newcastle trophy win would leave me miserably isolated in my still raw grief. Now I felt communal support for my feelings of real delight at the achievement, tempered with acute awareness of how much Ewan would have relished the day.

The Toon tribe now emerged from wherever it had been enjoying, or enduring, the match, and instinctively gathered. We headed into Newcastle city centre, where businesses were preparing themselves for an epic night. We were joined by Jane and also John Dales and his daughter Louisa. John had been a childhood friend who had shared my chagrin at our school's ban on playing football and was one of my closest companions supporting Newcastle in our London exile. We had also played football together in the 1980s at such exotic venues as a caged five-a-side pitch on the Isle of Dogs, pretending to be part of an all-conquering Toon team at a time when the club's performances had seemed as detached from the elite as were the East London locals from the Canary Wharf bankers newly towering over them.

Outside St James' Park we found fans swarming over the statues of Alan Shearer, who had stayed for many years as a player despite never winning a trophy, and Bobby Robson who would have so loved to have managed his boyhood club to glory. There was much speculation about whether they would soon be joined by an appropriately tall tribute to Dan Burn, the Blyth Colossus. 'Champions' was one of the evening's repeated chants which I remembered later when reading the autobiography of another player and manager who would have loved to have won something here, Kevin Keegan. Talking about the death of his father, a miner originally from the North East, Keegan recalled: 'Dad's favourite word was 'champion'. Even when the cancer took hold. I'd go, 'How are you today, Dad?' He'd reply, 'Champion, son'.'

The Sela-bration

In the days that followed, there were symptoms of a giant regional hangover ranging from a suspiciously high number of train cancellations to news that our local baker, an avid Toon fan, was temporarily and tearfully 'indisposed'. The club did its best to help its more affluent supporters avoid too much of an emotional crash by announcing that 'Newcastle United has launched a commemorative Champagne in response to requests from supporters following their Carabao Cup win at Wembley' and kindly offering 'United's passionate and loyal fanbase the opportunity to purchase their very own bottle!'. It felt as if we had come a long way from the days when the club, and the city, were thoroughly Brown Ale branded.

Attention now turned to how the city could celebrate with the players. The club's new shirt sponsors were a Saudi-based event management company called Sela that stated its ambition 'to be the most admired powerhouse that creates iconic experiences'. A traditional open-topped bus parade winding its way in and around the city did not seem to be considered practicable nor did its unpredictability probably fit the modern idea of a managed event. So what was devised instead in the time available was what might be called a Sela-bration: a short bus ride for the players to the Town Moor, where a crowd had been assembled for hours in front of a hastily constructed stage watching a re-run of the final on a large screen.

The images were designed to reach a global audience. Soon afterwards the club announced the launch of an 'official supporters' club' for those around the world. 'From Newcastle to New York, Blyth to Beijing, Wallsend or Wellington' all were now part of 'one Toon army'. Supporters' clubs that 'provide a sense of citizenship and a family way of life' could now receive an 'official seal of approval'. Soon afterwards I read an interview with Liverpool's American chairman stating his belief that 'there could now be as many as a billion people around the world who follow Liverpool'. Newcastle now aspired to reach that level of international recognition. But where, I wondered, would that leave the passionate local patriotism mobilised as so often before on the city's Town Moor?

I was not there for the parade as we were going to the wedding of Ewan's best friend James, a welcome opportunity to mark now much he had been supported by such relationships during his long illness. But the Newcastle event had anyway lacked appeal; the idea of ticketed (although free) entry to a fenced-off section of the Moor sat uneasily with its great traditions of open access. When I later watched a recording I enjoyed the players' attempt to show their version of local-global fusion. Brazilian captain Bruno Guimaraes led the singing and Dan Burn added vocal Northumbrian heft. But things petered out in front of a crowd chilled by hours of waiting as celebrities who could not remember everyone's names led over-prolonged cheers and gags.

It was no surprise that the moment many would remember most from that day happened elsewhere, shortly before the players left St James' Park. Wor Flags, the independent fans' group that had done so much to transform the St James' Park atmosphere, staged a breathtaking *coup de theâtre*. Two figures abseiled down a tall hotel building opposite the ground to unveil a huge banner with an image of the Newcastle manager Eddie Howe in clenched-fist delight. The day, Howe commented, had shown 'the power football possesses. It can change people's mood, can change the city's mood'. He too had reinforced the mood of celebration mixed with regret, saying straight after the Wembley win: 'Naturally you end up thinking of the players, the staff, but also the people who aren't with you – like for me, my mum, family members'. Howe, who faced perhaps his own brush with mortality when hospitalised with pneumonia later that season, would return to the inspirational story of his mother Anne who had sacrificed so much for him as a single parent before her death soon after he became a manager. 'I know that her spirit, her courage and her determination is with me in so many different ways in how I act and behave. I know she's willing me on from somewhere, and very proud' he said later that summer. 'I feel I have a duty to protect her legacy by how I conduct myself in what I do.'

THOSE NOT THERE

The theme of remembrance amidst celebration was a constant and sustaining presence at that time. When Alfie and I arrived to take our seats for the first home league game after the Carabao win, we were expecting much unrestrained revelling. But I was speechless with stinging eyes for several minutes after emerging into the ground to see across the East Stand, as the first thing all the players would see as they ran onto the pitch, a Wor Flags banner dedicated to 'All the Ones Who Didn't Make the Night'. It was a summer in which the flying of flags around the country would become became associated in many places with tension, hostility and division; these flags and banners were by contrast the most moving displays of a community's shared sense of its people and its past.

After the season had ended with Newcastle, just, making it back into the Champions League we were back in the stadium that summer for a concert by Sam Fender. He was swiftly becoming a global music superstar but remained proudly and loudly committed to his North-East roots. In his poetic lyrics there was lamentation about the region's tragic problems, such as the suicide rate among its young males. But there was uplifting love too, not least for Newcastle United. I was delighted to discover that, on the day of the Carabao final, he had been playing a concert in my beloved Berlin, the band clad in black and white shirts. The lyrics of one song were changed that evening to: 'What is God? His name's Dan Burn'. I pictured Ewan's eloquent eyebrows raised when it came to the theology of that one, but how he would have enjoyed it, nevertheless.

At Fender's concert in St James' Park the following June there was further rumbustious celebration of black and white rock and roll. But the moments that will resound forever in my mind where when he paused at one point for a complete change to tone and atmosphere as the Easington colliery band arrived on stage to become his accompanists. And then Fender sang 'Remember My Name', dedicated to his grandparents and written, Fender said, 'from the perspective of my Grandad who was looking after my Grandma when she was suffering from dementia'. And in that song were also the thoughts of parents remembering with pride their footballing son, amidst the fear of forgetting in the face of dementia's cruellest consequences:

> Remember my name
> Chasing a cross in from the wing our boy's a whippet
> He's faster than anything
> Remember the pride that we felt for the two of us
>   made him ourselves.

And there I was edging closer to Jane, swaying with the emotion of the moment, remembering our rapid winger called Ewan, whose name we will remember when we are in this stadium and in every other place we go to and live in. And just as he discovered so powerfully how culture can help those suffering from the most severe of disease, so we could find such consolation through a song in a football ground mined from the emotional depths to help us survive the greatest of grief.

CONTINUING THE CONVERSATION

The mood of commemoration as well as celebration after Newcastle's Carabao triumph extended even to the cemetery in Hexham where Ewan is buried as the staff there flew a Newcastle United flag. I passed it on one of my regular visits to his grave.

Every time I go there, I notice new things. There are the war graves, like that of Richard Dalzell Oliver, Northumberland Fusiliers and Army Cyclist Corps, killed on 22 November 1917 aged 23. I find myself wondering whether he played football and how his parents coped with the loss of their son in his twenties and how they perhaps hated the Germany I came to think of as my second home. When I pass graves of women who were young adults in the 1920s I wonder whether they were part of the first female football generation so cruelly banned. Then I carry on past the place where another young man is buried beneath a gravestone decorated with black and white stripes, the identity his family most wanted to give him in perpetuity. And finally on to the woodland section where Ewan lies and where we have spent such times since his death, emotions veering between rage and the calm of greater acceptance, sometimes immobilised by what has happened, sometimes busying ourselves with tending his grave and cultivating our memory, the grass and bulbs around his body watered by rainfall and tears.

And, if I can, I sometimes talk to him. Most recently about Gateshead surviving against the odds to play spirited football for fans who keep the faith. Or about Lionesses like Lucy Tough Bronze, who emerged from Lindisfarne and Northumberland, defied lingering FA restrictions on girls playing football, and eventually played a victorious tournament for England in 2025 with a broken leg and helped create a 'proper English' positive patriotism in a way that would have had all the lost lasses of the North East footballing past cheering.

And then, dear Ewan, with sighs, wry smiles and much eye-rolling, the latest on Newcastle. How they won a trophy, but the following summer, as black follows white, still seemed to be a club beset by uncertainty. The most extraordinary game I have ever attended at St James' Park, came early in the 2025/26 season. It was against Liverpool again, the team we had vanquished at Wembley, yet reigning Premier League champions and about to sign, amidst much acrimony, our star striker Alexander Isak, who was refusing to play.

That gave the pre-match atmosphere a special edge, and Wor Flags added their own trenchant commentary with a banner proclaiming: 'Nothing is Achieved Alone. We Are a City. A Whole Population. We Are Newcastle United.' The game began and a plot unfolded with twists and turns, surging emotional waves, that would have distinguished any great drama. Newcastle attacked with spirit, yet the absence of their top finisher told. Then Liverpool scored against the run of play, and frustrated stand-in centre forward Anthony Gordon took on the role of tragic villain with a rash challenge which VAR, after the traditional highly-charged hiatus, turned into a red card.

At half-time, the bravest Toon fans still dared to hope, but when Liverpool scored a second soon after the restart all seemed truly lost; the upstarts were surely about to be put firmly in their place by a thumping defeat as their assets, and aspirations, were stripped. But then an utterly unexpected revival. Orchestrated by one of our flamboyant yet steely Brazilians, brilliant Bruno Guimaraes, Newcastle's ten men went back on the offensive, and brought the score back to 2-2.

We were a minute away from an extraordinary draw but this was the Newcastle football stage where plot twists are never over until the final whistle. Pressing for a winner in the spirit of the wonderfully reckless Kevin Keegan teams of the mid 1990s, space was left fatefully for a final Liverpool counter-attack and the winning goal. I and many around me were stupefied and speechless, utterly torn between crushing disappointment and fierce pride.

The global audience was watching on too, a game like this in a place like this offering something no other kind of TV spectacular, sporting or otherwise, could rival that day. Among the admirers was the great German player Toni Kroos. 'I'm going to sign up as a Newcastle member today,' he said. '(It was not) just the atmosphere, but also the team. They completely captivated me.' Days later Newcastle sought to fill the Isak gap by signing a German striker, Nick Woltemade, adding to the German defender Malick Thiaw also recruited that summer. The Toon, I would have loved to joke to Ewan, were making us feel more at home than ever by finally embracing *Fussball*.

I was still trying to find words to make sense of all this visiting the cemetery soon afterwards, its peace the ultimate contrast to the volcanic emotion of St James' Park. And amidst the sounds of nature in this wonderful spot, the bees Ewan loved rescuing buzzing around their nearby hives, I tell him we can hear carried on the wind the distant shouts of the next generation of boys and girls in our town falling for football. And the nearby river Tyne brings us migrating salmon leaping like angels, and gulls gossiping about city and sea, their piercing cries mimicking the anguish and ecstasy from all Tyneside's footballing theatres further downriver.

Playing with Angels

Ewan's plot, and the ground we have reserved around it for our own burials when the time comes, is now precious to us. It is our eternal green space, about the size of the green space down the bottom of our road where I first kicked a ball around with my little boy, the space where with him I saw the potential of sporting joy, and then suddenly, when he collapsed as a teenager, life's fragility.

'I leave you these goals in my will,' begins a verse by Tyneside poet Keith Armstrong from a work entitled *Angels Playing Football*:

> snapshots of me on the run.
> I leave with you these pieces of skill,
> Moments of me in the sun
>
> Pass me my memories,
> pass me the days,
> pass me a ball and I'll play:
>
> play with the angels,
> play on their wings,
> play in the thunder and lightning.

Ewan is no longer on this earthly pitch but will always be with me as the game goes on, never knowing or assuming whether we will be facing win or loss, the sublime or the sorrow, black or white. 'No complacency' remained our watchwords when it came to football, and our team. And there should indeed be no complacency – about football, or anything else. But precisely because of that, because we all live if we are honest with the constant possibility of catastrophe and the knowledge of death, we need to celebrate the sublime every time and everywhere we find it. And then we can make the sadness brighter, remember that we had such moments with those who are no longer with us, and always win something even when we lose.

Acknowledgements

I OWE GREAT THANKS TO DAVID MOLONEY for spotting the potential for a book in our first conversation about grief and football and asking me to write it. And I am grateful to him and his colleagues at Herne for all their skilled work guiding the book towards publication.

For advice, interviews and other help for the book I would like to thank Mary Raine, Christine Hardman, Sarah Miles, Kal Singh Dhindsa, Patrick Brennan and, in Germany, Carmen Mayer and Chris Law.

Friends ever since schooldays, especially John Dales, Nick Rugg and David Haggie, have shared the resilience and good humour needed when supporting Newcastle United and have helped me remember what happened along the way. Fellow fans at Newcastle, Gateshead and other games have been an endless source of football wisdom and wit. Staff at the library of the Newcastle Literary and Philosophical Society and Newcastle City Libraries have been very helpful.

In my time working for the BBC Jim Frank and Chris Morris injected football-related relief into grappling with the likes of German history and Brexit. Smita Patel was a great collaborator as we investigated subjects including football fencing. I am also grateful to all those at the BBC who commissioned ideas and worked with me on a number of other football-related projects. At the *Times* newspaper obituaries desk, Ian Brunskill, Nigel Farndale and Anna Temkin have enabled me to write about many fascinating football lives.

I learned a lot about how to approach history and writing from my schoolteachers Alan Mitchell and Brian Davidson, and subsequently David Cannadine, Jonathan Steinberg and Simon Schama. In the US and India I benefited from wonderful conversations about all sorts of things, including football, with Abhijit Banerjee.

My Dad Ronnie took me to some of my first professional games and opened my eyes to the wider importance of North East football. My Mum Liz constantly encouraged me, stood on the school touchline and was an enjoyable commentator on some of football's crazier aspects. My father-in-law Tony Harrison taught me so much about embracing every kind of culture in art and sport and 'confounding their categories'. I am very grateful to my siblings Rachel, Rick, Anna and Tom for all their ideas, family stories, and support in difficult times. My daughter Laura has been a wonderful support too, as well as a tolerant and amusing observer of family football madness. My son Alfie has become my great football companion, seeking out adventures with his unique blend of curiosity and courage. I owe most of all to my beloved wife and soulmate Jane who has encouraged me so much and embraced football in her distinctive way (while rightly raising the occasional affectionate eyebrow at the extent of her husband's obsession).

In a strange and sad way, of course, I wish I had never had reason to write this particular book, as part of it is about the illness and death of our dear son Ewan. But I have come to think of it also as a celebration of what I was lucky enough to share with him, and a continuation of our conversation about the great game we both relished. I hope it can form part of his very special legacy and I dedicate it to him with unending love.

BIBLIOGRAPHY

Appleton, Arthur, *Hotbed of Soccer* (London, 1961)
Ardagh, John, *A Tale of Five Cities* (Secker and Warburg, 1979)

Bowlby, Ewan, *Borrowed Stories* (Darton, Longman and Todd, 2025)
Brennan, Patrick, *The Munitionettes* (Donmouth, 2007)

Chaplin, Michael, *Newcastle United Stole My Heart* (London, 2021)
Charleton, R. J., *A History of Newcastle on Tyne* (Newcastle n.d.)
Charlton, Cissie, *Cissie* (Berwick, 1988)
Clarke, Jed, *Fifty Years of Hurt* (Edinburgh, 2006)
Cole, Andy, *The Autobiography* (London, 1999)
Colls, Robert, *This Sporting Life* (Oxford, 2020)
Colls, Robert and Lancaster, Bill (eds) *Geordies* (Edinburgh, 1992)
Colls, Robert and Lancaster, Bill (eds) *Newcastle-Upon-Tyne* (West Sussex, 2001)

Ferris, Paul, *The Boy on the Shed* (Hodder, 2018)

Gascoigne, Paul, (with Hunter Davies) *Gazza, My Story* (London, 2004)
Goldblatt, David, *The Ball is Round* (London, 2007 edition)
Goldblatt, David, *The Game of Our Lives* (London, 2015)
Greaves, Jimmy, *This One's on Me* (New English Library, 1991)

Haigh, Gavin, *Black and White Stripes* (Leicester, 2022)
Harrison, Tony, *Continuous* (London, 1981)
Harrison, Tony, *'The Trackers of Oxyrhynchus'* (London, 1990)
Harrison, Tony, *V* (Newcastle, 1985)
Hesse-Lichtenberger, Ulrich, *Tor! The Story of German Football* (London, 2002)
Hopcraft, Arthur, *The Football Man* (Aurum, 2006)
Hutchinson, Roger, *The Toon* (Birlinn, 2010)

Jackson, Dan, *The Northumbrians* (London, 2019)

Jackson, Dan, *Howay the Lads!: A People's History of Newcastle United* (forthcoming)
Joannou, Paul, *Fortress St James* (Gateshead, 2000)
Joannou, Paul, *The Hughie Gallacher Story* (Derby, 1989)

Keegan, Kevin, *My Life in Football* (Macmillan, 2018)

Logan, Gabby, *The First Half* (Piatkus, 2023)

Mains, Brian and Tuck, Anthony, *Royal Grammar School, Newcastle Upon Tyne* (Oriel Press, 1986)
Macdonald, Malcolm, *Super Mac* (Highdown, 2003)
Milburn, Jack, *Jackie Milburn, A Man of Two Halves,* (Edinburgh, 2003)
Marples, Morris, *A History of Football* (London, 1954)

Niven, Alex, *The North Will Rise Again* (London, 2023)

Peacock, Gavin, *A Greater Glory* (Christian Focus, 2021)
Pearson, Harry, *The Far Corner* (Abacus, 1994)
Pearson, Harry, *The Farther Corner* (Simon and Schuster, 2020)
Pearson, Lynn, *Played in Tyne and Wear* (English Heritage, 2010)
Priestley, J. B., *English Journey* (Manchester, 2023 edition)

Robson, Bobby, *Farewell but not Goodbye* (Hodder, 2005)
Robson, Bobby, *Newcastle – My Kind of Toon* (Hodder, 2008)

Sharkey, Joe, *Akenside Syndrome* (Jajosa Books, 2014)
Smith, Dan, *An Autobiography* (Newcastle, 1970)
Srníček, Pavel, *Pavel is a Geordie* (Mojo Risin', 2015)

Walker, Michael, *Up There, The North East Football Boom and Bust* (London, 2014)
Williams, Jean, *A Game for Rough Girls?* (London, 2003)
Wilson, Jonathan, *Inverting the Pyramid* (Orion, 2009)
Wilson, Jonathan, *Two Brothers* (Hachette, 2022)
Withe, Peter, *All For the Love of the Game* (Goodyear, 2017)
Wrack, Suzanne, *A Woman's Game* (London, 2022)

Young, Percy, *A History of British Football* (London, 1969)

Websites:
The Blizzard
nufc.com
The Athletic
www.trauerundfussball.de

Interviews
Kal Singh Dhindsa
Carmen Mayer and Chris Law
Mary Raine

REFERENCES

1: A MOMENT WHEN EVERYTHING CHANGES

10   'like the Dutch': see Wilson, *'Inverting the Pyramid'*, p. 227

16   'as he wrote later': quotations taken from Ewan Bowlby, *Borrowed Stories*, p. 31

16   'a 2014 cup upset' reported in *Varsity*, Monday 17 November 2014

2: DRAWN IN

27   **Dad wasted no time:** His interview was in the *Newcastle Evening Chronicle* 6 January 1973

28   **My son Ewan:** Ewan's ideas on stories and facing illness are set out in his book *Borrowed Stories*

28   **RGS headmaster's** statement is from Mains and Tuck, *'Royal Grammar School'*, p. 125

29   **Niall Ferguson's** words are taken from his *Empire*, p. 260

29   **Harry Pearson:** see Jackson, *Northumbrians*, p. 157

30   **'people's park'** is from Charleton, *'Newcastle upon Tyne'*

30   **Robert Colls**, *This Sporting Life*, p. 145

30   **Lynn Pearson**, *Played in Tyne and Wear*, p. 26-8

31   **'Democratic Golf'** in *The Times*, 6 January 1919

32   **'sheep awaiting slaughter'** is from Appleton, *Hotbed*, p. 120

32   **Peter Withe** *For the Love of the Game*, p. 139

32   **Andy Cole** *The Autobiography*, p. 45

33   **Kevin Keegan**, *My Life in Football*, p. 4-5

33   **Paul Ferris**, *Boy on the Shed*, p. 152, 236

33   **Arthur Appleton**, *Hotbed of Soccer*, p. 18

34   **Jackie Milburn**, in *Milburn, Jack, Man of Two Halves*, p. 190

34   **Arthur Hopcraft**, *Football Man*, p. 189

34   **crash barriers:** see Joannou, *Fortress*, p. 54

34   **Macdonald**, *Super Mac*, p. 93-4

36   **Ardagh**, *Tale of Five Cities*, p. 189-90

38   **Smith**, *Autobiography*, p. 71-3

3: DRAWN AWAY

42   **In the Edwardian period** – Holt and Physick quotation is in Colls and Lancaster (eds.), *Newcastle upon Tyne*, p. 207

43   **Jackie Milburn** is from Colls and Lancaster (eds.), *Geordies* p. 124

43   **Alan Shoulder** – see my obituary published in *The Times*, 10 February 2025

44   **Jack Charlton comments**, see https://nufc-history.co.uk/misc/nufc-match-qpr-1984-85.html

49   **Ronald Amman's** article was in 'The World Today', August 1987. *Perestroika* stood for a kind of restructuring and *glasnost* for openness and honesty in dealing with the people

49   **largely unmodernised Palace** which I have written about at: https://www.bbc.co.uk/news/uk-politics-41650215

50   **David Goldblatt**: see his *The Game of Our Lives*, p. ix

50   **John Campbell** is from the second volume of his biography of Margaret Thatcher (London 2003), pp. 573-4

50   **'slum sport'** quoted by Matthew Syed in *The Times*, 18 November 2019

51   **Tony Harrison's** poem 'Divisions' is taken from his collection *Continuous*

53   *Daily Mail* article on 'V' was published on 12 October 1987. Bernard Levin's column was in *The Times* on 19 October

54   My **BBC documentary** on football fencing, produced by Smita Patel, was broadcast on Radio 4 on 8 May 2000 in the series *Why Did We Do That* (available for streaming from 2025 as a BBC Radio History series).

54   **Lord Taylor's report** is available at https://www.jesip.org.uk/wp-content/uploads/2022/03/Hillsborough-Stadium-Disaster-final-report.pdf

56-57 **Billy Whitehurst**: Alan Hansen's comments are in his *A Matter of Opinion* (London, 1999), p. 7

59   **Gazza's** comments on Gazzamania and at 10 Downing Street are from *My Story*, pp. 123, 127

4: FUSSBALL

63   **Helmut Schön** quotation used in my piece for BBC Online, 'Is Fussball coming Home?', published on 22 May 2013: https://www.bbc.co.uk/news/magazine-22609495

65   **Schalke 04** for more on the club's history and mining identity see Kit Holden, 'The Nostalgia Trap', in *The Blizzard*, issue 54

66   **Japanese Navy**: The fullest account of this relationship is in Marie Conte-Helm's *Japan and the North East of England* (London, 1989)

68   **John Keegan**, *The Face of Battle* (Penguin), p. 250

69   **Evening Chronicle** coverage published on 12 September 1984

69   **Northumbrian Brigade**: quotations taken from *The War History of the 1ˢᵗ Northumbrian Brigade, August 1914-July 1919* (Newcastle, 1927)

69   **Dan Dunglinson's** story, see https://www.newmp.org.uk/person/d-dunglinson-1916/ and also *Hexham Courant*, 19 July 2016

75   **Rehhagel** quotations are taken from the BBC TV documentary 'King Otto and Football's Greek Gods': https://www.bbc.co.uk/programmes/m002053h

76   **Olympic Stadium**: My documentary was broadcast as 'Stadium of Spooks' on BBC Radio 4, 9 July, 2006

79   **Angela Merkel** Radio 4 'Profile', 8 September 2013

81   **Uli Hesse** See 'Is Fussball coming Home?' above

82   **Walter Frankenstein** My obituary was published in *The Times* on 8 May 2025

83   **Werner Oscar Maier** – see the vivid memories of his son Daniel: https://medium.com/@DanielMaier/from-wartime-to-full-time-370620de5779

5: BEARING OUR STRIPES

88   **Peter Davidson** is from his book *The Idea of North* (London, 2005), p. 121

88   **Bobby Robson** 'black and white world' from his *Newcastle – My Kind of Toon*, p. 11

89   **love of alcohol** – on North East drinking culture see Jackson, *The Northumbrians* 148-151 and Sharkey, *Akenside Syndrome*, pp. 67ff

90   **People talked** is from Keegan, *My Life in Football*, p. 138. Club's lack of washing machines is p. 161.

92   **Jonathan Tulloch's** description of the Metrocentre is from his novel *The Season Ticket*, p. 87. On the Metrocentre see also Niven, *The North*, pp. 102-5

92   **Margaret Thatcher comment** on Metrocentre quoted in *Newcastle Evening Chronicle*, 13 October 1986

92   **Geordie Nation**: John Hall comments on this and mystique and passion of football from an interview in *The Independent*, 21 June 1994.

93   **Joe Sharkey** on shirt wearing in *Akenside Syndrome*, pp. 86-7

94   **Pavel Srniček** quotations are taken from his book *'Pavel is a Geordie'*

95   **Andy Cole** washing night is from Keegan, *My Life*, p. 179. 'Caressing' is from Cole, *The Autobiography*, p. 77

95   **Gabby Logan** memories taken from her book *The First Half*, pp. 178-9, 226

96   **'contorted with anger'** Keegan, *My Life*, pp. 196-8

96   **profile for BBC radio**: My profile of Hall was broadcast on BBC Five Live on 15 October 1995

96   **'blood stock'** is from Joannou, *Fortress St James*, p. 60

98   **Les Ferdinand** is quoted in Niven, *The North*, p. 280

98   **Devlin** on 1995-96 Newcastle kit at: **https://x.com/truecolourskits?lang=en)**

99   **'totally different organisation'** Keegan, *My Life*, p. 217

99   **'Fake Sheikh'** sting, see https://www.bbc.co.uk/news/uk-37555017

101   **'Bobby Robson'** quotations taken from Robson, *Farewell But Not Goodbye*, pp. 1-3, 190 and *My Kind of Toon*, p. 221

104   **'strangely addictive'** Keegan, *My Life*, pp. 280, 287

104   **Gavin Haigh** *Black and White Stripes*, p. 165

104   **BBC documentaries** My profile of Ashley was broadcast on BBC Radio 4, 23 February 2013

106   **'changed my feelings'** Keegan, *My Life*, p. 317

108   **'explore a controversial development'** I presented a documentary on 'The Lending Game', broadcast on BBC Radio 4 on 18 August 2013

110   **Peter Clarke** in his book *'Hope and Glory'* (London, 1996), p. 51

111   **profile of Denise Coates** broadcast on BBC Radio 4 31 December 2017. After Newcastle's Sandro Tonali was banned from playing for 10 months in 2023 for breaching betting rules as a result of his gambling addiction he spoke of meeting 'a lot of people with ordinary jobs, especially in Newcastle, who had this problem': https://www.bbc.co.uk/sport/football/articles/c93pnz5z3z2o

111   **Rafa Benitez** quotation from an interview published in the *Newcastle Evening Chronicle*, 15 March 2025

113   **new Saudi owners** For more on the on the new ownership and the Newcastle shirt see the chapter in Joey D'Urso's book *More Than a Shirt* (London, 2025). The broader 'sportswashing' issue in relation to Newcastle United and others is covered in Miguel Delaney's *States of Play* (London, 2024)

113   **Jackie Milburn** quotation is from Milburn, *A Man of Two Halves*, p. 24

114   **the crest** Newcastle United statement on 'updating our crest' on 9 May 2025 at https://www.newcastleunited.com/en/news/updating-our-crest-together

114   **Percy Young**, *History*, p. 56

115   **Hall had reflected**: see Sharkey, *Akenside Syndrome*, p. 80

115   **he was globalising Newcastle** quoted in *Shields Gazette* 22 October 2021. The Newcastle team was certainly globalised under Ashley, beginning the 2013/14 season without a single English-born player: Walker, *Up There*, p. 25

116   **endorsed the Reform party:** https://www.bbc.co.uk/news/articles/c3gejn3gkl4o

6: THE SOUL OF A STADIUM

117   **a site of memory** For example Dmowski, Seweryn. 'Lieux De Mémoire' in *Eastern Bloc Football (1945-1991): Integration and Decomposition, Resistance and Adaptation*

118   **Freddy Shepherd** comments in https://www.bbc.co.uk/sport/football/15672054

Siting of **Shearer statue** was reported in the Freemen's magazine: https://fon.org.uk/downloads/magazine/FreemenMagazineIssue20.pdf

119 **Bobby Robson** quotations from *My Kind of Toon*, pp. 17, 20, 151

120 **Lawrie McMenemy** *A Lifetime's Obsession* (Liverpool, 2017) p. 26

120 **correspondent of *The Times*** published in the paper on 22 April 1911. For more on Veitch see Chris Goulding's website: https://colinveitch.homestead.com/Colin-Veitch.html

121 **Lord Ridley** quoted in Ardagh, *Tale of Five Cities*, p. 231. **Keegan** is from *The Guardian* 14 February 2008

121 **Karel Čapek** is from his *Believe in People* (London, 2010) p. 23

121 **Labour council leader** Ardagh p. 231

122 **'a paintbrush of a left foot'** Robson, *My Kind of Toon*, p. 224

122 **Dabizas** in *Newcastle Evening Chronicle, 30 July 2020*; **Ian Wright** is from Dennis Bergkamp, *Stillness and Speed* (London, 2013), p. 218

123 **profile of Sir John Hall** on BBC Five Live on 15 October 1995

123 **Jonathan Tulloch** quotations are from *The Season Ticket*, pp. 112, 151-2, 216

124 **bogofs** were the 'buy one, get one free' offers popular then in supermarkets

125 **Matt Ritchie** interview in *The Athletic*, 4 July 2025: https://www.nytimes.com/athletic/6471369/2025/07/04/newcastle-the-challenge-of-attracting-top-players-and-why-this-summer-is-different/

127 **Granit Xhaka** https://www.standard.co.uk/sport/football/xhaka-interview-arsenal-newcastle-b1000425.html **Kevin Keegan,** *My Life*, p. 134

129 **football dystopia** Robot football has already reached China: https://www.bbc.co.uk/news/videos/c5ylkyrkjnzo

130 **Amazon documentary** entitled 'We Are Newcastle United'

130 **David Goldblatt** *The Ball is Round* (London, 2007), p. 23

130 **the ambassador** Interview with Prince Khalid in *The Times*, 16 October 2021

131 **Joannou,** *Fortress St James*, p. 75 on the quagmire and p. 61 on proposed theatre

133 **Peter Silverstone's** background and ambitions were set out by the club here: https://www.newcastleunited.com/en/news/newcastle-united-appoints-peter-silverstone-as-chief-commercial-officer

133 **milking of devotion** Walker, *Up There*, p. 190

134 **Percy Young** in his *History of British Football*, p. 198

135 **Eddie Rutherford** quoted in *Newcastle Evening Chronicle* 26 February 2013: https://www.chroniclelive.co.uk/news/north-east-news/scattering-ashes-st-james-park-1401879

135 **Wor Flags** statement quoted in *The Athletic*, 10 January 2025: https://www.nytimes.com/athletic/6006091/2025/01/10/st-james-park-newcastle-future/

136 George Caulkin is from Robson, *Farewell but Not Goodbye*, p. 299. **Bobby Robson** quotations are from *My Kind of Toon*, p. 147 and 185

7: KEEPING THE FAITH

137 **martial tradition** See Jackson, *Northumbrians*, chapter 2

138 **on the Sabbath** Marples, *History of Football*, p. 59

138 **George Ferebe** https://www.british-history.ac.uk/vch/wilts/vol7/pp187-197

138 **sporting parson** See Young, *History* p 33, III. The tradition lingered into the 1950s when Lawrie McMenemy was introduced to football by Father Hardie, a 'fine player' who taught at his Catholic Newcastle school (Lawrie McMenemy, *A Lifetime's Obsession*, p. 42)

139 **Carthusians** *The Times*, 29 April 1895

139 **Reverend Kenneth Hunt** see https://web.archive.org/web/20070823202332/http:/www.localhistory.scit.wlv.ac.uk/genealogy/KennethHunt/chapter4.htm. and Appleton, *Hotbed*, p. 136

Quotations are from his book Hunt, Kenneth R.G. *First Steps to Association Football* (London, Mills and Boon, 1924), p. 12, 55

140 **Basil Hume** on Milburn quoted in Colls and Lancaster, *Newcastle upon Tyne*, p. 209

141 **Cuthbert Bardsley** See *The Times*, 20 May 1967

141 **Christine Hardman** https://www.ukpol.co.uk/christine-hardman-2016-maiden-speech-in-the-house-of-lords/. The article on Benitez's decision to stay was in *The Times* on 26 May 2016

142 **Alan Hutchinson** was remembered in the official matchday programme for Newcastle v Liverpool 25 August 2025

142 **Kevin Keegan** quotations taken from *My Life*, pp. 134, 147, 158. Fan comments reported in *The Independent*, 9 January 1997

143 **The Messiah:** Alex Niven discusses his own internalizing of the Keegan 'fairy tale' and his fears of the 'tragic implication' of belief in a messiah in *The North*, pp. 281-2

143 **Les Ferdinand** quoted in Clarke, Ged *Fifty Years of Hurt* (Edinburgh, 2006), p. 278

143 **Peter Knowles** See Gordos, Steve, *Peter Knowles, God's Footballer* (Derby, 2009), p. 155

144 **Bobby Robson** 'sporting gods' is from *Newcastle, My Kind of Toon*, p. 41. His comments on monks come from an article by Sid Waddell in *The Times*, 1 August 2009 https://www.thetimes.com/sport/football/article/wor-bobby-affable-hero-of-the-working-man-r666zd0qsss

144 **Gavin Peacock** from his *Greater Glory*, pp. 112, 238

145 **Christian Atsu** My obituary of Atsu was published in *The Times* on 18 February 2023

145 On **John Wooden** see https://www.thewoodeneffect.com/pyramid-of-success/

146 **Jürgen Klopp** response to death of Diogo Jota: https://www.liverpool.com/liverpool-fc-news/features/breaking-liverpool-jota-jurgen-klopp-31985620

146 **Alex Bellos** *Futebol* (London, 2002) pp. 259. **Bruno Guimaraes** on his knees was reported by Keith Downie https://x.com/i/status/1928042297175732449. True Faith website is true-faith.co.uk.

147 **Ewan once wrote** Extracts are from a draft article Ewan sent me about football and religion

148 **Peter Clarke** from his *Hope and Glory* (London, 1996), p. 53

8: MEN AND THEIR MOODS

151 **Bundesgartenschau** – see Eric Sandelands https://ericsandelands.substack.com/p/what-happened-next-after-the-gateshead

151 **German region** For the territory of the former GDR overtaking the north of England economically see Tom Forth: https://tomforth.co.uk/humancapital/

151 **Priestley** *English Journey*, pp. 353-5

152 **Jonathan Tulloch** *Season Ticket* p. 104

152 **Brendan Foster: steeliness** quotation is from a piece by John Gibson in *The Times*, 8 April 1975. Other quotations taken from Brendan Foster and Cliff Temple, *Brendan Foster* (London, 1978), pp. 2-3

153 **Arthur Appleton** *Hotbed*, p. 63. On fans' **'deep and sore disappointment'** p. 17. On Gateshead FC generally see also Walker, *Up There*, pp. 227-232

157 **Morris Marples,** *A History*, pp. 214-5

158 **Harry Pearson,** *Farther Corner*, p. 1

160 **Arthur Hopcraft,** *Football Man*, p. 197

160 **Medical researchers:** article is W. Kirkup, D. W. Merrick, published in *Journal of Epidemiology and Community Health*, Vol 57, No 3 (June 2003)

160 **Bobby Robson** *Newcastle*, p. 27

161 **miners' leader** quoted in McCord, Norman, *North East England* (London, 1979), pp. 191-2

162 **wee fellow** is from Joannou, *Hughie Gallacher*, p. 37, and p. 74 for Gallacher on pay. **John Arlott** quotation is from his introduction to Appleton, *Hotbed of Soccer*, p. 15. **Bobby Robson** comment is from *Newcastle*, p. 219

162 **Keith Armstrong's** poem is called '36 Goals' from his collection *Angels Playing Football* (Whitley Bay, 2006)

163 **Jackie Milburn and Hughie Gallacher Junior** comments are in Joannou, *Hughie Gallacher*, pp. 110-12. For Shearer at Hall of Fame see: https://nationalfootballmuseum.com/halloffame/hughie-gallacher/

163 **Jimmy Greaves** quotations taken from his book *This One's on Me*, p. 13

164 **Dhindsa** quotations are from author interview with Kal Singh Dhindsa

165 **didn't make sense** Quotations from Gascoigne, *Gazza*, pp. 24, 44, 52. **'Fat ill-mannered'** from a *Daily Mail* piece (3 June 1998) is on p. 181. He discusses his suicidal thoughts on p. 349

166 **the precariousness** is from a piece by Oliver Brown in the *Daily Telegraph* 29 March 2025 https://www.telegraph.co.uk/football/2025/03/29/i-sat-front-row-for-paul-gascoigne-show-gazza-fragile-soul/?utm_source=substack&utm_medium=email

166 **De La Rue** job cuts: see https://www.bbc.co.uk/news/uk-england-tyne-48761570

166 **Antony Gormley** comments are from https://www.gateshead.gov.uk/article/5303/The-history-of-the-Angel-of-the-North

167 **Jonathan Tulloch** is from *The Season Ticket*, p. 125

167 **Ewan (Bowlby)'s** comments on levity are from his *Borrowed Stories*, p. 163

169 **Gateshead Yeshiva:** see https://www.theguardian.com/world/2019/dec/22/gateshead-torah-on-tyne-britains-orthodox-jewish-community

171 **J. B. Priestley,** *English Journey*, pp. 179-80

172 On **Charlie Rogers** see the book about him complied by Brian Rankin, *Pursued by Bulldozers* (Gateshead, 2025), pp. 17-19. Another excellent artist-footballer was Harold Riley in Manchester. My obituary of him was in *The Times*, 1 May 2023

173 **Thomas More** is quoted in Marples, *A History of Football*, p. 50

9: LOST LASSES

177 **David Goldblatt** *Ball is Round*, p. 783

178 **Rose Reilly** The BBC TV documentary was in the series *Icons of Football*, first broadcast on 16 June 2023

180 **Brennan quotes:** Labour official is in *The Munitionettes*, p. 42. **Letter allegedly written** is on p. 49.

180 On **James Welldon** see article from a Sheffield newspaper quoted here: https://static1.squarespace.com/static/5be45672e749406b1582ed88/t/5da11496ae38d1604184eb0f/1570837656300/Imitators+of+Men.pdf and also https://hindzeit.wordpress.com/2019/01/11/bless-his-cotton-socks-a-tale-of-two-bishops/

For more details on range of women's teams see Williams, *Rough Girls*, p. 32

180 **Alice Kell's** comments are from: https://www.irishtimes.com/sport/soccer/2022/06/16/dick-kerr-ladies-football-fa-goodison-ban/ For an excellent overview of all this history see Suzanne Wrack's *A Woman's Game: The Rise, Fall, and Rise Again of Women's Football*

181 **football comics** see Riches, Adam, *Football's Comic Book Heroes* (Edinburgh, 2009) pp. 47, 50

181 **Football Association** resolution is from the *Official History of the Football Association* (London, 1953), pp. 533-4

181   **Jean Williams**, *Rough Girls*, p. 4

182   **Matt Busby** is quoted in Joannou, *Hughie Gallacher*, p. 11

182   **Virginia Woolf** *A Room of One's Own*, pp. 70-1; *Three Guineas*, pp. 142-3

183   **kicking a turnip** is from the essay by Richard Holt and Ray Physick in Colls and Lancaster (eds), *Newcastle upon Tyne*, p. 211. On Mary Lyons see BBC report: https://www.bbc.co.uk/news/articles/c89gkdvk3pqo and also: https://shekicks.net/centenary-of-stars-footballing-debut-remembering-mary-lyons/

183   **Ellen Wilkinson** *The Town That Was Murdered* (London, 1939), p. 231

183   **local or national sites** see Williams, *Rough Girls*, p. 33

183   **Elizabeth Milburn** quotations from Charlton, Cissie, *Cissie*, pp. 12, 15, 24, 39, 56. **Jack Charlton** comment is from *Jack Charlton — the Autobiography* (Partridge Press, 1996), p. 3. **Bobby Charlton** is quoted in Jonathan Wilson's *Two Brothers* (London 2022), p. 29. **Teapot** story is in Hopcraft, *Football Man*, p. 90

185   **Arthur Appleton** *Hotbed of Soccer*, p 120

185   **Margaret Petrie in** Chaplin, *Newcastle United*, pp. 174-7

186   **Mary Raine**: quotations from my interview with her; see also https://www.bbc.co.uk/programmes/w3csym7d

186   **Lord Denning** is quoted in Williams, *Rough Girls*, p. 17. See p. 97 for her comment on **winter cold**

187   **as she told a BBC documentary**…. Carol Wilson interview is from a BBC *Storyville* documentary on *Copa 71*, first broadcast in June 2024

189   **Fran Kirby** comments are taken from https://www.bbc.co.uk/sport/football/31850624

189   Quotations from **Carmen Mayer** and **Chris Law** taken from my interviews with them in Hamburg, July 2025

191   **Cissie Charlton** coaching comments are from her *Cissie*. p 183

10: FLOODLIT MEMORY

194   **a solitary soul** from Ewan's *Borrowed Stories*, p. 90. His comment on the language of cancer treatment is on p. 134

195   **images of health** from *A Picture of Health* (Medical Research Council, 2022), p. 120

196   **Bobby Robson's** words are from his *Autobiography*, p. 310

197   **Arsène Wenger** quoted in *The Times*, 4 October 2020

198   **language of laughter** from Ewan's *Borrowed Stories*, p. 182

204   **force de frappe** French missile strike force, designed to get through any defences

205   **Dan Jackson** from *The Northumbrians*, p. 151

11: WINNING REDEMPTION

207 **Arthur Appleton** doldrums in his *Hotbed*, p. 220

208 **Reubens'** website is https://www.reubenbrothers.com/

209 **Aldous Huxley** I explored his interest in ICI and Teesside in a BBC Radio 4 documentary *Brave New Billingham*, broadcast on 7 June 2004

213 **Kevin Keegan's** Dad quoted in *My Life*, p. 132

213 **Newcastle United champagne**: https://www.newcastleunited.com/en/official-carabao-cup-24-25-winners-champagne. Launch of official supporters club: https://www.newcastleunited.com/en/fans/official-nufc-supporters-clubs

214 **a billion people** from interview with Tom Werner in *The Times*, 27 June 2025

215 **Eddie Howe** comments after cup final: https://www.bbc.co.uk/sport/football/articles/c5yp3lzvIgeo and on influence of his mother: https://www.bbc.co.uk/sport/football/articles/cIdx0qyy4640

216 **Sam Fender** on his ballad 'Remember My Name': https://www.nme.com/news/music/sam-fender-shares-soothing-new-ballad-remember-my-name-3838250

217 **to give in perpetuity**: Gabby Logan writes movingly about how her family buried her 15-year-old brother Daniel, who had collapsed and died in a kickabout, in his favourite Welsh football kit (*The First Half*, p. 140)

219 **Toni Kroos** comments in *Newcastle Evening Chronicle*, 25 August 2025: https://www.chroniclelive.co.uk/sport/football/transfer-news/toni-kroos-new-newcastle-united-32372585

220 **Armstrong, Keith,** *Angels Playing Football* (Whitley Bay, 2006). In Oldham there is a football team of men who have lost a child in pregnancy, birth or infancy. Their name? Angels United. See the article by Daniel Storey, 'Angels United: the club for Dads who have lost a child', in the *iPaper*, 13 November 2025.

Index

Also available:

When Ewan Bowlby was diagnosed with a brain tumour at the age of 17, he tackled the consequences head on. During the following, final decade of his life he recorded his experiences and searched for ways of approaching mortality with greater clarity, honesty and creativity than is found in contemporary healthcare.

Ewan discovered the power of culture – as diverse as Dostoevsky's *The Brothers Karamazov* and Dante's *Divine Comedy*, John Green's *The Fault in Our Stars*, and recent television dramas *Breaking Bad* and *Cold Feet* – to enable those confronting death and disease to map their own situations.

'The world is too full of shocking suffering and waste to do without a work of witness like this, a profoundly and persistently generous book in which the writer makes sense of what is happening by making a gift of his experience to those who might have to share it or something similar — or just those who need to know a bit more about living with dignity and vision through the end of a world.'
Rowan Williams

Borrowed Stories **can be bought from the publisher's website www.dltwritingforyou.com, or ordered through any bookseller.**